RESEARCH ON WRITING APPROACHES IN MENTAL HEALTH

STUDIES IN WRITING
Series Editor: Gert Rijlaarsdam

Recent titles in this series:

VAN WAES, LEIJTEN AND NEUWIRTH
Writing and Digital Media

SULLIVAN AND LINDGREN
Computer Key-Stroke Logging and Writing

HIDI AND BOSCOLO
Writing and Motivation

TORRANCE VAN WAES AND GALBRAITH
Writing and Cognition

ALAMARGOT, TERRIER AND CELLIER
Written Documents in the Workplace

HA AND BAURAIN
Voices, Identities, Negotiations, and Conflicts: Writing Academic English Across Cultures

Related journals:

Learning and Instruction
Educational Research Review
Assessing Writing
Computers and Composition
Journal of Second Language Writing

RESEARCH ON WRITING APPROACHES IN MENTAL HEALTH

EDITED BY

LUCIANO L'ABATE

Department of Psychology, Georgia State University, GA, USA

LAURA G. SWEENEY

Henry County, GA, USA

United Kingdom • North America • Japan
India • Malaysia • China

Emerald Group Publishing Limited
Howard House, Wagon Lane, Bingley BD16 1WA, UK

First edition 2011

Reprints and permission service
Contact: booksandseries@emeraldinsight.com

British Library Cataloguing in Publication Data
A catalogue record for this book is available from the British Library

ISBN: 978-0-85724-955-5
ISSN: 1572-6304 (Series)

Contents

PART III: AN UNACCEPTABLE WRITING APPROACH

List of Contributors

Jenna L. Baddeley Psychology Department, The University of Texas, Austin, TX, USA. E-mail:jennabaddeley@gmail.com; website: http://homepage.psy.utexas.edu/homepage/students/Baddeley

John F. Evans 1516 Great Ridge Parkway, Chapel Hill, NC, USA. E-mail: jfevans77@gmail.com

Luciano L'Abate 2079 Deborah Drive, NE, Atlanta, GA, USA. E-mail: llabate3@bellsouth.net; website: www.mentalhealthhelp.com

Thomas Mackrill Center for Alcohol and Drug Research, Aarhus University, Artillerivej 90, 2. 2300 København S, Denmark. E-mail: tm@crf.au.dk

Debbie McCulliss 5440 South Grape Lane; Greenwood Village, CO, USA. E-mail: dmcculliss@gmail.com; website: www.dmcculliss.com

James W. Pennebaker Department of Psychology, University of Texas, Austin, TX, USA. E-mail: pennebaker@psy.utexas.edu; website: www.psy.utexas.edu/Pennebaker

Lawrence Ressler Department of Social Science, Taylor University, IN, USA. E-mail: lwressler@taylor.edu

Brenda Stockdale 1025 Ambrose Avenue, Alpharetta, GA, USA. E-mail: brenda.stockdale@gmail.com

Laura G. Sweeney 401 Briarvista Way NE, Atlanta, GA, USA. E-mail: laurasweeneyworks@gmail.com

Foreword

Research on Writing Approaches for Mental Health comes at an historic juncture in the development of effective ways to treat mental health. Recently, the Internet has made it possible to deliver a cornucopia of mental health services. However, many of these services mimic face-to-face therapy and follow traditional processes common in conversational therapy. Some offer therapy through writing in chat rooms, a synchronous atmosphere, and some that offer email, a more asynchronous setting, which offers reflection. Both chat rooms and email offer a researchable base in the texts that can be saved from session to session and indeed over the whole history of the therapy. A field of words ripe for research exists here.

Future research needs to expand on methods of increasing the ability of the consumer to engage with the etherapy program. For example, we will be investigating what combination of interactive web-based components increase motivation and improve treatment outcome (e.g., interactive exercises to complete online and offline, journal keeping, personalized tailoring of information and the use of webcams, blogs, chat rooms, and message posting). In addition, we will also look at other information technology devices such as the use of virtual reality technology and mobile Internet/email messaging tools (2008).

Echoing some of the major findings of *Best Practices in Online Therapy* from authors, Jo-Anne M. Abbott, Britt Klein, and Lisa Ciechomski, L'Abate and Sweeney describe a broader range of therapeutic writing than what is found in online therapeutic writing and they make their own recommendation. After looking at research in automatic writing, expressive writing, autobiographies, diaries, bibliotherapy, and poetry, L'Abate and Sweeney assert why distance writing may be the preferred method of help and healing in the 21st century.

While professional resource catalogues and general bookstores, both online and in our neighborhoods, offer dozens of titles touting the benefits of writing therapy, few offer more than anecdotal evidence for the efficacious features of this practice. On the one hand are a few older works like James Pennebaker's, *Opening Up: The Healing Power of Expressing Emotions* (1990) and on the other hand are contemporary numerous works like, Elizabeth Maynard Schaefer's, *Writing through the Darkness: Easing Your Depression with Paper and Pen* (2008). Pennebaker's work provides a research base upon which to ground practice and generate new theory. Schaefer's work, part memoir and part self-help guide, provides an insider's story of managing depression. The former reports research; the latter reports anecdotes. It can certainly be argued that both works have a place, but they illustrate a gap in the literature.

This gap needs to be filled as L'Abate and Sweeney suggest within these pages. No matter how popular a treatment writing is now or may become, it will not serve the professional community and clients or fulfill its promising potential as well as it could until its research base is alive, healthy, and robust in the literature of the disciplines. The discipline demands that health-care workers such as psychologists, therapists, and counselors become reflective practitioners. How does writing therapy work and under what conditions? How does writing therapy compare with traditional therapies? How can writing therapy be standardized or modified as prescribed by client needs. Are there writing therapies supported by studies that can be duplicated?

Whatever your current wellness and writing practice, the following chapters offer illustrations of the current state of research, theory, and practice. Much remains to do. I agree with L'Abate and Sweeney that therapeutic writing needs more rigorous science, what Pennebaker calls the "big science, big medicine" approach applied to large samples of people with differing diagnoses.

I agree. I would also like to emphasize that a significant contribution to the science of writing-to-heal can come from individuals and professionals in settings large and small if they engage in reflective practices, carefully documenting their processes and results. If each mental health-care professional were part of a network documenting interactions with clients, but honoring privacy requirements, a rich database would grow quickly. From these records of reflective practitioners, a richer description and deeper understanding of writing-to-heal theory will emerge providing models of practice.

I am delighted that *Research on Writing Approaches for Mental Health* encourages its readers to expect more rigor and discipline from those who suggest writing is an effective tool for treating mental health challenges. My vision for future wellness practice includes writing as a mental health modality and extends beyond that application to other health challenges as well. Wellness and writing connections is a braided column. One braid suggests that expressive and programmed writing as effective methods for individuals. Another braid suggests a curriculum for training professionals who will include writing as a significant treatment modality. Joining the first two braids is one that suggests program guidelines for individuals who work in institutional settings like hospital wellness programs, cancer treatment clinics, trauma centers, prisons, counseling offices, schools, and universities.

John Frank Evans
Founder and Executive Director
Wellness & Writing Connections

Preface

Writing as a medium of professional help and healing in the various interventional tiers of self-help, education, promotion, prevention, and psychotherapy, and rehabilitation has expanded exponentially since the introduction of computers and the Internet in the last generation. Furthermore, the emphasis on homework assignments has created the conceptual, clinical, and empirical rationale for using writing at a distance between professionals and participants. One could conclude that distance writing without ever seeing participants is to this century what face-to-face talk was to the last century.

The purpose of this edited volume, therefore, is to include under one roof research on different types of writing and distance writing that have been or need to be used by the various mental health approaches included here. To obtain collaborators for this edited monograph, a call was made through appropriate online channels to well known and accomplished collaborators in one specific writing approach. Consequently, the following entries came to life.

The first part of this monograph includes two chapters that cover writing approaches normatively and nonnormatively. In Chapter 1, Laura G. Sweeney and Luciano L'Abate introduce various types of writing covering the wide and increasing range of conceptual and practical advances that have occurred in the last generation in mental health, all related to the use of writing in general and distance writing in particular. After introducing the various dimensions of writing (expressive, face-to-face, structured–unstructured. prescriptive–cathartic, abstract–concrete, and general–specific), these authors cover the advent of telehealth and the Internet in its various applications, including blogging, and social networks, such as Facebook, Twitter, and many others. All these applications imply that in this century distance writing will become the most common medium of communication and healing in this century, allowing through Skype or other forms of visual communication to supplant traditional face-to-face contacts. Working at a distance from participants does not mean that mental health professionals must remain passive. On the contrary, part and parcel of working at a distance involves also the assignment of homework. This approach allows participants a more active involvement in the process of healing that strengthens the process of self-help and health promotion. These sea changes in how mental health services will be delivered (at a distance) is being met by a great deal of resistance from the established mental health community that has been trained to rely on face-to-face personal contact and talk as the main means of communication. All of the above has important implications about how education and training in mental health will occur in the 21st century.

In Chapter 2, Brenda Stockdale reviews research about the use of writing in physical and concomitant mental illness by including the biological underpinnings of writing for healthy functioning and how the mind heals and hurts the body. Stress, inflammation, and early life experiences have a great deal to do with how much we are able to remember and to express, verbally as well as in writing. The body retains all of the unpleasant and painful experiences that we have not been able to express and to share with loved ones. One of the most important examples of how retaining unexpressed feelings is found in alexithymia, a disorder that produces a great many psychosomatic and physical illnesses. This condition leads to the importance of psychoeducation, biofeedback, and expressive and programmed writing as ways to help and heal people who are unable to express their feelings, as also found in the Asperger disorders. Considering the brain as a narrative organ, writing in depression, anxiety, and posttraumatic stress disorders will provide help to large numbers of people afflicted with these conditions who find it too expensive to be treated with traditional face-to-face, talk-based approaches.

Part II covers research about the various types of writing approaches available to date. Lawrence Ressler and Luciano L'Abate, after including an historical background about the research literature on autobiographies until 2006 in Chapter 3, review the considerable amount of research that has accrued since that year to date. The literature on autobiographies includes both qualitative and quantitative research that deals with addictions, autism, cancer, children, dementia, feelings and emotions, gender differences, heart disease, longevity and mortality, mental disorders, multiple sclerosis, obesity, retirement, senior citizens, and sex offenders. These authors lament the lack of theory to "explain" how autobiography helps most people who use it, whether they are functional or dysfunctional, suggesting that perhaps Relational Competence Theory may encompass autobiography as a self-help way to learn more about oneself.

Diaries, as covered in Chapter 4 by Thomas Mackrill, are another inexpensive, self-help way to keep track on one's self and discover about oneself aspects that may not emerge otherwise. The advantages of diary writing are so many, in addition to their cost-effectiveness, that is no surprise that diaries are still considered an important idiographic research tool by many scholars. One must differentiate between solicited and nonsolicited diaries because this differentiation may make a difference in the results. One of the many advantages of diary writing is their temporal extension over days, weeks, months, and even years. Of course, even though diaries are relatively easy to administer, there are rather time-consuming to analyze. Nonetheless, diaries have been administered to learn more about behavioral and existential therapies as well as anxiety and eating disorders, and substance abuse.

As reviewed by Debbie McCulliss in Chapter 5, bibliotherapy based on writing is an extremely popular either alternative or supplementary form of psychotherapy that is admired by both laypersons and mental health professionals. This approach has a long history going back to the beginning of the last century. However, over the last century this approach has differentiated itself in different types of bibliotherapy, such as clinical, developmental, and client-developed, as a form of self-help, among others. Biblionarrative, for instance, is a child-focused approach that combines stories with real-life events to facilitate conversation between a mental health professional and a child.

Both Brenda Stockdale and Debbie McCulliss, in their respective chapters, give credit to Jamie Pennebaker for what Jenna Baddeley and him modestly called the Expressive Writing Method, also known as the "Pennebaker's Paradigm." Known all over the world and supported by a plethora of evidence, this approach strikes at the bottom line of our existence: writing about traumas that many of us have experienced but kept inside and not expressed and shared with anybody. The content in many writings about traumas can be either rational or emotional or a combination of both. It can occur in front of a professional in a group or at a distance from a professional. Since both authors avoided controversial topics, we, the editors, added an editorial addendum to include references that were not considered by Baddeley and Pennebaker. We hope they will not mind our editorial inclusion.

In Chapter 7, Debbie McCulliss found that poetry therapy has not received a great deal of research, but it is extremely widespread to the point that even a journal is being published. Yet, even a journal does not assure that controlled research will be valued in this approach. After an early history of poetry therapy, considered as the oldest form of literature, this author indicates how many physicians and therapists from different disciplines use it in their practices as a palliative approach. Poetry therapy has evolved over the years into a recognized approach becoming organized as a discipline in its own rights but used by various medical and psychological disciplines. It really came to life in the second half of last century in an organized association with its own criteria for membership and even educational degrees. More often than not poetry therapy is combined with other healing approaches, making unfortunately difficult whether it produced real gains in its outcome. Eventually, various models of poetry therapy emerged that were amenable to empirical evaluation.

In Chapter 8 about interactive practice exercises or mental health workbooks based on programmed writing, Luciano L'Abate introduces what tantamounts to a simple transformation of most psychological tests, DSM-IV symptoms, and syndromes into active and interactive workbooks. This simple transformation allows to change static evaluation instruments and behavior and symptom lists into interactively dynamic interventions that allow to match interventions with evaluations in ways that would be difficult if not impossible to obtain in face-to-face, talk-based psychotherapy. Therefore, these workbooks cover the whole range of functional conditions and dysfunctional disorders in individuals (children, youth, and adults), couples, and families. Their printed nature makes them completely replicable ad infinitum allowing to combine research and interventions in less expensive ways than traditional psychotherapeutic approaches.

In Part III, by reviewing popular and professional literature about automatic writing, Laura Sweeney found that this technique is of questionable usefulness as a popular fad a century ago that still quite known to this day. Even though automatic writing is usually administered face to face, many popular books give instructions on how to perform it without additional help, indicating that this approach can occur at a distance from a professional or nonprofessional helper. In spite of many reservations about the usefulness of this approach, why would a mental health professional or researcher or one interested in writing studies be interested in reading this chapter's negative conclusions about this approach? This relevant question can be answered in terms of the popular, uncritically enthusiastic hype that surrounds this approach. Those very researchers or mental health professionals need to know about this approach as part and parcel of their knowing about what works and what does not work in distance writing. In their practices, these professionals might have to contend with charlatans or quacks who claim magic results about this approach without any evidence.

In a conclusive Epilogue, Luciano L'Abate and Laura G. Sweeney contend that the research-based writing approaches included in this monograph will influence the delivery of mental health services in this century. One major implication is the prediction that writing in general and distance writing in particular will become the preferred medium of mental health help and healing in this century. Writing is part of the information processing that will characterize mental health applications in this century. All the approaches included and reviewed in this monograph involve a public rather than a private health approach, the most good for the most needy. However, the Editors close their Epilogue as well as this monograph with a warning that any professional who wants to use distance writing as an online treatment approach should consult local and national rules and regulations protecting the vulnerable public from charlatans and hucksters who prey on needy and naïve people seeking help for their troubles.

What will be the readership of this monograph? We hope that researchers, scholars, and students in the various mental health disciplines will profit by reading these chapters. Perhaps, mental health professionals in their respective disciplines will be able to upgrade and update their practice skills to enter this century rather than remaining in the past one.

Luciano L'Abate
Laura G. Sweeney
Atlanta, GA
Editors

PART I

BACKGROUNDS FOR WRITING APPROACHES

Chapter 1

The Role of Writing in Mental Health Research

Laura G. Sweeney and Luciano L'Abate

> "*There is a compelling need for innovative approaches to the solution of many pressing problems involving human relationships in today's society. Such approaches are more likely to be successful when they are based on sound research and applications.*" (Cleveland & Fleishman, 2011, p. xiv)

During the last generation a great many changes have occurred in the delivery of mental health services, portending that in this century more and more psychological evaluations and interventions will occur in writing and at a distance between professionals and participants. Among these changes, one must consider the following: (1) structural dimensions of writing; (2) advent of telemental health via the Internet as the main medium of service delivery in mental health, with a phenomenal increase in the quantity of psychotherapy available online, including Skype and online conferencing; (3) professionals working at a distance from participants; (4) increased importance of and reliance on homework assignments; and (5) resistance from the mental health professions to adopt and adapt distance writing to their practices as an alternative, adjunct, or substitute for one-on-one (1on1), face-to-face (f2f), talk-based (tb) interventions. There is still a great deal of resistance from the established psychotherapeutic community to give up two traditional models of intervention: f2f, tb, one-on-one, one professional with one participant in personal, verbal contact (L'Abate, 2011d).

Additional relatively conceptual and practical advances include expansion of (1) conceptually the analogic to digital model applicable to both talk and writing; (2) the rise of structured interventions that will allow to specify which approach is

Research on Writing Approaches in Mental Health
Studies in Writing, Volume 23, 3–21

ISSN: 1572-6304/doi: 10.1108/S1572-6304(2011)0000023005

more effective for which specific issue or problem; and (3) the growth of a plethora of interventions that will increase the need for more detailed and wide-ranging evaluation of what intervention will be more effective for which problem and/or which individual(s).

Dimensions of Writing

Talk is too variable, uncontrollable, and not a replicable medium of communication and healing. It is essentially inefficient in producing replicable specificity as much more easily achievable through writing. Writing, and especially many distance writing approaches included in this volume, is replicable ad infinitum and the basis for the scientific evolution of mental health service delivery. Science progresses on the basis of replicable written records, not on the basis of talk (L'Abate, 2011d).

The various dimensions of writing are classified in Box 1.1 which in and of themselves should be self-explanatory, even though some may overlap with one another.

Box 1.1. Toward a classification of writing dimensions

1. *Expressive as in Creative/Spontaneous* (contextual, constructive of stories) versus *Contrived/Instructive* (grammar, syntax, logic and logical sequence of arguments, sentence construction and combination, vocabulary, and spelling).
2. *Face-to-face* in front of a professional helper through talk versus *at a distance* from a professional helper through computers, fax, regular mail, phones, or Internet.
3. *Structured–Unstructured* as a dimension can vary from *open*, as in diaries and journals, or *closed*, as in answering specific questions in writing on preestablished topics, either positive, happy, or unhappy events and/or memories, as in expressive and programmed writing (see Chapters 6 and 8 of this volume). A great deal of traditional f2f, tb, one-on-one psychotherapy is still occurring according to the unstructured extreme of this dimension, that is: e-therapists mimic online what most therapists do in their privacy of their offices, practically without any structure except time and fees. This approach, which L'Abate (2011d) calls "reactive psychotherapy," is usually immediate, without any clear, step-by-step, replicable plan except the personal and artistic intuitions and personal biases of the therapist without pre–post-objective evaluation and follow-up.
4. *Goals* could be *prescriptive* to produce specific outcomes via specific homework assignments, or *cathartic* to produce discharge of and release from tensions or traumas.
5. *Content* can be painful, traumatic, neutral, banal, or joyous, emotional, rational, problem-solving, individual, relational, or multigroup.
6. *Level of abstraction* ranging from very concrete, that is, "Write what you ate for breakfast," to very abstract, that is, "Write about the meaning of life."
7. *Specificity*, ranging from general, as in autobiographies and diaries, to extremely specific, concrete, and restricted, such as: "Write about all the clothes you have in your closet."

The Advent of Telemental Health via the Internet

By now the contribution of computers in delivering mental health services is increasing by leaps and bounds (Armstader, Broman-Pulks, Zinzow, Ruggiero, & Circone, 2009; Bloom, 1992; Cox, et al., 2003; Koocher, 2009; Lange et al., 2003; Ljotsson et al., 2007; Marks, 2007; Marks & Cavanagh, 2009; Mohr, 2009; Richardson, Frueh, Grubaugh, & Elhai, 2009; Ritterband, Ritterband, Gonder-Frederick et al., 2003) to the point that practically no psychological disorder can be left behind its influence. Of course, one must take into consideration possible misuses of the Internet (L'Abate & De Giacomo, 2003; Ruiz, Drake, Glass, Marcotte, & van Gorp, 2002).

It does not take a genius to predict that within decades most mental health services will be delivered through the Internet (Abbott, Klein, & Ciechomski, 2008). Furthermore, one must take into consideration how the present generation of children and youth will deal with professional help when they need it. How do children and youth relate with each other today? They perform extensively through texting and Skype. Looking into the not-too-distant future, how will children relate with others when they grow up? Will they accept f2f, tb, one-on-one psychotherapy after they have been texting and corresponding through Skype for years, as well as using other Internet communication channels to be together and communicate with peers? Why would they want to see a professional f2f if they can do it at a distance? Answers to these questions are given in one way or another through the chapters of this volume.

As Gallego and Emmelkamp (2011) concluded in their excellent review of research about the effectiveness of Internet treatments:

> "Internet-based treatments try to overcome some limitations of traditional CBT treatments: they diminish distance between therapist and patient, save therapist (and patient) time, reduce waiting lists, are available for disabled people, allow anonymity and help to face fear of stigmatization.
>
> Randomized controlled studies that test the efficacy of Internet-based treatments have found that these treatments are as effective as face-to-face therapy for anxiety disorders and depression. Furthermore, Internet-based treatments have shown to be significantly more effective than a waiting list control group in most of the studies into anxiety disorders, depression and eating disorders. It should be noted, however, that participants in these studies were volunteers who applied for psychological treatment through the Internet.
>
> There is some controversy about the need for some face-to-face therapist contact in computer-driven treatment. While there seems to be less need in mild depression, post-traumatic stress and panic disorder, it is questionable whether treatment without any face-to-face support is feasible with severe agoraphobic patients and severely depressed patients. For example, it is much easier not to keep a difficult

> exposure assignment with an Internet program than with a face-to-face therapist. In addition, contact with the therapist during the Internet-based treatment may prove to be more important than once thought, given that it may increase treatment compliance and improve outcome.
>
> Surprisingly, ethical concerns with respect to patients' safety and privacy associated with tele-assessment and therapy are hardly discussed. Clearly, tele-therapy is not suited for all patients (e.g. patients who dissociate, psychotic and suicidal patients) and adequate measures have to be taken that such patients are not enrolled in tele-therapy programs. Further, the system must allow appropriate actions to be taken in case of emergencies. There is a clear and urgent need of guidelines and formal regulation by professional associations of assessment through the Internet and tele-therapy." (p. 1)

For more information about the Internet technology and technology in general, the interested reader is referred to a complete chapter on Information Processing (De Giacomo, Mich, Santamaria, Sweeney, & De Giacomo, 2011) and a whole handbook on technological advances in psychology, psychiatry, and neurology (L'Abate & Kaiser, 2012).

Internet Applications (Apps)

As digital technology is embraced by the public in general and by most mental health professionals in particular, Internet applications or apps as well as portable devices and digital bulletin boards will soon provide mental health professionals venues for recording behaviors and observations in structured and unstructured interventions. Such technologies are attractive as professionals will be able to work asynchronously with participants while recording data in a precise timeline. Moreover, participant clients will be able to revise their work and have a chronological record of their revisions on digital bulletin boards. Such interventions will relate specifically to challenges facing clients.

More and more, we are communicating increasingly through the latest technologies including smartphones and iPads which, by the way, have begun to replace laptop computers. For this reason, the youth of today tends to feel more comfortable communicating digitally in synchronous and asynchronous time without frontiers. According to Qualman (2011, p. 269): "There will be more mobile consumption as technologies like smartphones, net books, and tablets improve. Wireless broadband penetration will make for an always 'on' world." Therefore, mental health will be expected to be available for their clientele more hours of the day. Individuals will be able to connect to iPads both through Wi-fi in homes, schools and places of employment, and through 3G on the go, in the United States and abroad (Levitus, 2010, p. 21).

One important consideration is that of the many ways people interact through social networks in addition to f2f interaction. According to Lerner and Steinberg (2009, p. 320), social interaction appealing to young people is manifested in 12 primary forms including: "e-mail, instant messaging, text messaging, chat rooms, bulletin boards, blogs, social networking sites (SSN), video sharing, photo sharing, massively multiplayer online computer games (MMOGs), and virtual worlds." There is no doubt these technologies will be utilized in mental health interventions in health promotion, illness prevention, psychotherapy, and rehabilitation while iPads will be utilized to educate students in the field through digital readings with interactive testing.

Working at a Distance from Participants

The process of helping and working with people at a distance through telehealth, without ever seeing participants face-to-face (f2f), is not too farfetched, given what has happened in medicine for decades. If one thinks about it, medical treatment occurs most of the time away from the eyes and face of the physician. This is how medical prescriptions came about: Medicine moved away from direct f2f treatment without prescriptions to indirect treatment through prescriptions. Being anesthetized during surgery produces another degree of separation from f2f contact. Most serious operations take place when the patient is not awake and aware of any physical interventions, except for the predictable physical pain that is a natural aftermath of the operation (L'Abate, 2007, 2008a, 2008b, 2008c).

However, the medical analogy is not the only example of working at a distance from participants. For instance, think about the construction of buildings. Architects and engineers create a structure on blueprints, which allow construction to take place away from their eyes; those blueprints serve as intermediaries between professionals and construction personnel. By the same token, many new memory-enhancing computer programs serve as direct interventions away from the eyes of their innovators (L'Abate & Kaiser, 2012). Can the approaches included in this volume furnish a blueprint for the delivery of mental health services in this century through the Internet? We leave an answer to these questions in the eyes and hands of mental health professional readers.

Expansion of Internet Applications

The last decade has seen a veritable explosion of Internet applications that come in to market every day. We are going to try to include as many as we can find. However, we have no doubt that we might have missed some applications. We are just covering the most important ones.

Blogging Anyone can be a journalist and publisher today through blogging. Blogger.com offers access to free sites or one can buy his or her own domain name. If one already has a personal website managed by a web designer, it is less costly to include a direct link from one's personal website to the free blog than it would be to have two domain names. Blogs are similar to hard copy journals in that the pages are published in chronological order, often beginning with the most current post moving backward to the least current post. Writers utilize blogs to support personal agendas, to teach, to coach, to share art and ideas, and to journalize life events in the form of memoir. The blog publisher has the option of letting readers reply to the posts; however, this function can be blocked for the reason that some replies are offensive or commercial, detracting from the main points of the blog. A blog memoir is often therapeutic although one must keep in mind that the blog is available to the general public. Again, one might abstain from forthright expression in the blog venue.

Quia.com This is a platform for creating multiple choice quizzes for students. The teacher writes both the questions and the multiple choice answers. Many English as a Second Language teachers write grammar quizzes for their students in which they try to identify the part of speech or missing word. Likewise, Quia.com would be an excellent venue for the administration of personality tests and questionnaires regarding personal preferences. These quizzes are instantly graded so that the teacher or counselor need not take the time to do so. Online quizzes through Quia.com, or a similar provider, are most effective to provide the teacher or counselor with an objective evaluation. Most students who have utilized these quizzes find them to be quite enjoyable, especially when they show their personality traits or when they understand what knowledge they need to gain in order to master a specific subject such as English grammar or a second language.

Social networks A quick search on Google will take researchers to a list of numerous social networking sites ranging from those sites that connect people with similar interests to sites that connect future employees with employers. One social networking site connects those whose main interest is small business, whereas another site connects vegetarians. Other sites exist with the explicit purpose of introducing potential partners. In numerous online venues, social networking enables poets and writers to critique one another's work before submitting it to publishers, which raises the question of who really owns the copyright for what writers share on social networking sites. There is a chance the site will claim ownership in the fine print or that publishers will not accept work that has already been published on a social networking site. Notwithstanding, the writing done in the social context is important as it allows writers to experience interconnectedness with regard to a specific cause.

It would be impossible to discuss all of the social networking sites here, and some of the sites mentioned will eventually become obsolete. Most notable are Facebook, MySpace, LinkedIn, Twitter, and Ecademy. Facebook currently has the most participants, having replaced MySpace as the leading venue for networking. A majority of Facebook users share their political ideas in this activist-friendly platform. Since users with similar viewpoints on issues are introduced through Facebook, this is the best venue in which to share causes like the need to "go green" or to vote for a specific candidate. Perhaps, Barack Obama can attribute his success as a presidential candidate to Facebook where he shared numerous messages of hope. Even in 2011, Obama continues to post important messages to those who have indicated they "like" his cause on Facebook. By liking a cause, the Facebook user attracts and befriends similar minds.

Writing on Facebook tends to consist of abbreviated status updates. These messages are much longer than those shared on Twitter. Pasting links to share with friends is quite popular. Such links are often accompanied with commentaries by the ones who shared the links. Rather than writing out an entire message, the participant might prefer to record a video message on YouTube to be linked to the Facebook post. Often, Facebook users merely update mundane facts such as what they were eating for dinner or which movie they saw and whether they enjoyed it. Facebook conveniently allows users to share important dates for events such as language "Meetups." One therapist promotes her books on psychopathology along with her lectures and group counseling. Readers receive free information each week for those who have an interest in the characteristics of psychopaths. As friends share newspaper articles and videos through Facebook, readers get to know more about what is going on in the world than they would have come to know when limited by local news. One of the drawbacks of Facebook is that people easily become offended by others' comments leading to online bickering and harassment by adults who would never behave so negatively when communicating in person. For this reason, one should not take the written offenses to heart or worry about others who "de-friend" them.

MySpace is basically a networking site to show off colorful web pages, backgrounds, photos, and descriptions of oneself. In a sense, MySpace includes an element of narcissism as it seems to express, "This is my little corner on the Internet. Here I am!" without going into much detail about causes. Above all, writers utilize MySpace to write glorified mini-autobiographies. MySpace is also used to promote authors' books and music.

LinkedIn is one of the best sites to meet others who work in the same or similar fields. More than 3000 members are already linked as writers in the LinkedIn group known as Writers' Cafe. This group is divided into subgroups for poetry, screenwriting, fiction, and nonfiction. There is another LinkedIn group affiliated with HigherEducation.com which allows participants to post about college teaching experiences and college job searches. Members of LinkedIn write primarily about hobbies, professions, and skills. Writers promote their books, while coaches offer retreats and coaching activities. Members find thousands of like-minds across the globe. More specifically, members from the United States, Canada, Ireland, the United Kingdom, Australia, and New Zealand all participate together as though they were interacting on the same continent. Of course, LinkedIn is also available to other nationalities and in other languages.

Ecademy is much more popular in Europe and abroad than it is in the United States. Some of the fees attached to this business social networking site have been a deterrent to Americans signing up, but it is okay to sign up for free. Most fascinating is the way participants may take a personality test determining the color that fits one's personality. After discovering one's type, he or she has the opportunity to join groups of people with the same personality type. Most members write to befriend others, promote themselves, and make international sales connections in the Ecademy social network.

Skype and video conferencing To some extent, Skype is a form of social networking since users can accept video messages and chat messages even, from people they do not know. Although Skype provides valuable opportunities to communicate, mostly free of charge, one never knows whom he or she will encounter on the other end of the video. One should beware of sexters, pornographers, and abusers in the Skype venue. However, Skype permits linguists to practice their languages and chat-writing skills across the globe. Teachers, coaches, and counselors nowadays share their services via Skype. Of one concern might be the need for licensing when counseling others through Skype.

Mailing lists E-mail messages become viral when the author encourages recipients to spread the message to others either for a personal benefit or to make life better. Almost every day, readers with e-mail accounts receive these forwarded e-mails requesting that the recipient sign a petition or that he or she donate money or that he or she vote in a particular manner. Receiving and forwarding messages to like-minded friends creates feelings of interconnectedness while bringing about change.

eCampus eCampus and other collegiate platforms are by far the best venues for counseling online including interventions from afar. Whereas the other venues previously described were public, eCampus permits privacy. Typically, instructors form small classes with various discussion boards in which members post questions and respond to them. The teacher or therapist moderates. eCampus allows participants to send personal messages via e-mail to the teacher and to receive confidential replies. A common scenario is that the leader asks a question. Participants respond to the question and then everyone expresses an opinion to at least three of his or her peers. eCampus allows the leader to administer multiple choice quizzes and to provide instant feedback if necessary. Written exams can be taken on eCampus with a limited amount of time to respond. Links, videos, and e-books are easily shared in this format so that the learning, coaching, or counseling experiences are ultimately multimedia experiences available even in smartphones and tablets. It will be interesting to see what will come next as technology improves in these exciting times.

Twitter Twitter provides an excellent venue for sharing brief messages to many people at once, conveniently, since one need not write the same message many times. The focus is on communicating clearly with the brevity of 140 characters or less. This is possibly a new artistic writing form due to its brevity. The drawback is that one tweet must compete with hundreds of other tweets; thus, the message should be fiery enough to catch the attention of readers. The messages that one writes on Twitter become public material, and therefore, the writer must always keep this in mind when publishing in this format. For those who wish to utilize Twitter but who have longer messages, linking to a blog or one's own website gives them the chance to share additional information. Therapists and coaches can promote their services through tweets of uplifting daily thoughts linked to other sites advertising their practices. Readers will have the opportunity to re-tweet (forward) the tweets of writers whom they follow.

Tablets One of the most delightful features of tablets is the "Notes" application. With the touch of a fingertip, this application opens up along with a digital keyboard. If one continues to type with a feather touch, notes will appear in legible handwriting that rests neatly upon each of the lines of the digital notebook paper. Once the paper is completed it can be immediately uploaded in the form of an e-mail for later use. Notes written on tablets are more legible than traditional handwriting. For this reason, one questions the extent to which hard copies written by hand in ink will be useful in the future. It is possible that youths will cease to learn handwriting skills because these will be substituted with writing done on tablets and smartphones.

Androids and more to come ... Android 3.0, also known as Honeycomb, is an alternative to the iPad. The Motorola Xoom with 3G, superior to many competing tablets, was the first commercial model in the United States. Most of the tablets distributed today include Android operating systems. These tablets often include 3G which, if the user is willing to pay a monthly fee, will enable him or her to access the Internet and e-mail during travels. It will be interesting to see whether the tablets or the cellulars will be most popular. Perhaps, the two versions will be integrated into a model that meets the demands of both markets (Cisotti, 2011, pp. 16–22).

The Android application market continues to grow. There are currently 206,000 Android applications divided into practical apps and games. Each application in the Google Store includes a rich description with comments by users and comparisons to similar products. Almost everything the user wants is to be found in the Google Store. Users can load free apps with the light touch of the finger. Other apps may be purchased with a credit card which only needs to be entered into the system once. As the applications are improved upon, users will be permitted to click on upgrades for free (Galvani, 2011, pp. 8–9). Such availability of enticing apps might lead to Internet addiction if one does not choose apps wisely.

Internet Dependence

According to a study at the University of Maryland's International Center for Media and Public Agenda, a 24-hour absence from the Internet was enough to create stress and feelings of addiction (Cheng, 2011, p. 28). Although 10 countries participated in the study, the United States and China were impacted the most with at least 22 percent of the participants from these two technologically advanced countries showing signs of addiction. The students who had the most difficulty coping with no access to the Internet were the ones who utilized media for work or studies, those who depended upon it for their career success. Above all, students craved new information and felt a bodily connection with the devices. The bodily connection was described by students with the same terminology that addicts would use to describe their medications. Susan D. Moeller pointed out that *The Daily News* literally finds students by sending them news alerts on iPhone pop-ups, Twitter, Facebook, e-mail, and sidebars (Cheng, 2011, p. 30). Since news seems to search the reader, a greater issue of how to filter so much information, deciphering what is important, enters into the bigger picture of media overload. Certainly, no health care professional or therapist can make the decision for the client as to how to decide that which he or she values in terms of the vast incoming knowledge base, and it becomes complicated for clients to decide how to react to their friends' disappointment when they are not sending or receiving regular updates in the forms of tweets and other postings.

This study is representative of a great deal of research about Internet dependence as another expression and type of addiction. One goal of therapists will be to work with clients in a manner that enables them to utilize all the healthy benefits of digital technology while avoiding addictions to social network communities.

The Importance of Homework Assignments

Only during the last two generations has the importance of homework assignments in the delivery of mental health services reached its prime (Deane, Ronan, Kazantzis, & L'Abate, 2005; Detweiler-Bedell & Whisman, 2005; Kazantzis & L'Abate, 2007; L'Abate, 2011c). However, this practice has not yet reached the level of being standard operating procedure in most mental health disciplines, such as clinical psychology, counseling, psychiatry, and social work. As discussed at greater length below, thus far those disciplines have resisted changing f2f, tb, 1 and 1 practices, avoiding reliance on potentially more cost-effective practices, including distance writing. This resistance has continued to perpetuate the mystique of f2f, tb, 1 and 1 contacts, one professional, one patient (L'Abate, 2011d).

Research indicates how helpful homework assignments are. Gonzales, Schmitz, and DeLaune (2006), for instance, found a significant relationship between homework compliance and cocaine use as moderated by readiness to change. Homework compliance predicted less cocaine use during treatment but only for participants higher in readiness to change. For those lower in readiness to change, homework compliance was not associated with cocaine use during treatment. Homework compliance early in therapy was associated with better retention in treatment. Homework compliance was not predicted by level of education or readiness to change.

Kazantzis and Dattilio (2010) surveyed 827 psychologists to assess the definition of homework, use of homework tasks, and perceived importance of homework. Theoretical orientation distinguished practitioners' responses. Cognitive-behavioral therapists rated homework as being closer to empirically supported therapy, whereas psychodynamic therapists rated homework as less characteristic of a process that embraces client responsibility and adaptive skills. Cognitive-behavioral therapists did not limit their choices to activity-based tasks, and psychodynamic therapists reported the use of behavioral tasks "sometimes." Monitoring dreams and conscious thoughts were also used among the entire samples surveyed. Psychodynamic therapists rated homework as "somewhat" or "moderately" important, whereas cognitive-behavioral therapists rated homework as "very important." These results suggest that the use of homework assignments may be common to different psychotherapeutic approaches but may vary according to empirical/nonempirical orientations of various therapeutic schools.

A meta-analysis of homework effects (Kazantzis, Whittington, & Dattilio, 2010) of 46 studies ($N = 1072$) replicated and extended Kazantzis, Deane, and Ronan's (2000) classical early review and a pre–post-treatment effect size of $d = 0.83$ for control conditions and a larger $d = 1.08$ for therapy conditions of homework. A pooled effect size of $d = 0.48$ favoring homework was obtained when the analysis was restricted to controlled studies contrasting the same therapy. No evidence was found for outlier or publication bias effects. In a meta-analysis of mental and physical health workbooks administered at a distance without f2f contacts with administrators, Smyth and L'Abate (2001) found effect sizes of 0.44 for mental health and 0.25 for physical health workbooks. These results suggest that it is possible to produce significant changes in participants through programmed distance writing, as discussed at greater length in Chapter 8 of this volume.

Written homework assignments in an outpatient setting may also increase significantly the number of therapy sessions for individuals, couples, and families, compared with comparable numbers of participants who do not receive homework assignments (L'Abate, L'Abate, & Maino, 2005). However, a problem-solving workbook administered to decompensating, behaviorally disordered women in a charity hospital in Buenos Aires (L'Abate & Goldstein, 2007) cut in half the number of days in the hospital for women who completed the workbook compared with women who did not. Consequently, the setting and the specific context of a setting in and of themselves may attract different kinds of dysfunctionalities and may interact with the types of workbooks administered. This is a completely open area for research.

If an empirical orientation were to prevail, then psychotherapy could consist of a systematic assignment of homework specifically tailored to deal with the referring concern, diagnosis, question, or problem. The availability of hundreds of workbooks or interactive practice exercises (L'Abate, 2004, 2011c) makes it possible to tailor and target specific exercises for specific conditions in a way that is practically difficult, if not impossible, to achieve with unstructured f2f, tb, 1 and 1 paradigms. However, for the therapist to match those workbooks with a specific condition or referral question, a thorough evaluation, before, during, after, and follow-up is not only necessary but mandatory (L'Abate, 2011b).

One major issue in distance writing and telepsychotherapy is the importance of the therapeutic alliance as a necessary condition for positive outcome. This issue was confronted by Germain, Marchard, Bouchard, Guay, and Drouin (2010), who evaluated the therapeutic alliance through videoconferencing therapy or f2f psychotherapy with 46 participants with posttraumatic stress disorder. Seventeen participants received cognitive-behavioral therapy by videoconferencing and 29 by f2f psychotherapy. A variety of questionnaires evaluating the quality of the therapeutic relationship was administered at five different times during treatment. Each session was assessed by the therapist and by each participant immediately afterward. These results indicated that a therapeutic alliance developed very well in both treatment conditions, and there was no significant difference between the two in outcome. Given the same results from two different methods, the least expensive method should be used over the most expensive one.

Self-Help and Low-Cost Promotions

The self-help movement (Harwood & L'Abate, 2010; Latner & Wilson, 2007; Watkins & Clum, 2008) as well as low-cost approaches to promote physical and mental health (L'Abate, 2007) indicate how it is possible to help troubled people help themselves. The major issue here is to identify individuals who are motivated to ask for help from those who do not. Once identification of these individuals is accomplished, it remains to be seen who will profit by simple physical exercise, who will benefit by writing at a distance, who will benefit by f2f tb psychotherapy, and who will need medication in order to function. Individual differences in attitudes toward mental health help, education, gender, motivation, and personality make the process of identification difficult but not impossible (Fonagy, Target, Cottrell, Phillips, & Kurtz, 2002).

Objective evaluation on a pre–post-intervention basis with follow-up after termination has not yet reached the level of standard operating procedures necessary to separate artists/charlatans from professionals/scientists in the mental health and psychotherapeutic disciplines (L'Abate, 2011a, 2011d).

Additional Conceptual and Practical Advances

An important conceptual advance that is relevant to both talking and writing in mental health has been the expansion of Pennebaker's Analogic to Digital Model (De Giacomo, L'Abate, Pennebaker, & Rumbaugh, 2010). This model posits that there is an internal, ambiguous, amorphous, undefined, and, therefore, analogic mass composed perhaps of painful and hurtful experiences that may well constitute the unconscious. This process may occur at various levels of awareness, from below consciousness, that is, completely unconscious, semi/quasi-conscious, consciously admitted but not expressed, consciously admitted and expressed. Both talking and writing may allow the emergence of such a mass by providing specific, digital words and concrete terms that match in some ways some aspects of that mass that will allow their emergence, providing some relief and perhaps some solution and/or resolution in f2f tb psychotherapy as well as in writing (Hillix, Rumbaugh, & Savave-Rumbaugh, in press; L'Abate, 2011d).

Another important advance has been the rise of and need for structured interventions in mental health, especially with severe illnesses, rather than online therapy mimicking unstructured traditional f2f tb psychotherapy. Structured intervention allows matching a symptom, concern, or disorder with a specific structured program specifically developed to deal with that symptom, concern, or disorder for a specified length of time, and cost given beforehand (L'Abate, 2008a, 2008b, 2011c). This issue will be expanded in Chapter 8 of this volume.

An important practical advance pertains to the evaluation of which approach, among a plethora of approaches, is more relevant for which individual, couple, or family. Who is going to evaluate whom, how, and how much and which methods of evaluation should be used (L'Abate, 2011b)? A great many instruments to evaluate functionally and dysfunctionality have been developed in the hundreds. However, most of them have been validated empirically without any link to or connection with any theory or to any clinical or preventive practice. A possible solution to fill in this gap between theory, research, and practice will be presented in Chapter 8 of this volume.

Consequently, a whole battery of validated, theory-derived, relational instruments has been developed by L'Abate, Cusinato, Maino, Colesso, and Scilletta (2010). Most of these instruments take only a few minutes to administer and to score. Combined with other ecologically oriented, but still experimental self-report, paper-and-pencil tests (L'Abate, 2008a, 2008b), such a battery, combined with the Brief Psychiatric Symptom List, and the Beck Depression Inventory should allow to determine what preventive, psychotherapeutic, or medical approach may be necessary according to a stepped-case approach discussed in Chapter 10 of this volume.

Inevitable Resistance and Maintenance of Status Quo in Mental Health

This resistance lies on not giving up two seemingly magical paradigms in mental health: f2f tb and 1on1 interventions (L'Abate, 2011c, 2011d). Apparently, both uncritically and normatively accepted paradigms are believed and considered as the main, if not the sole, ways to improve maladjustment or even deal with psychopathology. These paradigms are by now so pervasively ingrained in our clinical evaluative, preventive, and therapeutic practices that to propose otherwise is akin to being viewed as a traitor and risking alienation from the mainstream establishment of most mental health communities (Barlow, 2010; Castonguay, Boswell, Costantino, Goldfried, & Hill, 2010; Dimidjian & Hollon, 2010). The dissemination and implementation of evidence-based f2f tb psychological treatments have contributed substantially to the legitimacy of both paradigms.

Of course, there is no denying that evolutionarily and historically f2f tb and 1on1 paradigms have been major breakthroughs in helping people at all levels of functionality and dysfunctionality during the last century, preventively, psychotherapeutically, and rehabilitatively. However, critical issues must be raised about the cost-effectiveness of both paradigms in comparison with less expensive approaches and interventions, such as online distance writing, that would allow mental health professionals to reach and help more people per unit of professional time than through f2f, tb, 1 and 1 personal contacts.

The issue here is cost: How are mental health professionals going to make effective use of their limited time? As long as f2f, tb, 1 and 1 contacts are the norm, the effectiveness of professional time will be limited to 8 hours a day, plus or minus however many hours a professional wants to use. Commonly, a professional may see between 20 and 30 participants a week, depending, of course, on how much extra time is needed to write notes, send out reports, answer phone calls, and so forth.

With the advent of the computer and the Internet, a sea change is taking place in how mental health services will be delivered and how mental health professionals may increase their effectiveness above and beyond f2f, tb, 1 and 1 contacts. The professional impact of using both traditional paradigms is going to be limited, given the great need for mass-produced interventions rather than for f2f tb and 1on1 approaches (L'Abate, 2011c).

Consequently, how are mental health professionals going to make more effective use of their time and expertise to help a greater and wider number of participants than is possible through f2f, tb, 1 and 1 contacts? *The answer to that question lies in relying more than heretofore on homework assignments administered at a distance through writing and through a hierarchy of professional, semiprofessional, and technical personnel, using computers and the Internet with a minimum of f2f, tb, 1 and 1 personal contacts.*

This answer suggests that this change is not only possible but within the grasp of most mental health professionals who are willing and able to expand, upgrade, and update their clinical skills and practices to enter into this century and make an impact on the urgent and expanding mental health needs here and abroad (L'Abate, 2007, 2008a, 2008b, 2011a, 2011b). These growing needs are not going to be met by f2f tb 1on1 paradigms.

Resistance to Change: Reasons for Keeping the Status Quo in Mental Health

In addition to a hierarchical mechanical/technical/paraprofessional/professional distinction in mental health and psychotherapy, there is another important dichotomy that is still pervasive in mental health and psychotherapy, and that is the creative artist versus the professional scientist. The main goal of the former is personal creativity without regard to cost and without pre–post intervention, evaluation, and follow-up. The main goal of the latter is cost-effectiveness, evaluated with pre–post intervention evaluation and follow-up some time after termination.

Changes in professional practices are very difficult to effect. The very profession that is dedicated to producing changes in others is the one that is very resistant to change, very resistant to moving on from f2f, tb, 1 and 1 to more cost-effective ways to practice (L'Abate, 2011b, 2011c). Resistance to change and fear of change are predictable in our profession as well as in our participants. This resistance occurs through various rationalizations for keeping the status quo in mental health and psychotherapy. We will include the most common ones we have heard from various professionals over the years since the laboratory method was implemented (L'Abate, 2008a, 2008b, 2008c). Here is a sample of statements made by representative mental health professionals to justify the status quo in psychotherapy: Each reason answers the stem sentence

> **"The main reason for keeping f2f tb one-on-one approach in mental health and psychotherapy is ..."**
>
> ***"To establish rapport or keep a therapeutic alliance"***

This argument no longer holds water when we consider the establishment of a plethora of relationships occurring online every day. The therapeutic alliance was predicated on talk between one therapist and one participant being the main if not the only medium of communication and healing available in the past. This assumption, however, is no longer tenable as we change over from talk to writing at a distance as the main medium of communication and healing.

> ***"This is the best way I know to help; I do not know of other ways."***

This is perhaps the most honest answer to the question about keeping f2f tb in evaluation and interventions. However, this answer indicates how inadequately and how restrictively most mental health professionals in general and psychotherapists in particular have been trained up to the present time; mental health training thus far has been conducted as if f2f tb and 1on1 practice were the only ways to help people in distress (Castonguay et al., 2010), as a nonreplicable art rather than a replicable, professional–scientific method. That is regressive training for the past rather than progressive training for the future.

As DeMaria (2003) indicated, for instance, most psychotherapists are completely ignorant of (or more charitably, one could say that they choose to be uninformed about) less expensive and perhaps more effective ways to help, such as self-help (Harwood & L'Abate, 2010), low-cost promotional approaches, nonverbal, physical approaches, and preventive and psychotherapeutic interventions based on homework assignments (Kazantzis & L'Abate, 2007; L'Abate, 2007) available to them and to their participants (L'Abate, 2011b). Unfortunately, the myths and mystiques of the f2f, tb, 1 and 1 approach as the only way to help troubled people are so ingrained, especially in current training practices, that it will take a revolution to help most training programs enter this century rather than remaining regressively fixated in the past century. Cost-effectiveness, as required by most insurance companies, may require abandoning less cost-effective practices such as f2f, tb, 1 and 1 approaches.

"If I listen closely, I will be able to help any individual."

Listening implies that the professional possess some magical knowledge or intuition that will allow him or her to identify what approach to use to help distressed individuals, couples, and families. This process means that the professional relies on his or her personal and professional experience and training to reach some kind of plan to treat the symptoms or reason for referral, concern, or complaint. This process, therefore, is entirely subjective and completely dependent on the professional's opinion, no matter how faulty or incomplete, making the whole process close to artistry and as unprofessional as possible.

The issue here is not just to listen subjectively but to evaluate intersubjectively and objectively the immediate and distant contexts of the complaint (L'Abate, 2011a, 2001b). Listening implies that if the participant continues to talk, eventually the professional will come up, through some mysterious, intuitive, and nonreplicable route, with the correct solution for any problem. F2f, tb, 1 and 1 therefore, remains the only solution for all psychological problems, real or imagined, either in professionals or in our participants.

"No one else can replace my scintillating personality, my effervescent style, or my insightful, intuitive evaluative and therapeutic approach."

This conceit is the natural outcome of the three previous explanations, making the professional the ultimate problem solver of all problems or complaints. No external, objective instruments or methods are necessary because they would diminish the omnipotence projected by the professional. This conceit may be excusable in psychotherapists not trained as clinical psychologists, but, as I argue elsewhere (L'Abate, 2011b), it is inexcusable and downright unethical in clinical psychologists who have received extensive psychometric training to evaluate people.

All of the above reasons hide one major phobia in psychotherapists, and that is the avoidance of structured interventions and uncritical overreliance instead on unstructured interventions that would maximize the role and importance of the uniquely distinct and uncontrollable personal contribution of the therapist. The bottom line of professional resistance to change is the desire to be "creative" and avoid anything that sounds or looks like uniformly prepackaged, already canned, or prescribed psychotherapy by replicable written prescriptions or recipes rather than through nonreplicable words. This desire separates the professional as artist/charlatan from the professional as scientist (L'Abate, 2011b). This desire will disappear only when professional associations will judge it for what it is: an unethical excuse for unchecked variability and inexcusable, vainglorious, unnecessarily self-centered conceit.

"I need to observe all the nuanced non-verbal behavior that is relevant to my evaluation."

In the second author's experience with the laboratory method (L'Abate, 2008c), Pink Ladies volunteers and graduate students, trained to record verbal and nonverbal behaviors, were just as good as any doctorate-level psychologist we have met. The Ph.D. degree in and of itself does not grant more specific powers of observation and recording than responsible and responsive individuals can achieve with proper training.

Implications for Future Education and Training in Mental Health

The best source of information about the context of writing and information processing we could find was Knoop's visionary chapter (2011). He made a great many qualified predictions that, if they would not occur soon, there is little doubt that they will occur because the future is "rapidly approaching" (p. 98), perhaps faster than we thought possible in our wildest dreams. Who would have thought a generation ago that we would correspond, keep in contact, transfer information, help and even heal the sick, and innovate through so many apps that are created literally every day and night of the week? Knoop asserted almost idealistically that "The fitness of any society depends on the quality of its institutions" (p. 99). This quality depends on how competitive societies are, especially in their educational institutions. Schools, therefore, will need to be *competitive* in order to survive and help the nations they represent to survive. Effective learning depends on self-reinforcing meaning, engagement, and positive emotions. Who is happy and comfortable with oneself is more likely to learn more and faster than someone who is not that comfortable. Hence, schools have to be "happy places" to learn, and even more importantly, teach students how to learn by ourselves.

Within the context of these predictions, Knoop (2011, pp. 101–103) proposed 15 hypotheses about how learning will be much the same in 2025 as it is now:

- The more physically and mentally healthy learners are, they more they will learn.
- The more autonomy and control over their own situation that learners experience while learning, the more they will learn.
- The better role models for learning and creativity that teachers are the more learners will learn. By creative Knoop means being more curious, innovative, socially caring, and technologically skilled. It is no wonder that one publishing house recently produced a two-volume encyclopedia of creativity (Runco & Pritzker, 2011), a handbook of organizational creativity (Mumford, 2011), and a third volume about theories, themes, research, development, and practice in creativity (Runco, 2006). Competition and comparative outcome in societies and their academic institutions will be based on how creative and innovative teachers are.
- The more intrinsically motivated learners are (i.e., the more they enjoy learning), the more they will learn and to contribute to the greater good of their society.

- The more positivity — specifically joy, gratitude, serenity, interest, hope, pride, amusement, inspiration, awe, and love — learners experience in their lives, the more they will learn.
- The more of an attractive future learners see for themselves, the more they will learn and more likely to learn how to learn.
- The better the teaching matches the intellectual strengths of learners, the more they will learn.
- The better the teaching matches character strength of learners, the more they will learn.
- The better the teaching matches the style of learners, the more they will learn.
- The more aesthetically rich and sense stimulating the teaching, the learning environment is, the more learners will learn.
- The more teaching and learning resemble a journey of discovery in which the learner is involved, the more learners will learn.
- The more creative learners are allowed to be, the more they will learn.
- The more authentically and socially connected the learners are, the more they will learn.
- The more learners experience a combination of being socially differentiated as unique individuals, the more they will learn.
- The more learners will experience a combination of positive support and challenge, the more they will learn.

At the conclusion of this list, Knoop integrated them (p. 103) into a model of general, processual ideals that predict academic and social success across political spectra, disciplines, and personal aspirations.

Afterwards, Knoop (pp. 103–107) introduced 13 scenarios about what will be very different in 2025:

- By 2025, there will be a great many new ways to improve physical and mental health by acquiring writing skills that will allow one to find as much information online to make education and psychotherapy based on 1on1, f2f tb interventions irrelevant or too expensive.
- It will be much easier than in 2010 to teach precisely enough to accommodate late learners' need for autonomy and control over their education.
- Teachers by then will be more curious, innovative, socially caring, and technically skilled to be good role models for their students.
- Schools will be organized to accommodate a very high degree of learner enjoyment through learning.
- Digital, technological evolution will presumably happen at least a thousand times as fast as in 2010.
- It will be possible to tailor learning quite precisely in accord with learners' intellectual strengths through brain scans and advanced psychological testing.
- Most learners will have a solid understanding of their own preferred styles across a variety of relevant settings.

- Both physical and virtual learning environments will be aesthetically rich and sense stimulating.
- It will be possible to take advantage of digital media to stimulate almost everything during teaching.
- There will be fantastic possibilities for creativity in almost all settings.
- It will be possible to be online everywhere and in constant contact with anyone, anywhere, anytime, thus strengthening commercial, educational, industrial, and personal connectedness.
- It will be generally acknowledged that the overall aim of any school worth its name will be to reinforce and stimulate the flourishing of individuals learning above and beyond what can be imagined in the present.
- Complementary values of science: openness to innovation but critical skepticism about whatever comes down the pike of creativity and innovation.

Conclusion

Knoop (p. 107) concluded his visionary list of present and future educational practices by predicting that: "The education of the future will be concerned not only with optimizing the experience of the individual learners because it is subjectively the best, but also because it is materially/economically the most sustainable." Whether all these predictions will come to pass will be left to those who will live and survive until 2025. There is no doubt, however, that most education will be digital and relying mainly on writing rather than on talking.

Chapter 2

Writing in Physical and Concomitant Mental Illness: Biological Underpinnings and Applications for Practice

Brenda Stockdale

> "*Illness is the night-side of life, a more onerous citizenship. Everyone who is born holds dual citizenship, in the kingdom of the well and the kingdom of the sick.*"
>
> — Susan Sontag

Even though some introductory parts of this chapter may overlap with those of Chapter 3 in this volume, emphasis will be on physical and mental illnesses that may have not received there the emphasis given here. We are mindful that: "At least half of all deaths in the United States have behavioral and social factors as significant causes ..." due, in part, to "the interaction of psychological, social and cultural factors with biochemistry and physiology," according to the Associate Director of Behavioral and Social Sciences Research at the National Institute of Health (NIH) (Ray, 2004) resulting in an emergent biopsychosocial model of health care. Accordingly, health psychologists and other clinicians actively promote the utilization of evidence-based methods that reduce stress and upgrade quality of life through a variety of practices and techniques. The efficacy and cost-saving potential have not been lost on insurers who have added behavioral medicine codes to reimburse for the treatment of heart disease, diabetes, autoimmunity, pain management, and overall wellness. Recent findings in multiple disciplines including neuroscience, immunology, and epigenetics shed light on how

Research on Writing Approaches in Mental Health
Studies in Writing, Volume 23, 23–35

ISSN: 1572-6304/doi: 10.1108/S1572-6304(2011)0000023006

behavioral medicine techniques, including soft interventions like expressive writing (EW), can influence physiological processes and strengthen coping mechanisms. (For the purpose of simplicity, the phrase "expressive writing" will substitute for all variations, denominators, and categories of writing for health unless otherwise specified.)

The Biological Underpinnings of Writing for Health

The practicality and potential benefit of EW as a viable technique for those facing a chronic or catastrophic diagnosis are offset by a general lack of awareness among health care providers along with contradictory findings resulting in a comparatively limited utilization of this low-cost medium. Fundamental to the expansion of EW in medical settings is an appreciation of mind/body mediation systems; namely, that the nervous, endocrine, and immune systems "... have receptors on critical cells that can receive information (via messenger molecules) from each of the other systems" (Ray, 2004). Since the limbic system, an area of the brain that regulates emotion, is 40% richer in neuropeptides (than other nervous tissue) that connect in lock and key fashion to immune cells, psychoeducational tools and methods that enhance emotional integration can be potent immunological modulators. Immune cells also secrete their own neurotransmitters that likewise connect back to the limbic system. The feedback loops are systemwide and include the cardiovascular system, neuroendocrine system, and enteric nervous system, each playing an active role in the conversation between mind and body. While our exposure to toxins and our diet affect the way our genes are expressed, our thoughts, feelings and the way we respond to stress are also potent immune and genetic modulators. Thus psychosocial interventions, including EW, that enhance emotional regulation have emerged as key players in brain and immune physiology (Hölzel et al., 2010; Lepore, Greenberg, Bruno, & Smyth, 2002; Smyth & Argo, 2009). Within that framework, this chapter attempts to evaluate findings both positive and negative in order to further critical methodologies apropos to a chronic illness population, including the recognition of personality constructs presenting particular risk and the value of expanded instruction in the form of psychoeducation and EW strategy.

How the Mind Hurts and Heals the Body

More than a decade ago even minor daily hassles were shown to be "strongly related to somatic symptoms ... even after the effects of major life changes were statistically removed" (Wickramasekera, 1998). Today we have even stronger evidence that chronic stress is a "... major way of upsetting important health-related homeostatic systems ..." (Ray, 2004). Stressful events trigger fight-or-flight responses due to activation of the sympathetic-adrenomedullary (SAM) axis, releasing catecholamines such as epinephrine and norepinephrine which in turn mobilize a variety of organ and tissue adaptations. Desirable and beneficial to survival in the short term, prolonged activation of the sympathetic nervous system increases susceptibility to morbidity (Cohen, Janicki-Deverts, & Miller, 2007). Strong evidence pinpoints chronic stress as a correlative factor in a wide range of medical conditions, including hypertension, cardiovascular disease, autoimmunity, infectious illnesses, diabetes, ischemic heart disease, chronic obstructive pulmonary disease and even cancer (Brown et al., 2010; Dube et al., 2009; Felitti et al., 1998; Sherman, Bunyan, & Creswell, 2009). While no single mechanism has been identified, the cumulative toll of chronic stress has been found to lower antioxidant levels, reduce natural killer cells, shrink telomeres (a biomarker of aging), degrade bone, shrink the hippocampus (due to neuronal death), negatively affect insulin sensitivity, increase platelet aggregation, and negatively impact epigenetic expression. At the very least, maladaptive coping mechanisms and patterns contribute "to allostatic load — the cumulative burden of coping with repeated stressors which instigates negative changes in physiological processes, leading to disease initiation and/or progression" (Temoshok et al., 2008, p. 787). Additionally, high-stress individuals present an exaggerated inflammatory response (increase in Interleukin 6, one of several inflammatory cytokines) found in a broad range of health disorders including depression, which can accompany and even contribute to morbidity and mortality (Miller, Maletic, & Raison, 2009; Pace et al., 2006; Ray, 2004). Depression itself releases inflammatory cytokines — promoting inflammation — precisely the same as in physical illness. Over time, proinflammatory cytokines reduce hippocampal volume (the memory center of the brain) and promote diabetes, depression, cancer and even heart disease (Miller et al., 2009; Raison et al., 2010).

The contributory allostatic load of chronic stress is compounded by massive sympathetic arousal that can occur when confronting mortality in life-threatening situations. Hence, means by which individuals can enhance their coping skills — achieving a balance between over- and underreacting — have neuroendocrine, immune, and epigenetic correlates. The role of EW, and disclosure, takes on particular significance in view of the impact of stress, neglect, and family dysfunction in childhood on adult health.

Stress, Inflammation, and Early Life

Bearing this out is a watershed study of over 17,000 participants from the Centers for Disease Control (CDC). The Adverse Childhood Experiences (ACE) Study (Dube et al., 2009; Felitti, 2009; Felitti et al., 1998) established that stress in childhood is a stronger predictor of serious illness in adulthood than smoking history, cholesterol, or obesity. An increase of disease (ischemic heart disease, chronic obstructive pulmonary disease, autoimmunity, lung cancer, and other leading causes of death) in the hundreds of percents was found in those with elevated ACEs *after* accounting for all other traditional risk factors (Brown et al., 2010).[1]

Unexpected clinical significance was discovered post-publication when a company specializing in neural net analysis offered two years of follow-up on 120,000 participants who had undergone a comprehensive medical evaluation using the ACE-based questionnaire. The result was a 35% drop in doctor's office visits, an 11% drop in emergency room visits, and a 3% drop in hospitalizations compared to the year before. Felitti, one of the lead authors explains "... what all of us associated with this work believe. We were asking, and people were telling us the worst secrets of their lives, and they were still accepted as human beings" (Stockdale, 2009, p. 160).

Secrets Kept from the Mind but not the Body

The physiological effects of disclosure as measured on a variety of indicators were well documented by Pennebaker and Chung (2007) more than two decades ago. Hundreds of later studies though bear contradictory findings. For example, a meta-analysis of 146 randomized studies (Frattaroli, 2006) found salutary but modest effects, whereas other studies failed to find benefit (de Moor et al., 2008; Honos-Webb, Harrick, Stiles, & Park, 2000) including a meta-analysis of 30 randomized controlled trials representing 2294 participants (Harris, 2006). Smyth and Pennebaker's (2008) examination of the data conclude that "expressive writing works some times and not others and that methodological features, mediators and moderators and outcome measures need to be 'revisited' 'in search of the right recipe' for, or 'boundary conditions' of, expressive writing" (Nicholls, 2009).

---

[1]Examining factors predictive of becoming a creative writer Kohányi (2005) found a correlation between mood disorders and an atypical amount of stress in childhood. Nevertheless, Kohányi suggests that potential developmental influences such as an enriched environment, verbal fluency, and a rich imaginative life lead to resilience and are collectively protective of adverse stress in childhood. The risks of allostatic loading, however, do not appear to be offset by an enriched environment but are, in and of themselves, linked to increase in mental (and physical) illness (Edwards, Holden, & Felitti, 2003) contraindicating an association with resilience. In a matched control study of female writers, Ludwig (1994) found, as Kohányi did, higher rates of multiple mental disorders among writers; but unlike Kohányi, higher rates of drug abuse were also noted. In this limited sample of 59 writers and 59 matched controls the dysfunction was indicative of physical and/or sexual abuse in childhood. Wisely, the authors acknowledge the relationship between creativity and mood disorders is a complex one. (Indeed, Andreasen (1987) further suggests a genetic determinant.) Rounding out the picture is the phenomenon of dissociation, which has been linked to creativity (Zoler, 2008). While dissociation is found in healthy populations, in one sample of more than 1000 individuals an elevated dissociative rate was five times higher than average for children who had been physically abused (Mulder, Beautrais, Joyce, & Fergusson, 1998). While creative writers may have enriched environments as noted by Kohányi, those factors — while likely stimulating literary genius — do not appear to correct for the mental and physical sequelae documented in this population. Bearing this out is an investigation of more than 8000 individuals in a relatively well-educated, upper middle class environment (one that would not preclude "enrichment") documenting a strong graded relationship between ACEs and mental illness (Edwards, Holden, & Felitti, 2003).

Equivocal findings can, in part, be explained by the fact that until the year 2000 few studies focused on outcome moderators. Since then — although more research is clearly needed — numerous moderators have been evaluated and those linked to enhanced outcome will be summarized later in this chapter. It is critical to note, however, that none of these analyses included the ACE Study and the follow-up findings of 120,000 individuals. The author believes the exclusion results from the unfortunate but common separation of psychological and medical research and the data should be acknowledged as potentially representing the largest sample to date on the medical benefits of disclosure. Important, too, is that while beneficial effects of Frattaroli's meta-analysis (2006) were relatively modest overall, a number of conditions positively affected are extensive and frequently found to be statistically significant. For example, asthma and rheumatoid arthritis patients showed improvements in lung function and joint mobility (Smyth & Argo, 2009), whereas "significant improvement in disease severity" was documented among patients with irritable bowel syndrome (Halpert, Rybin, & Doros, 2006). EW also proved effective in regulating sinus rhythm (Sloan & Epstein, 2005). Multiple studies involving cancer patients also report health benefits described as "significant" including general improvement in physical health, reduction in physical symptoms, medical appointments for cancer-related morbidities, a reduction in pain overall, better sleep (which has anti-inflammatory effects), and higher daytime functioning (de Moor et al., 2002; Henry, Schlegel, Talley, Molix, & Bettencourt, 2010; Low, Stanton, & Danoff-Burg, 2006; Rosenberg et al., 2002; Stanton & Danoff-Burg, 2002). In an even-handed review Baikie and Wilhelm (2005) summarizes further findings:

> "Patients with HIV infection showed improved immune response similar to that seen in mono-therapy with anti-HIV drugs (Petrie et al., 2004) and individuals with cystic fibrosis showed a significant reduction in hospital-days over a 3-month period (Taylor et al., 2003). Women with chronic pelvic pain reported reductions in pain intensity ratings (Norman et al., 2004) and poor sleepers reported shorter sleep-onset latency (Harvey & Farrell, 2003). Benefits have also been found for post-operative course after papilloma resection (Solano et al., 2003) and for primary care patients (Klapow et al., 2001; Gidron et al., 2002) ..." **Baikie concludes**, "... there is sufficient evidence for clinicians to begin applying expressive writing in therapeutic settings with caution. Indeed, Spiegel (1999) noted that a drug intervention reporting medium effect sizes similar to those found for expressive writing (Smyth, 1998) would be regarded as a major medical advance ... given its simplicity, expressive writing appears to have great potential as a therapeutic tool in diverse clinical settings or as a means of self-help, either alone or as an adjunct to traditional therapies." (Baikie & Wilhelm, 2005, p. 342)

The dichotomy is also due, in part, to that few studies have focused on who would most benefit from EW. The last decade has seen an increase in such investigations but they are still relatively rare and not necessarily well integrated with mind–body constructs. This challenge is compounded by the written disclosure paradigm itself which assumes an ability to identify and distinguish between a wide range and mix of emotional states (Kennedy & Franklin, 2002). This is of critical import as individuals limited in this regard are found in statistically greater numbers with chronic illness than in the general population. As identifying and expressing emotion appears to be protective against physical illness (Kennedy & Franklin, 2002), those with difficulty in discerning feeling states may be particularly vulnerable to illness and likely poor candidates for short-term EW. "Beneficial outcomes occur when people recognize and acknowledge personally stressful experiences, access and activate emotional memories of those experiences, identify and put into words their emotions, and eventually think differently about the experience" (Lumley, Tojek, & Macklem, p. 75).

Alexithymia and Repressive Coping

Not surprisingly then, alexithymia and the related construct of repressive coping have emerged as distinct risk factors for certain chronic conditions. A relatively recent term, alexithymia was coined in 1972 and is described as having "no words for feelings" (Uher, 2010) or "a lack of words to express emotion (a: absence of; lexi: words; thymia: emotions, affects)" (Guilbaud, Corcos, Hjalmarsson, Loas, & Jeammet, 2003). The inability to recognize and accurately identify feelings leads to maladaptive responses directly contributing to allostatic load (Temoshok et al., 2008). Alexithymia is not only considered a factor of vulnerability for a variety of medical conditions (Baikie & Wilhelm, 2005) but also now associated with a number of illnesses including asthma, cancer (de Timary, Roy, Luminet, Fillee, & Mikolajczak, 2008), autoimmune-inflammatory diseases (Bruni et al., 2006), progression of HIV (Temoshok et al., 2008), reduced levels of natural killer cells (Dewaraja et al., 1997), idiopathic hypertension, poor metabolic control among diabetics and proved predictive of all-cause mortality even after controlling for medical risk factors (Lumley et al., 2002; Wickramasekera, 1998). The denial of distress appears to skew the delicate balance of the two arms of the immune system (Th-1 or "cellular"/Th-2 or "humoral"), resulting in overactivation of the sympathetic nervous system, further disrupting autonomic, neuroendocrine, and immune systems, thereby increasing inflammation and an individual's overall risk for stress-related disorders and disease (Corcos et al., 2004; Guilbaud, Corcos, Hjalmarsson, Loas, & Jeammet, 2003; Uher, 2010). For a more detailed, theory-derived account of research about alexithymia, the interested reader may consult Cusinato and L'Abate (in press).

Emotional identification exercises that assist an individual's ability to identify, experience, and discriminate between emotional states have been found to be beneficial for those high in alexithymia (Baikie & Wilhelm, 2005; Kennedy & Franklin, 2002). In Kennedy and Franklin's (2002) work, psychoeducation included a discussion of what feelings are and why they are important along with identification of eight primary emotional states: fear, anger, joy, sadness, acceptance, disgust, expectancy, and surprise. EW homework included writing about how feelings were handled in their family of origin, exercises designed to develop an emotional vocabulary, keeping a "feeling journal," and relating feelings to physical symptoms and sensations. Over time, patients were less ambivalent about emotional expression and were able to experience and identify a range of feelings. Without such specific training alexithymics may be inclined to "vent" when instructed to write their innermost thoughts and feelings [a typical experimental assignment considered counterproductive in terms of health (Baikie & Wilhelm, 2005)] skewing EW outcomes as well, since screening for alexithymia is rare. (For written and structure interactive practice exercises about feelings and emotions, please consult references contained in the previous Chapter 7 of this volume.)

Psychoeducation, Biofeedback, and Expressive Writing

Psychoeducational programs have been established in a number of domains including cognitive behavioral therapy (CBT) with attendant physical benefit. Low-cost psychoeducation and homework that increases the ability to accurately label feeling states reduce physiological arousal and may improve outcome measures in all EW groups whether or not alexithymia is present (Creswell et al., 2007a; Graham et al., 2009; Simha-Alpern, 2007). Functional neuroimaging reveals labeling one's emotions through words, as in mindfulness-based cognitive therapy, attenuates responses in the amygdala, promotes cognitive reappraisal, reduces anxiety and negative affect, and lowers inflammatory cytokines (Creswell et al., 2007a; Hölzel et al., 2010; Miller, Maletic, & Raison, 2009). At least one study shows that feeling identification exercises reduce the risk of cardiac problems and suggests that neurocognitive mechanisms improve health outcomes (Creswell et al., 2007a; Lumley et al., 2002). The link is not surprising considering that factors such as hostility, anxiety, depression, overregulation, and inhibition or suppression of emotional responses are implicated in asthma, arthritis, coronary artery disease, and cancer (Lepore et al., 2002). Although alexithymics have difficulty in identifying a range of specific emotions they may acknowledge that they feel "upset"; in contrast to repressors who insist despite the evidence that "everything is fine" as disclosure "threatens their self-image" (Lumley et al., 2002, p. 80). Repressors, as measured by the Marlowe–Crowne or Lie scale are at further risk for serious health effects since denial can dysregulate autonomic nervous system (ANS) functions (Wickramasekera, 1998). Patients may not consciously feel disturbed by low levels of depression or anxiety, but their cold hands, back pain, or headache may signal otherwise. The denial of psychological distress is also linked with physiological arousal as measured by biofeedback (Electroencephalogram (EEG), Electromyogram (EMG), temperature, moisture, and/or blood pressure). Visible measures of reactivity can effectively remove the denial of emotional distress, encourage curiosity (about the change in blood pressure, for example), and open a window to resolution with physiological and psychological benefit. Inexpensive and easy-to-use Biodots (recommended in Harvard's Mind–Body Medicine) can accompany feeling identification and writing exercises with positive outcomes. As patients track their hand temperature (or muscle tension, etc.) along with their thoughts and feelings, patterns emerge and the ability to deny physiological distress is reduced.

Even so, writing about distressing experiences can result in a temporary increase in negative affect. Specific instructions, such as those found in *Interapy* (Lange, van de Ven, Schrieken, & Emmelkamp, 2002) where EW is flanked by alternative activities along with distinct recommendations that integrate cognitive aspects of the experience can reduce the likelihood of a patient being overwhelmed and create a "container" (Nicholls, 2009) for the process. However, and without apparent conflict, gratitude emerges as a positive influence on all counts even affecting heart rate variability, which "provides a powerful, noninvasive measure of neurocardiac function that reflects heart–brain interactions and autonomic nervous system dynamics, which are particularly sensitive to changes in emotional states" (Emmons & McCullough, 2004, p. 233). Writing prompts focused on the recognition and cultivation of gratitude would have potential benefit in most patient populations.

The Brain Is A Narrative Organ

Mindfulness practice, supported and fine-tuned with cognitive restructuring in expressive and narrative writing is rarely used in research settings. Yet, the integration of emotional and cognitive aspects of an experience has biological implications for as we change our "... minds, we are changing our biology" (Creswell et al., 2007a; Ray, 2004, p. 32). The stories we create about our lives, and who we are, affect the very architecture of the brain, stimulating neurogenesis when inspired and negatively affecting neuronal health when adversely challenged (Lipton, 2005; Rossi, 2002). The shift in thinking is evidenced by Columbia University's "narrative evidence-based medicine" (NEBM) program in recognition of "... the narrative features of all data and the evidentiary status of all clinical text" (Charon, 2008, p. 297).

Establishing or reestablishing a coherent and supportive narrative is an established component of trauma treatment (Baikie & Wilhelm, 2005; Simha-Alpern, 2007) as well as wellness paradigms. The narrative format (including a beginning, middle, and an end) that includes emotional and cognitive elements — as opposed to fragments of disjoined feelings more commonly suited to poetry — may have further benefit. Kaufman and Sexton consider "... an abundance of evidence that professional poets have poorer health outcomes relative to both other writers and to the population at large" and conclude, "The formation of a narrative, an element often missing in poetry, may provide the answer" (2006, p. 268). The narrative function can also assist in meaning making, and mobilizing defenses (Willig, 2009). Pennebaker (2001), through a computerized program (the Linguistic Inquiry and Word Count) analyzed 82 language categories and found that participants using insight words such as "understand" and "realize" and causal words such as "because" and "reason" had improved outcomes (Baikie & Wilhelm, 2005). In like manner, EW can provide a framework for the examination of deeply held beliefs, including familial and cultural, about treatment and the potential for recovery. This can be of critical import as expectations of medical procedures and treatment influence outcomes (Mondloch, Cole, & Frank, 2001; Ray, 2004). An outgrowth of EW is the emerging trend of developmental creative writing (DCW) which seeks to bridge the gap between expressive and creative writing (Nicholls, 2009). While DCW frees itself from the standard experimental confines characterizing EW research by promoting long-term and open-ended creative writing projects, data is currently limited. Patients may be unable, or unwilling to participate in ongoing creative writing groups. The time involved in shaping a narrative or autobiographical piece in DCW may be unsuited to those who have little interest in writing as a hobby. Yet it is exciting to see how future research plays out in NEBM and DCW over time, increasing the spectrum and utilization of EW in a variety of settings. The recent cultural phenomenon of Internet support groups (Murray, 2009) may meet the need for connection and solve the problem of isolation experienced by many with chronic illness. The method of connecting through a narrative where written disclosure connects individuals with similar diagnoses in a supportive way could provide benefits only recently explored. A promising investigation found *women with breast cancer benefited from written disclosure in online support groups resulting in greater improvements in health, self-efficacy, emotional well-being, and functional well-being* (Shim, Capella, & Han, 2011). Online forums may offer the opportunity of gradually and safely "open up" and disclose, while receiving altruistic benefit by offering supportive feedback to others in the group.

On Mood and Mortality

Since EW is an accepted tool in enhancing self-regulation (cognitive, behavioral, and affect) by extension its potential for enhancing coping and quality of life cannot be underestimated. For example, EW proved to be of particular benefit to women with metastatic breast cancer who had little emotional support (Low, Stanton, Bower, & Gyllenhammer, 2010) and in a randomized group of 93 early-stage breast cancer patients EW enhanced perception of social support along with greater levels of subjective well-being up to six months post-intervention (Gellaitry, Peters, Bloomfield, & Horne, 2008). Approximately half of 71 leukemia and lymphoma patients reported that "writing resulted in changes in their thoughts about their illness" and were "significantly associated with better physical quality of life at follow-up (Morgan, Graves, Poggi, & Cheson, 2008, p. 59). While a positive attitude is a cliché in mind–body medicine, and not without conflict in the current debate over positive psychology, longitudinal studies spanning decades indicate explanatory style to be a significant predictor of longevity (Maruta Colligan, Malinchoc, & Offord, 2002; Peterson, Seligman, & Vaillant, 1988; Steptoe, O'Donnell, Badrick, Kumari, &

Marmot, 2008; Xu & Roberts, 2010). Pennebaker's findings that word choice (an indicator of explanatory style) is not fixed across the life span (Pennebaker & Stone, 2003) make this an especially compelling topic. Yet findings investigating posttraumatic growth and its sister construct, benefit finding, are conflicting and warrant caution over EW methods focusing on these constructs exclusively is a concern for multiple reasons (Aspinwall & Tedeschi, 2010; Slavin-Spenny, Cohen, Oberleitner, & Lumbley, 2010). The psychological constraints previously discussed, of alexithymia and repressive coping, may be at play. For individuals who have processed a range of emotions, a description of "benefits" resulting from diagnosis (i.e., "I learned who my real friends were," "I re-discovered a spiritual perspective in life," etc.) may indeed be therapeutic. But for those unable to define and differentiate feelings or who are actively suppressing, a similar focus may be counterproductive.

Implications for Depression, Anxiety, and PTSD

A key element of therapeutic writing as an intervention in health-related disorders is improvement in quality of life and mitigating emotional disturbance; therefore, it has potential application for anxiety, depression, and posttraumatic stress disorder (PTSD) occurring concomitantly or secondary to the disease itself. This presents a significant challenge in physically ill populations and particularly in PTSD in which symptoms can be mislabeled to suppress the trauma. The unfortunate result is that concomitant psychiatric illness often remains undiagnosed — and hence untreated — as symptoms can mirror side effects of the physical condition and/or treatment with each compounding and exacerbating the other.

The awareness that a chronic illness can trigger PTSD is a relatively recent one. In an average population, according to the National Institute of Mental Health, about 1 in 30 adults in the United States suffer from PTSD not including war veterans. But the third edition of DSM-III "... specifically excluded chronic illnesses from among the traumatic events that might elicit PTSD," until overwhelming evidence revealed a "... significant percentage of cancer survivors exhibited the re-experiencing, avoidance, and arousal symptoms that are characteristic of PTSD," and an astonishing "26% met all criteria for current or lifetime diagnoses of PTSD." Using a conservative analysis of heart transplant recipients, "10.5% met full criteria for the disorder and an additional 5% were probable cases" (Stukas et al., 1999). As a result, the DSM-IV (1994) specifically includes chronic illness as a risk factor for PTSD.

It is helpful to keep in mind that while a genetic component can predispose a patient to PTSD the genes involved are more likely to be expressed in those with a history of neglect or trauma in childhood. As indicated earlier in the chapter, this is no small matter as childhood trauma or neglect, chronic anxiety and depression are distinct risk factors for physical illness in adulthood; likewise, PTSD, in particular, poses a health threat associated with a significant increase in all-cause mortality (Ladwig et al., 2008). Bearing this out, nearly 90% of women diagnosed with PTSD have been diagnosed with at least one serious medical condition (Fennel, 2008) and recent research found veterans with PTSD have a significant increased risk of autoimmune conditions and cardiovascular disease (Boscarino, 2004).

The damage inflicted by PTSD is believed to shrink telomeres, a crucial component of chromosomes, and is "associated with an increased risk of cancer, cardiovascular disease, and autoimmune and neurodegenerative diseases, as well as early death" (O'Donovan et al., 2011). For an already at-risk population, early identification and intervention are critical. As health care providers become more aware that concomitant psychiatric disturbance can negatively impact recovery, more patients may be screened for affective and cognitive symptoms.

Although EW "findings for emotional health are not as robust or as consistent as those for physical health" (Baikie & Wilhelm, 2005), as noted earlier, therapeutic writing is of particular benefit in individuals scoring high in alexithymia along with those "... high in splitting (Baikie, 2003), characteristics often seen in patients with psychosomatic disorders and borderline personality disorder respectively, suggesting potential for the use of expressive writing in these populations" (Baikie & Wilhelm, 2005). In a seldom cited but significant study, Bloom (1992) found that even psychotic participants profit from writing. These findings further support the possibility that psychotic participants in remission respond to objective, written tests, a process that seems to increase rapport with the examiner (L'Abate et al., 2010).

Likewise, while findings for EW as an intervention in anxiety, depressive disorders and PTSD are mixed (Baikie & Wilhelm, 2005; Frisina, Borod, & Lepore 2004; Sloan, Marx, & Greenberg, 2011; Smyth et al., 2008) there are strong reasons to include therapeutic writing in this population. For example, in a small but provocative study of 22 people with PTSD and concomitant psychosis, 12 of the 22 wrote about the most stressful aspects of their illness and 10 recorded emotionally neutral topics. Five weeks later, evaluations revealed a reduction in symptom severity and avoidance among those writing about their psychotic experiences compared with the neutral writing group, while anxiety and depression remained unchanged (Bernard, Jackson, & Jones, 2006). However, in a study of 25 individuals diagnosed with PTSD, EW resulted in a significant decrease in dysphoric mood along with a reduction in cortisol levels but had no effect on PTSD as a whole (Smyth et al., 2008). The reduction in cortisol, however, is clinically significant since elevated cortisol levels negatively affect hippocampal volume (an area of the brain devoted to memory) and proinflammatory cytokines which, together, are predictive not only of depression but diabetes, heart disease, and cancer. In that case interventions such as therapeutic writing that enhance coping, decrease depression, anxiety and PTSD can be physiologically beneficial and vice versa.

Baikie and Wilhelm (2005) notes that some studies documented longer-term benefits of EW in emotional health outcomes, "including mood/affect, psychological well-being depressive symptoms before examinations, and posttraumatic intrusion and avoidance symptoms." While the precise mechanisms behind such salutary effects remain unknown Baikie summarizes three potential pathways: (1) confronting previously inhibited emotions which could reduce physiological stress resulting from inhibition; (2) cognitive processing which could assist in the development of a coherent narrative useful in reorganizing and restructuring traumatic memories; and (3) repeated exposure to the trauma.

Reducing psychological distress resulting from inhibition is further evidenced by the relationship to working memory capacity. As EW improves working memory it has been linked to a decrease in posttraumatic intrusion. For example, among adolescents who wrote about their emotional reactions to the death of a classmate, those whose writing revealed a progressive movement from a factual perspective to an integrated emotional and cognitive restructuring of the event had less inhibition (Margola, Facchin, Molgora, & Revenson, 2010). Among individuals suffering from generalized anxiety disorder those assigned to a written exposure condition (writing specifically about the trauma) reported significant improvement in anxiety, depression and related somatic symptoms compared to the control group (Goldman et al., 2007).

Inhibition and working memory capacity have also been linked to depression. Redick, Heitz, and Engle (2007) summarize, "Another clinical condition believed to be related in part to impaired thought suppression is depression … . Depressed patients may focus on negative thoughts to a greater degree than healthy individuals, and similar to those with PTSD, people with depression may … (have) a reduced ability to allocate attention resources to processes such as inhibition … depression may act as a cognitive load that affects performance on tasks requiring WMC (working memory capacity)" (Redick et al., 2007). Although Kacewicz, Slatcher, and Pennebaker and Chung (2007) acknowledges the lack of EW studies with clinically depressed samples, this could explain why "… several studies have found drops in self-reported depression or distress among people who have been classified as formerly depressed … among mixed psychiatric, medical and community samples" (Kacewicz, Slatcher, & Pennebaker & Chung, 2007). This, in part, underscores why cognitive processing therapy (CPT) and CBT are recognized interventions in the treatment of PTSD and both support written exercises as a standard component of effective treatment. As a testament to the efficacy of both CPT and CBT the availability of these interventions is mandatory for veterans with PTSD according to Veteran Affairs (U.S. Medicine, 2009).

Echoing this therapeutic potential is that "… central to many theories of depression is the idea that people process information with regard to self through a negative filter (i.e., Beck's cognitive triad)" (Cacioppo et al., 2007; L'Abate, 2011a). Indeed, among women newly diagnosed with breast cancer an increase in anxiety and depression could be predicted based on the prevalence of negative emotion in writing (Smith, Anderson-Hanley, Langrock, & Compas, 2005). The therapeutic writing accompanying CBT requires the identification and labeling of self-limiting and inaccurate beliefs, which are then countered by recording accurate and self-supportive statements. Highlighting this approach, a novel investigation of essays written by women with early-stage breast cancer showed self-affirmation to have a significant positive effect on psychological and physiological well-being when compared with other factors. The authors suggest "that self-enhancing views buffer the deleterious effects of threatening events and positively affect mental and physical health … lower distress and biological response(s) to stress …" and overall demonstrate greater resilience and emotional stability (Creswell et al., 2007a; Creswell, Way, Eisenberger, & Lieberman, 2007b).

Equally impressive is a randomized controlled trial of over 100 individuals with acute stress disorder (ASD) or PTSD. The ASD group participated in either CBT or structured writing therapy (SWT) for five 1.5-hour sessions and the PTSD groups (both CBT and SWT) for ten 1.5 hour sessions. At posttest and follow-up, both treatments were associated with lower levels of intrusive symptoms, depression, and state anxiety (Van Emmerik, Kamphuis, & Emmelkamp, 2008). This intervention has even proved promising in children with PTSD. Using cognitive behavioral writing therapy (incorporating exposure, cognitive restructuring, and social sharing) with 23 children, pre- and posttesting revealed a significant reduction in PTSD, depressive symptoms, and trauma-related cognitive distortions (Van der Oord, Lucassen, Van Emmerik, & Emmelkamp, 2010).

Nevertheless, while more research is needed, Pennebaker offers a noteworthy recommendation:

> It has been our experience that traumatic experiences often bring to the fore other important issues in people's lives. As researchers, we assume that, say, the diagnosis of a life-threatening disease is the most important issue for a person to write about in a cancer-related study. However, for many, this can be secondary to a cheating husband, an abusive parent, or some other trauma that may have occurred years earlier. We recommend that writing researchers and practitioners provide sufficiently open instructions to allow people to deal with whatever important topics they want to write about (Pennebaker & Chung, in press, p. 7).

Conclusion: A Multimodal Perspective

As there is no one-size-fits-all formula, novel strategies, rigor, and methods utilizing a multimodal therapeutic writing approach are warranted. Up until now, primary methods of evaluation have precluded some of the most salient variables found to enhance outcome; accordingly, Stanton and Danoff-Burg suggest "... building into the instructions for the intervention some of the ingredients presumed to be mechanisms for its benefits, such as narrative coherence, causal thinking, and positive emotion ..." (2002). An expanded EW paradigm can also include: privacy (the need to feel free from censure or prying eyes); flexible writing periods (as opposed to a standardized 20-minute session); further duration (continuing over weeks as opposed to a few days) (Frattaroli, 2006; Nicholls, 2009); feeling identification exercises; assessment of physiological arousal and techniques to reduce distress that can be tracked by the patient through biofeedback/psychophysiological methods; explanation of narrative features; inclusion of gratitude; and elements of mindfulness and cognitive behavioral methods. Findings in neuroscience and mind–body medicine can be more readily integrated in progressive writing paradigms. Although methodological problems remain considerable, significant evidence supports therapeutic writing as a key component of a biopsychosocial approach to wellness. This low-cost intervention is best achieved by integrating a variety of approaches including psychoeducation to reduce risk and enhance outcome.

PART II

SPECIFIC WRITING APPROACHES

Chapter 3

Autobiographies

Lawrence Ressler and Luciano L'Abate

> "... *knowledge of life histories is a means of self-analysis first and foremost for the one who writes about himself and herself: every man and woman mindfully grows in relation to his or her ability to reprocess the past as a resource for the present.*" (Demetrio & Borgonovi, 2007, p. 251)

The purpose of this chapter is to review research about therapeutic writing using autobiographic methodology. This methodology differs substantially from the use of diaries reviewed in Chapter 5 of this volume. Autobiography is oriented toward the past, whereas diaries are oriented toward the present. Furthermore, conceivably autobiographies can be written with or without a schedule, at any time the writer chooses to write. Diaries, however, require some kind of schedule, even if irregular.

Historical Background

Most research about this approach to writing was reviewed by Demetrio and Borgonovi (2007) who concluded the following:

> In spite of its widespread use and enthusiastic endorsements by its advocates, the evidence for the use of autobiography as a vaccine relies mostly on the results of the Nun Study (Snowdon, 2003). In addition to being easy to administer to large masses of people, that study, fortunately for its advocates, is one of the best pieces of evidence to demonstrate the long-term outcome of writing autobiographies at an

Research on Writing Approaches in Mental Health
Studies in Writing, Volume 23, 39–53

ISSN: 1572-6304/doi: 10.1108/S1572-6304(2011)0000023007

> early age. However, one needs to look at *the kind of writing* before making a pall-mall declaration of universal applicability for autobiographies as vaccines. The evidence from that study shows how autobiographies can be used diagnostically to predict how long and how well one will live, on the basis of idea density and the use of positive emotion words, as supported by other research (see Chapter 3 of this volume). Consequently, on the basis of the definition of a vaccine as an easy to administer, low-cost intervention to large groups of people, with some benefits for a certain few, the use of autobiographies will benefit from research on individual differences on how and why some individuals will benefit by it and why some will not. (p. 267)

Since that conclusion came from a review covering research in the autobiography literature until 2006, this chapter will cover relevant research since that year to date with one exception not included in that chapter. Tenni, Smith, and Boucher (2003), for instance, explored the ways researchers go about analyzing (qualitatively, n/a) autobiographical data. Using a journaling, anecdotal approach in a focus-group setting, those authors suggested "using theory to challenge one's assumptions about oneself." They stated:

> Writing of our biographical data is inexorably informed by the theoretical constructs that we use in our daily practice. Data (sic) is never theory-free. What we choose to write and how we choose to write it is constructed based on the ways we understand the world, our practice, and ourselves. (p. 4)

We shall come back to this point after we have critically reviewed evidence to support the use of autobiography to improve mental health.

Qualitative Studies of Autobiographies

Thornton (2008) discussed the proposition that learning is an unexplored feature of the guided autobiography method and its developmental exchange (see also Demetrio & Borgonovi, 2007). Learning, conceptualized and explored as the embedded and embodied processes, is essential in narrative activities of the guided autobiography method leading to psychosocial development and growth in dynamic, temporary social groups. The chapter is organized in three sections and summary. The section "Qualitative Studies of Autobiographies" provides a brief overview of the guided autobiography method describing the interplay of learning and experiencing in temporary social groups. The section "Research Studies on Autobiography (2006–2010)" offers a limited review on learning and experiencing as processes that are essential for development, growth, and change. The section "The Importance of Theory in Autobiography" reviews small group activities and the emergence of the "developmental exchange" in the guided autobiography method. Two theoretical constructs provide a conceptual foundation for the developmental exchange: a counterpart theory of aging as development, and collaborative-situated group learning theory. The summary recapped main ideas and issues that shaped the guided autobiography method as learning and social experience using the theme, "Where to go from here."

In a combination of expressive writing (see Chapter 2 of this volume), as an addition to lectures and discussions on mental disorders, Segrist (2008) in his abnormal psychology course incorporated an overview of the literature on the therapeutic value of expressive writing. Students read, discussed, and wrote about four full-length autobiographies related to mental illness and rated each on five dimensions: perceived therapeutic value to the author, degree to which the book increased understanding of mental illness, degree to which the book increased understanding of the personal experience of mental illness, enjoyment of the book, and likelihood of recommending the book. Strong associations emerged between perceived therapeutic value to the author and the other ratings. Books rated highest in terms of perceived therapeutic benefit to the author were also the books from which students perceived learning the most.

Taking a formal, sociocognitive approach to narrative analysis, DeGloma (2010) explored autobiographical stories about discovering "truth" in political, psychological, religious, and sexual realms of social life. Despite (1) significant differences in subject matter and (2) conflicting or oppositional notions of truth, individuals in different social environments tell stories that follow the same awakening formula. Analyzing accounts from a wide variety of social and historical contexts, DeGloma showed how individuals and communities use autobiographical stories to define salient moral and political concerns and weigh in on cultural and epistemic disputes. Awakening narratives are important mechanisms of mnemonic and autobiographical revision that individuals use to redefine their past experiences and relationships and plot future courses of action while explaining major transformations of worldview.

Awakeners use two ideal-typical vocabularies of liminality to justify traversing the social divide between contentious autobiographical communities. Further, awakeners divide their lives into discrete autobiographical periods and convey a figurative interaction between the split personas of a temporally divided self. Individuals use this autobiographical formula to reject the cognitive and mnemonic norms of one community and embrace those of another. Advancing a "social geometry" of awakening narratives, I illuminate the social logic behind our seemingly personal discoveries of "truth."

Hughes (2009) explored how autobiographical narrative about everyday activities can stimulate critical reflection. A reinterpretation of Schön's stages of reflective practice is used to explore some examples from autobiographical writing about the everyday practice of carrying a bag to illustrate literary devices which enable self-interrogation and internal dialogue. Such writing can mimic the dialogue with a peer or coach to generate new perspectives and sometimes change in habitual practice. Implications of using both reflection on everyday life and creative autobiography for the development of professionals are finally discussed.

Research Studies on Autobiography (2006–2010)

Research studies on autobiography before 2006 were covered by Demetrio and Borgonovi (2007). Here we are covering research on autobiography between 2006 and 2010. The psychological aspects of the biography–autobiography phenomenon have been attracting varying interest from the beginning of the last century (Dilthey, Bühler, Allport) (Ferenc, 2006). Autobiographies inspired by systematic self-reflection can be considered as reactions to the individuals' epoch of modernism (Baumeister). They may be presented as a chronicle-like document as well as a piece of literature (autobiographical novel). Presenting the self to the public, the diary and the autobiography are reflecting different personality constellations in the context of openness and inclination to self-presentation. There exist certain "sensitive periods" of diary writing and autobiography composition (midlife crisis, life review).

According to Ferenc (2006), recent research in the field of autobiographical memory has given a fresh impulse to the analysis of the biographical factors of the personality, that is, "the identity as a life story" approach, the narrative expansion, and the "affective revolution." Ferenc is convinced that the study of life history's psychological universe and that of the autobiography in particular is leading to a kind of integrative area of major psychological research trends, such as self-reflection, autobiographical memory, self-knowledge, and self-presentation.

Ferenc systematically examined these problems in the context of autobiography writing devoting special attention to the motivational pattern of written self-disclosure. The principal components of this pattern are the transcendence of one's limited personal existence, the assertion of one's individuality, and the legitimization of the actual self and self-esteem. He also touched upon self-reflection practices and the varying forms of autobiographies and additionally raised issues about autobiographical time and the limits of self-knowledge. One can only write about what one knows about oneself.

The quantity and quality of research about autobiography since 2006 are such that it will be possible to separate studies about autobiography according to different categories and conditions. Most of this research covers the area of individual differences left practically untouched by the previous review (Demetrio & Borgonovi, 2007).

Addictions

Illegal drug use in Hungary became a mass phenomenon after the political changes of 1990 (Rácz, 2006). It is only recently that autobiographies of recovered drug users and their family members have been written and published. Rácz suggests that since the Alcoholics Anonymous (AA) approach has no traditional roots in Hungary, recovery stories are obliged to follow another master narrative. All of these stories were published in book form. The author analyzes the various narratives partly through the lens of Frank-style illness narratives and partly using self-pluralistic theories. The latter (primarily using Herman's notion of the dialogic self) provide a good theoretical basis for analyzing the processes active in the personality of a drug user and for showing the "retrospective" construction work that accompanies recovery (which in fact takes place at the same time as recovery). In this case, the spatial interpretation of individual self-positions and the dialogical relationship that developed between them proved particularly useful.

Autism

Assumptions of difficulties with social interaction, or lack of interest in social interaction, are central to many definitions and conventional understandings of autism (Causton-Theoharis, Ashby, & Cosier, 2009). However, many individuals with autism describe a strong craving social interaction. This chapter uses autobiographical accounts written by individuals who identified as autistic as a source of qualitative research data and specifically explores the ways these texts address issues of social relationships. Using narrative inquiry, the authors explored how individuals with autism described their own notions of and experiences with social interaction. This chapter discusses the broad themes of (a) the desire to have connections and (b) navigation through the world of people. Lastly, implications for the education of individuals with autism are considered.

There is a wealth of autobiographical material produced by people who describe themselves as experiencing autistic spectrum disorders (Barrett, 2006). Increasingly, these writers and academics are suggesting that professionals should be using this material to help develop understanding. Barrett described a small-scale, qualitative research project that explored ways in which video- and audio-autobiographical material could be used by Experimental Participants (EPs) with teaching professionals. It suggests that a collaborative, conversation-based approach to the material can help develop understanding, empathy and lead to practical teaching and learning outcomes.

To date, few studies have focused on the viewpoints of autistic persons themselves despite an increasing number of published autobiographies. The aim of a study by Chamak, Bonniau, Jaunay, and Cohen (2008) was to highlight their personal experiences, and to compare them to scientific and medical knowledge and representations. Adopting an anthropological approach, these investigators analyzed 16 autobiographical writings and 5 interviews with autistic persons. They systematically screened this material and explored the writers' sociodemographic characteristics, cognitive skills, and interests with a focus on their sensory-perceptual experiences and their representations of autism.

The authors' ages (22–67 years), their countries ($N = 8$) and backgrounds were varied, and most of them were high-functioning individuals with autism or Asperger syndrome. The most striking observations were that all of them pointed out that unusual perceptions and information processing, as well as impairments in emotional regulation, were the core symptoms of autism, whereas the current classifications do not mention them. Their results suggested that what has been selected as major signs by psychiatric nosography is regarded as manifestations induced by perceptive peculiarities and strong emotional reactions by the autistic persons who expressed themselves. These considerations deserve to be taken into account by professionals to better understand the behavior and needs of autistic persons. We propose to include this point in the reflection on the next psychiatric classifications.

Cancer

Cancer survivors often compare their situations to other survivors' situations (Bellizzi, Blank, & Oakes, 2006). However, types of social comparison processes used and resulting outcomes are not clearly delineated. This study explores usage and consequences of three social comparison styles (downward, upward, and parallel) of adult cancer survivors in free narratives, using content analysis of 30 autobiographical books by survivors ranging in age from 30 to 70 years ($M = 54$, SD = 10.04); 43 percent prostate cancer, 17 percent breast cancer, and 40 percent other cancers. Overall, cancer survivors used more parallel comparisons than directional comparisons, followed by upward comparisons. Each type of comparison was associated with different kinds of positive and negative consequences.

Herndl (2006) explored four volumes of collective autobiography in which women who have had breast cancer simultaneously struggled with writing a new identity and creating an ethical narrative. Overwhelmingly, writers of breast cancer autobiography constructed narratives that attempted to paint a positive picture of recovery and healing, but are such narratives unproblematically true? What are their political consequences? In what ways do the body, its inadequacies, and its fragmentation become part of a new narrative identity? Herndl came to these questions as a feminist critic who had been writing about women, illness, and narrative for more than 15 years but also as a 6-year survivor of breast cancer. In this essay, she wanted to embody the tension between the immediate purpose (or even need) of narrative and the larger structural and cultural politics of it.

Coping with cancer presents a formidable challenge. Finding meaning, or making sense of the disease, has been shown to have positive benefits for the individual. Leung (2010) introduced an innovative qualitative method — the autobiographical timeline interview — in research on the illness experience, as demonstrated in a study to understand the meaning-making process for Chinese women with breast cancer. This method integrates narrative technique and life story approach in facilitating research participants to explore and articulate the meaning they constructed of their cancer experience. It allows in-depth understanding into a phenomenon with adherence to methodological and scientific rigor. The emphasis of this chapter is on the discussion of the research method and how it elucidates participants' subjective realities in light of their cultural, temporal, and social contexts. The research process not only promotes evidence-based reflective practice but is also an empowering experience for the participants.

Children

Learning conceptions may be studied as specific implicit theories based on theory of mind. Previous studies suggest that a developmental shift from a direct implicit theory of learning to an interpretative one occurs during childhood. Here Scheuer, de la Cruz, Pozo, and Neira (2006) explored the development of children's autobiographies of learning to write by adopting this framework. These investigators aimed at studying children's autobiographical accounts of learning to write and whether these accounts change according to the mentioned developmental shift and sociocultural environment. The sample consisted of 60 children attending public schools in Argentina who were equally distributed according to school level (kindergarten, first grade, fourth grade) and sociocultural environment (middle and marginal).

Children were interviewed individually at school and requested to write "as you used to when you were just beginning to write." This question was repeated for 1-year intervals until the child's current age was reached. The anticipation of writing next year was also requested. Children's responses were coded into descriptive categories. A multiple correspondence factorial analysis studied the relations among response categories, school grade, and sociocultural environment. On the basis of these results, categories were ordered into a Guttman scale.

Results showed developmental shift from a focus on isolated products to the integration of procedural and representational changes was evident. School grade and sociocultural environment were statistically significant. From these findings, Scheuer et al. concluded that children's writing autobiographies showed developmental differences that suit the shift from a direct to an interpretative theory of learning on the basis of hierarchical integration rather than conceptual replacement.

Dementia

People with dementia are finding increasingly creative and diverse ways of making their voice heard in society and one such method is through the publication of autobiographical accounts. Following set inclusion criteria, Page and Keady (2010) in a meta-ethnographic analysis compared and contrasted the contents of 12 books written by people with dementia and published between 1989 (the year of publication of the first text) and the end of 2007 (the selected cutoff point for inclusion). Of the 12 books, three authors were published twice, five were male, eight were from the United States of America, one was Australian, and all nine had a professional background. Eight of the authors had Alzheimer's disease and one had frontotemporal dementia. The average age of the narrator was 51.5 years (age range 38–61 years). Meta-ethnographic analysis of the 12 books inductively generated five themes that linked each story and these were: (a) awareness of change, (b) experiencing loss, (c) standing up and bearing witness, (d) sustaining continuity, and (e) liberation and death. The importance of reconstructing identity appeared a pivotal process in living with the onset and progression of dementia together with maintaining key social relationships and networks.

Diabetes

Piana et al. (2010) introduced a narrative-autobiographical approach in the care and education of adolescents with type-1 diabetes and observe the effects of this novel approach on adolescents' self-awareness, concern for self-care, and well-being. Ninety-four adolescents with type-1 diabetes attending one 9-day summer camp in 2004, 2005, or 2006 participated in structured daily self-writing proposals on diabetes, integrated with daily interactive self-management education. After some months, these investigators sent participants interview-like questionnaires, and two independent researchers performed a qualitative analysis of the 50 answers that were mailed back.

They found that writing about the discovery of diabetes was, for many, a stressful experience, but with a strong liberating effect. One relevant point was change which occurred: (a) in the perception of self; (b) in the relationship with others; (c) in the relationship with the disease. On the basis of these findings, these investigators concluded that by integrating autobiography in diabetes camps and by adding the value of sharing individual stories to the liberating power of self-writing, adolescents can be helped to overcome their feelings of diversity. They also concluded that integrating autobiography can initiate several changes reflecting increased self-efficacy, maturity, acceptance of the disease, and responsibility in self-management. The practical implications of these conclusions are that self-writing is feasible and well accepted, and provides health care professionals a proper way to patient-centered care.

Feelings and Emotions

Autobiographical narratives ($N = 97$) of guilt and shame experiences were analyzed to determine how the nature of emotion and context relate to ways of coping in such situations (Silfver, 2007). The coding categories were created by content analysis, and the connections between categories were analyzed with optimal scaling and log-linear analysis. Two theoretical perspectives were tested: the view that shame generally is a more maladaptive emotion than guilt; and the view that in situations where responsibility is ambiguous, both guilt and shame feelings are likely to be maladaptive. In line with the latter, chronic rumination was more likely to occur in situations where responsibility was ambiguous compared to situations where the respondent's responsibility was clear, regardless of emotion. In addition, reparative behavior was less frequently reported in shame situations than in situations where the respondent felt guilty or both guilty and ashamed. The findings supported the view that the nature of emotional reaction and the nature of the situation both affect the ways of coping.

Experiential avoidance (EA) is the unwillingness to remain in contact with particular private experiences, and higher levels of EA are associated with increased psychopathology (L'Abate, 2011a). Robertson and Hopko (2009) explored relationships between EA, age, and the use of emotion words in positive and negative autobiographical narratives. Participants included younger ($N = 60$) and older adults ($N = 60$) who completed a measure of EA and described a positive and negative autobiographical narrative. In the positive autobiographical narrative, there was a significant interaction between age and EA, whereby among low EA participants, younger adults used more emotion words than older adults. In the negative autobiographical narrative, there was a main effect of age in which older adults utilized fewer emotional words and a significant interaction, whereby among high EA participants, younger adults used more emotion words than older adults. These results can be explained in the developmental context of socioemotional selectivity theory (Carstensen), which posits that older adults may be more likely to verbally communicate in a style characterized by emotion regulation.

Gender Differences

Food and its emotional and political significance pervade autobiographical writing by lesbians (Lindenmeyer, 2006). The author traces the connections between food, sexuality, and identity through four exemplary texts — Jeanette Winterson's Oranges Are Not the Only Fruit, Audre Lorde's Zami, Dorothy Allison's "A Lesbian Appetite," and Anna Livia's "Tongues or Fingers" — where food is crucial in both defining and contesting lesbian identity, sexuality, and community. Food memories and histories are portrayed as constitutive of the self, reaching back to childhood, and images of "home." However, they are also related to the social context of class inequalities and gendered hierarchies. Within these autobiographical narratives, food both constitutes and expresses a sense of self, playing a crucial part in the construction of the writers' complex, multilayered narratives of identity.

Heart Disease

Heart disease is the leading cause of illness, disability, and death among women in Canada (Bowers & Buchanan, 2007). Myocardial infarction (MI) accounts for almost half of these deaths yearly. The purpose of this study was to understand younger women's experience of recovery from MI. A purposive sample consisting of six younger women diagnosed with MI participated in an 8-week guided autobiographical (GA) group intervention where they engaged in weekly reflection, writing, and group dialogue. The experience of loss, uncertainty, changes in self-perception, self-care, health care and support from others, and caring for others emerged from the data analysis. GA was shown to be an effective psychosocial intervention to facilitate emotional recovery following a significant cardiac event as all participants described the GA group as a therapeutic component of their recovery process.

Longevity and Mortality

Pressman and Cohen (2007), in an attempt to replicate Snowdon's findings (2003), analyzed the relationship between social word use in autobiographies and longevity. Although there is substantial evidence that our social relationships are associated with mortality, interpretation of this work is weakened by the limitations of assessing the social environment with structured questionnaires and interviews. By analyzing the word content of autobiographies, we could assess spontaneous indicators of important social relationships and relate them to longevity. This technique is less subject to social desirability reporting biases and more sensitive to aspects of the social environment that are central to how one experiences his or her social world.

The autobiographies of 96 psychologists and 220 literary writers were digitized and scanned for social relationship word frequency via a computerized word counting program. Archival data were collected on birth and death dates, year of publication, place of birth, age when the autobiography was written, and sex. After controlling for sex, year of birth, and age at the time of writing, Pressman and Cohen found that higher use of words indicating social roles/integration (e.g., father, sister, neighbor, coworker) was associated with an increased life span in both samples. Specific social categories assessing the use of family role terms (e.g., aunt, family, brother) and references to other individuals (e.g., they, we, us, everyone) also predicted longer life, but only in the sample of psychologists.

The conclusions from these important findings show that assessing social word use in autobiographies provided an indirect measure of social relationships that predicted longevity. The technique of analyzing writing samples may be useful in future archival research as well as in studies where it is desirable to study social relationships in an indirect fashion.

Drawing on terror management theory, Landau, Greenberg, and Sullivan (2009) proposed that maintaining a coherent autobiography protects the individual from mortality concerns by imbuing experience over time with significance and order. Two studies tested whether mortality salience combined with a threat to autobiographical coherence (induced by an alphabetical organization of past events) prompts compensatory bolstering of the significance and orderliness of temporal experience.

In Study 1, whereas exclusion-primed participants led to organize past events alphabetically perceived their past as less significant, mortality salient participants showed a compensatory boost in perceptions of their past's significance. In Study 2, mortality salience and an alphabetic event organization led participants high in personal need for structure to parse their future into clearly defined temporal intervals. This research is the first to experimentally assess the role of existential concerns in people's motivation to defend the significance and structure of their temporal experience against threats to autobiographical coherence.

Mental Disorders

Smorti, Risaliti, Pananti, and Cipriani (2008a) explored how the autobiographical process can lead to a transformation in the quality of psychiatric patients' self-narrative. Fifteen participants, with ages ranging from 25 to 40 years and affected by Axis I psychiatric disorders (DSM IV), were selected to participate. A 10-question interview referring to 10 autobiographical cruxes was used to collect autobiographical data; the interview was readministered 2 weeks later. A coding system (the N.O.I.S.) was used to analyze each participant's two autobiographical productions.

Results from the second interviews showed significant and positive transformations in the quality of patients' autobiographical representation. This study is an important first step toward discovering whether autobiographical writing will improve behavior. The authors failed to demonstrate that "transformations in the quality of patients' autobiographical representations" were linked to improvements in the patients' behavior.

The goal of this study was to explore how the autobiographical process involves a transformation in psychiatric patients' self-narratives (Smorti, Risaliti, Pananti, & Cipriani, 2008b). For this study 15 participants were selected, aged 25–40 years, affected by a psychiatric disorder of Axis I in the DSM IV. An autobiographical interview was used consisting of 10 questions referring to 10 autobiographical cruxes. The interview was repeated after 10 days. Both autobiographical productions were analyzed with a coding instrument (N.O.I.S.) created for the purposes of this study. Results evidenced a significant transformation of autobiographical report between the first and the second interview. It should be noted that a control group was not used making the study qualitatively incomplete.

However, in a follow-up to the previous study by Smorti et al. (2008a) that evaluated possible changes in behavior due to this experience, Smorti, Pananti, and Rizzo (2010) explored how the autobiographical process can lead to a transformation in psychiatric patients' lifestyle, well-being, and self-narrative. Nine participants, aged between 20 and 42 years and affected by Axis I psychiatric disorders (DSM IV), were selected to participate in an autobiographical laboratory. Eight to 10 meetings took place, each lasting about an hour, during which autobiographical accounts were collected.

At the beginning and end of the autobiographical laboratory, the medical staff completed the Social Functioning Scale to evaluate each patient across six dimensions: social engagement, interpersonal ability, prosocial activities, recreation, independence-competence, and independence-performance. The Language Inquiry and Word Count (Yi-Tsi Seih & Pennebaker, in press) was used to analyze patients' autobiographical accounts. A comparison between the first and second compilation of the Social Functioning Scale showed significant positive changes across the six social dimensions. The analysis of language in the narratives collected in the first and seventh meeting showed how inpatients passed from a narrative that was more centered on the memory of the past to a narrative that was more similar to a conversation and enriched with "insight" terms and the use of verbs in the conjunctive form. The authors interpreted these outcomes as being consistent with the improvement that was observed in inpatients' social functioning. To our limited knowledge, this is the first study to demonstrate significant improvements in psychiatric patients' behavior. The only missing factor would be using a control group of similar patients required to write about neutral or nocuous topics.

Multiple Sclerosis

Musical autobiographies consist of a powerful therapeutic tool by which individuals define themselves. The use of this technique may help (re)construction of personal identities and improve quality of life of patients with multiple sclerosis (MS) (Moreira, França, Moreira, & Lana-Peixoto, 2009). Eight adult patients on treatment at CIEM Multiple Sclerosis Investigation Center after selecting 10–15 pieces of music most significant in their lives were interviewed. The data collected were classified according to Even Rudd categories, which reveal how a person expresses his or her personal, social, temporal, and transpersonal identities. The authors observed that recall of musical history makes MS patients get better perception both of their feelings and body awareness, as well as provide them with an alternative way to express themselves, activate and contextualize affective memories, and achieving a sense of life continuity in spite of the disease.

Obesity

Maldonato, Piana, Bloise, and Baldelli (2010) reviewed recent results of the current approaches to the education of obese people, focusing on the motivation for healthy behaviors, and to present the narrative-autobiographical approach as a possible tool in the education of obese people. These authors admitted that their overview was necessarily partial, and limited to some studies that succeeded in improving the motivation for healthy lifestyles in people with overweight or obesity. They also described the use of the autobiographical approach in the "Io-muovo-la-mia-vita" project.

Maldonato et al. (2010) found that many of the studies induced relevant behavioral changes mainly by using intensive interventions. Weight loss maintenance has been difficult and usually has required proactive follow-up interventions. The use of self-writing may allow overweight and obese people to reveal their inner feelings to themselves and to peers, and may reinforce their motivation for self-care. They concluded that the association of weight loss with intensive interventions and the need for follow-up proactive interventions to maintain results make one wonder whether the inner motivation of participants is usually fostered as recommended. Practice implications suggest that the narrative-autobiographical approach appears to be a proper way to patient-centered care, but for an effective practice, the human and relational attitudes of health care professionals should be integrated with specific educational skills.

Prosopagnosia

Prosopagnosia is a selective impairment of the visual learning and recognition of faces. The congenital type, which is not accompanied by detectable brain damage or malformation, was recently found to be far more common than previously known. Therefore, one should expect that at least a few biographies or autobiographies would reveal a prosopagnosia. In this study, an autobiography and a biography describing five cases of congenital prosopagnosia are presented. These biographic descriptions of prosopagnosia add further evidence to the assumption that the congenital type of prosopagnosia is not a rare condition, and not as socially crippling as one might expect (Grüter & Grüter, 2007).

Retirement

The aim of this study was to examine the means by which men on the verge of retirement create continuity or bridges between their past and present in their autobiographical narratives (Nuttman-Shwartz, 2008). Based on Whitbourne's "life span construct model of adaptation," 56 Israeli men on the verge of retirement were asked to relate their "life stories" and "life scenarios" (their vision of the future). Their bridging strategies were examined using qualitative structural analyses, focusing on the "crossovers" to the future in the "life stories," and those to the past in their "life scenarios." The findings show three main bridging patterns in the life stories and three in the life scenarios. Each was associated with differences in the ways that the men were coping emotionally with the transition to retirement, and pointed to the different ways by which they used continuity to cope with the anxieties aroused by their impending retirement. After trying to account for the greater frequency of bridging attempts in the "scenarios" than the "life stories," the discussion elaborates on the different bridging strategies and their associated features. The findings suggest that the identification of crossover patterns in life stories and life scenarios may be a useful tool for assessing a person's coping abilities and adjustment to difficult transitions.

Senior Citizens

Subjective memory complaint is a self-reported memory impairment which affects elderly people. This problem does not interfere with daily living activities but could decrease quality of life. Grossi et al. (2007) aimed at verifying whether a specific, newly developed, autobiographical recall training could modify self-perception of memory of participants with subjective memory complaint. Seven elderly participants (four women and three men; mean age 65.5 years, $SD = 11$) with such complaint, evaluated through a specific questionnaire, attended the training course and were prospectively assessed on standard neuropsychological tests, depressive symptomatology, and self-perception of memory. Self-perception of memory, as assessed by scores on a formalized questionnaire, improved significantly after the training, whereas depressive symptoms did not change. Neuropsychological performances were normal before and after the training, but a statistically significant improvement was observed only on the phonological fluency test. Thus, the present pilot study suggested that training may be effective in improving self-perception of memory and metamnestic capacity in elderly people with subjective memory complaints but not in changing participants' depressive symptoms. These suggestive findings require replication of this work with a much larger sample so that statistical power is adequate.

Trunk and Abrams (2009) investigated younger and older adults' communicative goals and their effects on off-topic speech for autobiographical narratives. Participants indicated their communicative goals by rating preferences among paired goals, for example, focus–fascinating, one of which was designated as an expressive goal, appropriate for producing elaborative speech, and one of which was an objective goal, suited to producing concise speech. The participants then told stories about episodic and procedural topics which were rated by groups of younger and older listeners. Age differences emerged in communicative goals where younger adults clearly favored expressive goals for episodic topics and objective goals for procedural topics. In contrast, older adults' goals were more diverse, consisting of a mixture of expressive and objective goals for both topic types without a clear preference. Younger adults' goals predicted ratings of off-topic speech assessed by listeners: Younger and older adults were perceived as equivalently focused, coherent, and clear for episodic topics, but older adults were perceived as less focused, less clear, and more talkative than younger adults on procedural topics. These results suggest that age-related changes in off-topic speech emerge as a result of younger adults selecting goals designed to produce more succinct stories.

In a pilot study, de Medeiros, Kennedy, Cole, Lindley, and O'Hara (2007) examined whether participation in a structured autobiographic writing workshop positively influenced memory performance in a group of community-dwelling older adults. Eighteen participants, aged 62–84 years, were enrolled in an 8-week writing workshop. At baseline and follow-up, they completed five memory assessments and submitted two writing samples, which were evaluated for linguistic complexity. The authors found a significant increase in follow-up scores on tests of verbal memory and attention, indicating a possible positive influence of the writing workshop. The authors also found a decline in idea density, suggesting that more research is needed to better understand how interpretation of the language assessment tool may be affected by improvements in writing.

Sex Offenders

Imprisoned sexual offenders undergoing treatment are expected to deduce and follow a treatment schema constructed on the foundations of cognitive behavioral therapy (CBT). A key element of their treatment program is the presentation of a core narrative, their autobiography, to treatment staff and peers. Examining this form of prison-based treatment through the lens of narrative theory, Waldram (2008) argued that the autobiographies and other stories that are developed and performed as part of this treatment process are largely the product of the imposition of this treatment schema in combination with dynamic group processes. Ironically, the treatment schema and the prevailing dynamics work to subvert the fundamental forensic goal of having inmates disclose aspects of their lives and crimes as an essential stepping stone toward rehabilitation. The narratives that emerge, both in detail and in meaning, cannot be seen as simply reflections of any single individual's life but, instead, as composites built on, and reflective of cultural processes somewhat unique to the forensic context. Narrative, a fundamental mode of thinking and communication, necessarily challenges the directed nature of autobiographical presentation derived from CBT. In such circumstances, the effectiveness of CBT for sexual offenders is questionable.

The Importance of Theory in Autobiography

As can be surmised by past and present research, the importance of theory in studies of the autobiographical process is either absent, neglected, or selective. Even when empirically based coding systems, content analyses, or word counts were used, in and of themselves they did not seem to be linked with any theory. This is an important issue because in order to link autobiographies to a theory, the theory needs to be comprehensive enough, highly specific, and sufficiently validated to be able to produce such a link. To our knowledge, possibly relational competence theory (L'Abate et al., 2010) may possess those three qualities. However, such a possible link will need to be demonstrated with more than wishful thinking.

Conclusion

From this review of the qualitative and quantitative research about autobiographical writing we can conclude with a high level of confidence that this approach: (1) is highly versatile — it can be administered to a wide range of healthy, unhealthy, and disordered populations; and (2) is relatively easy to administer. We can additionally conclude that autobiographical writing is not easy to evaluate in its process and outcome. However, since the last review (Demetrio & Borgonovi, 2007), important steps have been taken in the analysis of its process and outcome. Adding controls matched with experimental groups in future research would be the capping stone for a promising approach to addressing mental health needs. The addition of control groups would allow us to learn more about individual differences regarding writing and improve mental health in populations varying in degrees of functionality.

Chapter 4

Diaries

Thomas Mackrill

> "*In diary studies, people provide frequent reports on the events and experiences of their daily lives. These reports capture the particulars of experience in a way that is not possible using traditional designs.*" (Bolger, Davis, & Rafaeli, 2003, p. 579).

The history of diaries as a tool in mental health intervention research and the history of writing are intertwined. Chronicles describing significant events have been kept for over 500 years in Europe by the church that once held a monopoly on writing. Chronicles are, however, not personal and reflective descriptions of events, which are a characteristic of the modern diary. In Japan, there are examples of personal reflective diaries dating back to the tenth century (Alaszewski, 2006). Personal reflective diary writing first became more common when the following two interconnected historic changes had taken place. With the introduction of formal schooling and the increased availability of the instruments of writing, pens and paper, writing became more commonplace among certain classes of people who were not clergy or monks. The second important historic development was the rise of individualism. Individualism is generally associated with the development of Protestantism and capitalism (Alaszewski, 2006; Symes, 1999). Protestantism stressed the significance of the individual person's relationship to God. Formally, the church had claimed responsibility for mediating people's relationship to God. As the individual's development of their relationship to God became more significant, some people started writing about their personal religious life and development in diaries. Protestantism also stressed the significance of personal diligence. The diary offered a technology for monitoring diligence; for organizing and reflecting about one's life in relation to time (Symes, 1999). The rise of capitalism was also central to

Research on Writing Approaches in Mental Health
Studies in Writing, Volume 23, 55–65

ISSN: 1572-6304/doi: 10.1108/S1572-6304(2011)0000023008

the development of individualism. As the legal bond that once tied peasants to certain lords and masters was broken at various different times across Europe (Asplund, 1985), even more peasants had to move to sell their labor to make a living. Life as a peasant had been tied to a specific place, and peasants typically carried out tasks similar to those their parents had carried out before them. Personal development and questions of identity were not central to life under these conditions. Moving from place to place, however, challenged the way people thought about themselves. People started to have to fit into a range of differing contexts and they began to meet more people from other places, who they also had to fit in with. These new conditions meant that people had to think far more about who they were, and how they behaved, than they had done as peasants (Asplund, 1985). Making sense of who one was, and getting one's life to hang together became a more central feature of people's lives. Diaries offered a technology that some people with writing skills used to conduct reflections about such issues.

After the rise of secularism, personal development was no longer necessarily tied to religious or spiritual development. With the development of new scientific participants, such as ethnography and psychology, secular ways of understanding and reflecting about personal development became more commonplace. As formal schooling became available to all in many countries and notions of the individual, individual freedom, and personal identity became increasingly widespread, diary writing gradually became more commonplace and less tied to elite groups.

The development and availability of new technologies also changed the form and the content of diaries. Where there once were but few accessible diaries, and diaries were generally considered a personal or private document and few diaries were published, the World Wide Web and blogs have now made many personal diaries available to others. It has now become far easier to write diaries together with others, and to write diaries for others to read. Diaries are no longer just read by others after the diary is completed and perhaps after the author is deceased. Other peoples' diaries can now be read on a daily basis. The Internet diary or blog as a technology enables a new form of interpersonal communication. This highlights a significant change in diary formats. The boundary between what was once kept private and what is in the public sphere is undergoing a change. Social media, reality television, the mobile phone (with or without a camera), video surveillance, web cameras, and blogs are just some of the new technologies that are bringing what was once kept private more frequently into the public domain.

Within the social sciences, diaries have long been employed as a research tool. The early ethnographer's field notes had a diary format (Malinowski, 1989). Historians have long used diaries as a source of data (Sheridan, 1993). Within psychology, Gordon Allport is usually credited with first emphasizing the significance of diary data.

> "In its ideal form, the diary is unexcelled as a continuous record of the subjective side of mental development. The first stirring of an interest, its growth, perhaps to the state of an absorbing passion, and its decline, can be traced. The turning points in a life are exposed to

view, set, as they ought to be, in the everyday frame of unaccentuated routine." (Allport, 1942, p. 95)

Technological developments have played a central role in the development of diary research methods. Pen and paper are still sometimes employed (Jacelon & Imperio, 2005; Ross, Rideout, & Carson, 1994), but personal computers and palm held computers (Armeli, Todd, & Mohr, 2005) are steadily making their way into the field. Diaries can now be stored on the Internet (Armeli et al., 2005; Neff & Karney, 2005; Sinadinovic, Berman, Hasson, & Wennberg, 2010), sent in by e-mail (Engels, Wiers, Lemmers, & Overbeek, 2005), or texted in using a mobile phone (Rönka, Malinen, Kinnunen, Tolvanen, & Lämsa, 2010). Diary methods also cater for those who have difficultly expressing themselves in writing as diaries, may be recorded in audio (Jacelon & Imperio, 2005; Monrouxe, 2009) or visual form (Holliday, 1999). Diarists can record themselves or they may phone their logs in (Bailey, Gao, & Clark, 2006). New technologies have been used to deal with diarist forgetfulness and fatigue, which has long been considered a problem in diary research (Bolger et al., 2003, p. 593). Where some researchers used to call participants by telephone to remind them to complete diaries (Jacelon & Imperio, 2005; Keleher & Verrinder, 2003), participants may now receive text messages (Day & Thatcher, 2009), or palm held computers may be programmed to remind or "beep" participants to complete diaries at specific times (Shiffman, Stone, & Hufford, 2008).

Technological developments have not just facilitated the gathering of good quality diary data; they have also contributed to new ways of analyzing diary data. For methods regarding the analysis of quantitative diary data, read Bolger et al. (2003), Thiele, Laireiter, and Baumann (2002), and Shiffman et al. (2008).

Solicited versus Nonsolicited Diaries in Research

Grasping the difference between solicited and nonsolicited diaries is essential when considering dairy approaches. The solicited diary is basically a research tool for gathering data, just as survey questionnaires, experiments, interviews, and fieldwork are methods of gathering data. Once a researcher has chosen a topic or question to study, the researcher considers how best to gather data that address the research question/topic. Researchers may at this point choose to use solicited diaries as a data-gathering tool among the various options. Conducting a solicited diary study involves asking participants to write or complete diaries about one's area of research interest.

Nonsolicited diaries are completely different. They are diaries that somebody happens to have written, but that provide data relevant for a specific study. Nonsolicited diaries have usually been studied within the fields of history and literature (Alaszewski, 2006), although there are examples relating to mental health (e.g., Lester, 2004; Peters & Beveridge, 2010). Nonsolicited diaries are used within the social sciences when a researcher finds accessible diaries with relevant data. Despite the similarity in name, the differences between solicited and nonsolicited diary studies are considerable. A solicited diary is: "an account produced specifically at the researcher's request, by an informant or informants. Solicited diaries (…) are written with the full knowledge that they are for external consumption" (Bell, 1998, p. 72). Solicited diaries are written with the researcher in mind (Elliott, 1997). Solicited diaries must therefore be viewed as co-constructed by the soliciting and analyzing researcher and the diarist (Alaszewski, 2006; Bell, 1998; Meth, 2003; Milligan, Bingley, & Gatrell, 2005). A solicited diary is a way of accessing the research participants' lived world.

Like interview formats, solicited diary formats can be structured to a greater or lesser extent. Diary researchers may pose open or closed questions or a mixture of the two. Less structured diary studies generally employ diarist guidelines for writing (e.g., Elliott, 1997; Mackrill, 2011). Diary guidelines are similar to interview guides, but the guide is handed over to the diarist in the hope that the participant will complete the diary elsewhere. Interviews allow immediate dialogue in the gathering of data, whereas diary methods do not. Guidelines are therefore often used to regulate the data gathered. When employing guidelines, diarists may be given examples of the data that researchers are hoping for (Alaszewski & Alaszewski, 2005; Mackrill, 2011). A constant dilemma for the diary researcher is attaining relevant data without restricting the diarists' writing flow unnecessarily (Alaszewski, 2006, p. 80). Qualitative interviewers face the same dilemma. More structured diary studies typically give diarists questionnaires to be filled out regularly (Bolger, DeLongis, Kessler, & Schilling, 1989; Chepenik et al., 2006; Milligan et al., 2005). Diarists may also be asked to respond to self-report scales (Bolger et al., 1989; Chepenik et al., 2006; Milligan et al., 2005). Thus diary methods can be employed to gather a wide range of data types.

Diary methods may be employed as the sole source of data, but they may also be used in connection with other methods. Diaries have been used as memory aides to improve participants' recall of events for later interviews (Carter, 2002; Keleher & Verrinder, 2003; Zimmerman & Wieder, 1975). The data from participant diaries may also be used as a primary source of data after which they may be triangulated or cross-checked against interviews (Jacelon & Imperio, 2005; Waddington & Fletcher, 2005) or visual observational data (Milligan et al., 2005). In mental health intervention research, diary data can also be triangulated against data from session recordings (Mackrill, 2011), or against pre- or post-intervention assessments (Piasecki, Hufford, Solhan, & Trull, 2007).

What Do Diary Formats Have to Offer Research into Mental Health Interventions?

This question has been answered comprehensively in an article by Mackrill (2008a), who identified seven structural features of mental health interventions that render diary research methodologies particularly relevant. First, mental health interventions generally take place over a course of time, and diary studies are particularly appropriate for gathering data that occur across time. Second, a central characteristic of many mental health interventions is that they occur across contexts. Clients go to sessions with mental health professionals or nonprofessionals to improve the quality of the life that they live elsewhere (Dreier, 2008); or they undertake mental health activities alone rooted in their everyday life contexts. Gaining access to clients' life contexts is therefore central when trying to understand mental health interventions. Diary studies can access the specific contexts where mental health professionals and nonprofessionals participate in mental health interventions with their clients, and they can also access the contexts of clients' lives, where clients strive to make changes. In their everyday life contexts, participants may do "homework" relating to mental health interventions (Kazantzis & L'Abate, 2005); carry out various formalized self-help activities, or carry out their own personal nonformalized mental health interventions to improve the quality of their lives (Dreier, 2008; Mackrill, 2008b, 2009). Essentially, mental health change transpires across the contexts of clients' lives as they strive to change the way they conduct their lives. Third, a person's reflexivity is central to his or her participation in most mental health interventions (Rennie, 1990), and diary methods offer a way of accessing a person's reflections as he or she works to make changes in his or her lives. Fourth, participating in mental health interventions is still a taboo in many parts of society. Even participants who seek professional mental health support can find revealing their problems to the professionals they consult, difficult. Diaries are a good way of accessing data that participants otherwise conceal. Fifth, the field of mental health intervention research encompasses a wealth of theoretical approaches and interests.

Diary studies offer a high degree of methodological and theoretical flexibility. Many aspects of a participant's life can be tracked in a diary, for example, topics or symptoms (Bolger et al., 1989; Burton, Weller, & Sharpe, 2007), activities or behaviors (Jacelon & Imperio, 2005), routines and coping mechanisms (Milligan et al., 2005), or a participant's pursuit of personal agendas or concerns (Mackrill, 2011). Sixth, the relationship between the client and the mental health professional has long been considered central to professional mental health interventions. Diary studies can be employed to highlight differences in perspectives between participants as both clients and professionals may complete diaries (Mackrill, 2011; Yalom & Elkin, 1974). Seventh, most clients take part in mental health intervention to "enrich" their lives or to be empowered. Diary research can be carried out as a form of participatory research, where diarists become coresearchers, investigating their own lives. Thus participating in a diary study may contribute to empowering diarist participants.

Mackrill (2008a) noted that the strengths of diary studies lie not just in the individual aspects presented in the above list but in the range of ways that these strengths may be combined in specific studies. For example, diaries offer a way of gathering data that enable an analysis of the relationship between a person's emotional states and his or her participation in contexts over time; or an analysis of a person's reflections about his or her mental health over time in relation to the contexts he or she inhabits. The many combinations of the above strengths offer the creative researcher a wide range of options when designing studies of mental health interventions.

What Are the Key Drawbacks of Diary Research in Relation to Mental Health Intervention Research?

Diary approaches have a series of limitations. Diary methods involve researchers relinquishing control of part of the research process. Clients may, for example, back fill diaries or even forward fill diaries before they are due (Stone, Shiffman, Schwartz, Broderick, & Hooford, 2002). Diarist may lose his or her motivation with regard to a diary project or simply forget it (Bolger et al., 2003, p. 593). Diary researchers must carefully consider the effort and time involved for diarists, if diarist compliance is to be assured. Diary projects are more susceptible to participants' selectivity (Meth, 2003, p. 202; Plummer, 2001, p. 50). Some experiences will be over-recorded; some will be under-recorded; and some experiences will go unregistered (Jones, 2000, p. 556). The irregularity in the type of data produced in some diary designs may be viewed as a sign of methodological weakness by scientists working within certain epistemologies. Some diary approaches only work with within certain nonrepresentative samples, as they may rule clients who lack writing skills, or lack the skill to employ new technologies, or participants whose level of reflective abstraction is limited, out of studies. Diaries are thus more appropriate to ideographic rather than nomothetic approaches. Diary research methods can be considered a secondary form of intervention that affect and some would argue contaminate the data concerning the mental health intervention in a range of ways (Quinn, Pascoe, Wood, & Neal, 2010). For more information on diary methods as a form of intervention read, for example, Levine and Calvanio (2007) and Heron and Smyth (2010). Diary researchers have developed methods for avoiding or restricting the consequences of many of these limitations. The problems of clients back or forward filling diaries can, for example, be countered to a certain extent by employing electronic diaries which time stamp entries (Shiffman et al., 2008).

Diary Studies of Mental Health Interventions

The following review of diary studies focuses on studies of professional or self-help mental health interventions. It includes studies that employ researcher-solicited diaries. Solicited diaries are here defined as some form of regular, but not necessarily fixed interval, self-monitoring conducted by participants within the contexts of their everyday life, over a period of time, and in connection with participating in or carrying out some form of mental health intervention. While some researchers still refer to their work as a diary study, others employ brand names such as ecological momentary assessment (Shiffman et al., 2008), experience sampling (Csikszentmihalyi & Larson, 1992), or a term that combines both, ambulatory assessment (Trull & Ebner-Priemer, 2009). Day reconstruction methods can also be employed, whereby the diarist reconstructs his or her day at the end of the day (Kahneman, Krueger, Schkade, Schwarz, & Stone, 2004). Other retrospective time frameworks may also be employed, for example, weekly or fortnightly reconstruction. Reconstruction may also be event contingent and, for example, occur in connection with interventions (Mackrill, 2009).

Thiele et al. (2002) reviewed quantitative diary studies in clinical psychology and in psychotherapy. Their review contained few examples of studies where diaries were used to gather data about psychotherapy or other mental health interventions. The primary focus of the studies they reviewed was the everyday life of participants suffering from a range of clinical phenomena such as pain, mood and affectivity, somatic complaints, psychophysiological symptoms, sleep disorders, anxiety disorders, eating disorders, and dependency disorders. There are very few quantitative diary studies of mental health interventions. Most clinical psychological diary studies investigate the phenomenology or variability of particular psychopathological symptoms and behaviors. Such studies are highly relevant, as psychopathology is typically variable over time (Myin-Germeys et al., 2009), and as the relationship between psychopathology and participants' participation in contexts is under-researched.

Traditionally, mental health intervention research has been divided into two strands, outcome and process research. Outcome research focuses on measuring the efficacy of interventions and process research focuses on describing and developing the nuts and bolts of interventions and describing and interpreting participants' experiences of using interventions. A third category of studies related to mental health interventions also exists. This category encompasses studies of the everyday lives of participants who participate in mental health intervention activities, but where the mental health intervention is not the topic of the study. There exist quite a few diary studies of this type, where persons who have been recruited due to their participation in a mental health intervention, but where the mental health intervention is not the topic of the study.

Diary data have long been an important component of assessment in behavioral therapy (Kanfer, 1970). Behavioral therapy has traditionally conducted efficacy case studies by employing continual measurement of target behaviors or symptoms (McLeod, 2010). Some of these studies have employed diary data. The following review focuses on the type of study (outcome, process, or neither) and the type of diary data gathered.

Diary data have been used in studies of anxiety disorders. In an outcome study of the behavioral treatment of panic disorder, Barlow, Craske, Cerney, and Klosko (1989) used diaries to monitor participants' daily fluctuations in anxiety, depression, and pleasantness four times a day (morning, afternoon, evening, and bedtime), and to note the intensity of the panic and whether the panic was associated with an event. Participants' intake of medicine was also monitored. Murphy, Michelson, Marchione, Marchione, and Testa (1998) used diaries to study the outcome of cognitive therapy, relaxation training, and therapist-assisted exposure in the treatment of panic disorder with agoraphobia. Participants kept systematic behavioral diaries of their self-directed exposure practice. Participants recorded the frequency of their practice, the duration of practice, the distance they traveled, and they monitored their levels of anxiety. The diary data were analyzed across and within treatments. Ruwaard, Broeksteeg, Schrieken, Emmelkamp, and Lange (2010) conducted a random controlled trial of a web-based therapist-assisted cognitive behavioral treatment for panic symptoms. A primary outcome measure was a one-week panic diary, where participants following each panic attack described the situation, their accompanying thoughts and bodily sensations, and rated the intensity of their fear on a 10-point scale. Clients maintained this diary throughout the 11-day treatment. For a nonintervention-orientated review of diary data and panic disorders see Alpers (2009). Allen, Blatter-Meunier, Ursprung, and Schneider (2010) recently tested the feasibility and validity of a separation anxiety diary, which might be used in future outcome studies.

Diary data have regularly been employed in studies of eating disorders. Self-monitoring is a standard part of cognitive behavioral treatment for eating disorders. Grange, Gorin, Dymek, and Stone (2002) modified cognitive behavioral therapy for binge eating disorder by asking participants to monitor their eating more intensively using diaries. Participants completed detailed pocket diaries about their mood and events when signaled at random by programmable wristwatches, as well as at all times when eating. The study concluded that the incorporation of the diary assessment method did not improve the efficacy of the treatment and that diary methods were a feasible way of gathering data about treatment. Munsch et al. (2009) tested the suitability of a diary assessment of the outcome of cognitive behavioral treatment for binge eating disorder. They found that binge eating outcomes could be equally accurately assessed by diary assessment as by retrospective self-report questionnaires. In another study of eating disorders, Tasca et al. (2009) employed a weekly eating behavior diary, in which participants recorded the frequency of urges to binge, vomit, overexercise, restrict, and/or abuse laxatives. Participants were asked to monitor their binge eating both according to time-contingent and to event-contingent modes. This study concluded that the method was a valid and reliable approach of recording symptom severity, and predicting treatment outcomes.

Diary data have also been employed in relation to mental health interventions for substance abuse. Shiffmann (2009a) compared three ways of assessing cigarette consumption: global reports of average smoking, timeline follow-back recall for the preceding week, and two weeks of monitoring cigarette use with electronic diaries. Shiffman concluded that diary methods were superior, suggesting that diary methods were highly suited to measuring outcomes in relation to smoking cessation. Diary approaches have also been widely used to gather data about alcohol and drug use and related behaviors. In a study of participants in an eight-week behavioral drinking moderation training program, Collins et al. (1998) used electronic diaries to investigate the role of drinking restraint, and of negative and positive affects. In relation to each episode of excess drinking, participants monitored the occurrence of the drinking episode, the number of drinks consumed, and negative and positive affects before and after the episode. Participants also interacted with the electronic diary in response to multiple random prompts each day, and at the start of each day the previous evening was assessed. The focus of this study was not the intervention, but behavior between interventions.

Another study of a treatment sample that did not focus on the significance of the intervention was conducted by Litt, Cooney, and Morse (1998). They studied the extent to which drinking urges occurred in participants' home environments after treatment for alcohol problems. They also focused on participants' mood states and alcohol-related stimuli associated with urges. This study employed a paper diary and found that the level of self-monitoring deteriorated when participants drank. Husky, Mazure, and Carroll (2008) used cell phones to sample the everyday life of participants in contingency management treatment for cocaine abuse. Participants were contacted five times a day randomly within specific time periods. Participants were asked about their contact with drugs users, their exposure to drug use, and their behavior. Participants reported using a range of drugs other than cocaine. This study was a mental health intervention process study in the sense that it focuses on the contingency management of participants in contingency management treatment. It was however not a typical process study, as the significance of the participants' participation in the treatment was not investigated or analyzed.

Sinadinovic and colleagues (2010) presented an innovative Swedish online mental health intervention where participants free of charge could monitor their drug and alcohol use and keep a personal diary. The study described the intervention and its users, but did not investigate the participants' experiences of using the service or the effects of using the service. Freedman, Lester, McNamara, Milby, and Schumacher (2006) used cell phones to study homeless crack cocaine-addicted adults in treatment. During a two-week period, participants recorded their current states of cocaine craving and using episodes. Participants indicated that the survey made them more aware of phenomena leading to cravings and use. Once again, this was not a study of the mental health interventions' processes or outcomes. It was a study of the feasibility of using cell phones to study a vulnerable sample. The study found that cell phones were a reliable way of gathering data. Johnson, Barrault, Nadeau, and Swendsen (2009) carried out a similar study that confirmed the feasibility and validity of using electronic diaries to study the everyday lives of drug-dependent women who were in treatment. For an overview of ecological momentary assessment studies relating to substance abuse see Shiffman (2009b). While there, to my knowledge, are no diary-based mental health intervention studies of mood disorders, Wenze and Miller (2010) have suggested that they are feasible and that even participants with symptoms are often able to adhere to study procedures.

As well as these quantitative diary studies of mental health interventions, there exist a few qualitative solicited diary studies. Rogers (1951) published extracts from a client's diary about her experiences of psychotherapy. The client was encouraged to write "a completely honest account, whether this meant positive or negative statements" (*ibid.*, pp. 88–89). Rogers comments on material in the diary that highlights his theoretical and practical approach to counseling, but there is no systematic analysis of the diary as it is considered "largely self-explanatory" (*ibid.*, p. 89).

Existential psychiatrist, Irving Yalom and his client, who is given the pseudonym, Ginny Elkin, also jointly published their individual diaries of over a year and a half of therapy with logs written after each session (Yalom & Elkin, 1974). Elkin wrote as a form of payment for sessions and Yalom viewed Elkin's writing as a part of a treatment for her writer's block. Elkin was asked to "write an honest summary of each sessions, containing not only her reactions to what transpired, but also a depiction of the subterranean life of the hour, a note from the underground – all the thoughts that never emerge in the daylight of the verbal intercourse" (Yalom & Elkin, 1974, xvii–xviii). By self-disclosing Yalom hoped to challenge Elkin's view of him as "infallible, omniscient, untroubled, perfectly integrated" (*ibid.*, p. xviii). They exchanged diaries every six months and discussed the experience of reading each other's diaries. Yalom reflected on the use of diaries as a therapeutic method, but not as a method of research. There was no systematic analysis of the diaries. The diaries were presented verbatim with a few comments.

A third diary study was carried out by Wosket (1999). The diaries were guided by a series of incomplete sentences concerning sessions that the diarists completed within 48 hours of sessions. The sentences concerned significant aspects of sessions, helpful/unhelpful events, unfulfilled wishes regarding sessions and sentences inquiring about the therapeutic relationship and themes in the session. Where the other diary studies merely present diary data verbatim, Wosket also presented summaries of the diaries related to five themes. Etherington (2000) presented diary data in a book on the treatment of men who have been sexually abused as children. Etherington encouraged two of her male clients, brothers who had both been sexually abused by their paternal grandfather throughout their childhood, to keep diaries during the period of time when they and their whole families were beginning to face up to and come to terms with the grandfather's abuse of them and other family members. Etherington encouraged the brothers to "to write down the story of what their lives were like at that time, while at the same time they were telling their stories orally" (*ibid.*, p. 152). One brother's diary is presented verbatim and the other brother has written an account based on his diary. The brothers' accounts offer a rich and moving case description of the dynamics of a whole family facing up to and beginning to come to terms with incest.

Etherington's book (2000) also contains a range of ideas about how to work on such cases as well as insights into Etherington's personal perspective on the counseling process. Though interesting, the diary data in themselves offer little information about how the counseling was used by the brothers and there are no analyses that link the contents of the diary data with the counseling processes in sessions. Thus, as in the other qualitative diary studies, this study also revealed a reluctance to analyze and interpret the diary data. All the above qualitative diary studies primarily present data verbatim and contain no systematic analyses of the diary data. This can be contrasted with the work of Mackrill (2011), whose research focused on the links between psychotherapy sessions and clients' everyday lives. Mackrill conducted a process study of psychotherapy with adult children of problem drinkers, where clients wrote diaries about significant events in sessions, and about new and different experiences in their everyday lives between sessions. Therapists also wrote diaries about significant events in sessions, and how they imagined these events might influence clients' everyday lives. Mackrill developed a method of analyzing these diary data qualitatively. Mackrill presented a series of findings, for example, about how clients were already changing prior to entering psychotherapy (Mackrill 2008c); about how clients employed a series of strategies for change in their everyday life that were not derived from psychotherapy sessions but that were modified in sessions (Mackrill 2008b); and about how clients used mental health interventions to corroborate perspectives on life issues that they had encountered elsewhere (Mackrill, 2009).

Conclusions

A series of conclusions can be drawn from the above diary studies. First, diary approaches offer a feasible and valid way of studying the outcomes of mental health interventions. Second, though diary approaches are a feasible and valid way of studying the outcomes of mental health interventions, they are very rare. This is probably because diary studies are more costly than outcome studies that use retrospective rating scales. Such studies offer a cheaper way of gathering more data and thus increasing the power of studies. Third, diary studies have as yet hardly been used in process studies of mental health interventions. This is surprising as they offer many exciting possibilities. Understanding the links between mental health interventions and the everyday life of participants is central to understanding the processes of mental health interventions. Diary approaches have much to offer in this respect. Diary process studies of mental health interventions can, for example, focus on the phenomenology of being a participant in a mental health intervention. They can focus on the interpersonal and intrapersonal variations in how mental health interventions are used. They can focus on the relationship between mental health interventions and the contexts of participants' lives; for example, by investigating how interventions are incorporated by participants into their everyday life contexts and how the contexts of clients' everyday lives influence participants' participation in and interpretations of interventions.

As mentioned earlier, a key strength of diary methods is that they enable researchers to gather data about personal reflections, and a key feature of participation in mental health interventions is personal reflection. The increased need for personal reflection was also what historically led to the development of the diary. This match has clearly not yet been employed to its full potential in diary studies of mental health interventions. The relationship between the types of reflections encouraged in interventions and clients' everyday reflections can be explored both quantitatively and qualitatively. Surprisingly few researchers have so far used solicited written diaries when studying mental health interventions. The use of written diaries challenges methodological tradition. Though diary approaches can be employed by both ideographic and nomothetic approaches, diary methods clearly favor ideographic approaches. Regardless of whether one favors ideographic or nomothetic approaches, developing theory and methods for analyzing complex courses of events across time and across contexts is clearly central to mental health intervention research.

Chapter 5

Bibliotherapy

Debbie McCulliss

> *"Come, and take choice of all my library,*
> *And so beguile they sorrow."*
>
> William Shakespeare.
> Titus Andronicus, Act 4,
> Scene 1, lines 34–35.
> (Hughes, 1994, p. 120).

Bibliotherapy is guided reading for the therapeutic purpose of gaining an understanding or solving problems of behavioral or emotional issues (Riordan & Wilson, 1989). This chapter provides an overview of bibliotherapy, the application of self-help books and computer-aided therapeutic interventions, as well as the emerging role of writing and research related to bibliotherapy. In 1904 in the United States, bibliotherapy was an aspect of librarianship. In 1906, libraries began to serve as therapeutic agents in "hastening convalescence and restoring health" (Hannigan, 1962, p. 184). The librarian served as a bibliotherapist, and books assumed a leading role in therapy (Jones, 1939). Over subsequent years, as libraries and information media evolved, nontraditional roles in librarianship have emerged. Bibliotherapy now provides an alternative career option to librarians. Two types of bibliotherapy have been described. *Reading* bibliotherapy occurs when books are read and there is no facilitated discussion of the reader's personal reaction to the material. *Interactive* bibliotherapy occurs when sessions concentrate on a dialogue led by a facilitator about assigned literature. Categories of reading and interactive bibliotherapy include: clinical, developmental, and client-developed.

Research on Writing Approaches in Mental Health
Studies in Writing, Volume 23, 67–83

ISSN: 1572-6304/doi: 10.1108/S1572-6304(2011)0000023009

Clinical bibliotherapy, on the one hand, is implemented by professionals who work in psychiatric units, community mental health centers, or chemical dependency units with patients dealing with significant emotional or behavioral problems. For example, selected works by Shakespeare, Proust, or Rilke may be prescribed by physicians, mental health practitioners, and/or social workers, often in consultation with a librarian (Sautter, 2010). Therapeutic goals for patients range from insight to letting go of resistance to initiating new ideas to a change in behavior.

The following is an example of how clinical bibliotherapy has been used with poetry as the vehicle for therapy. Bibliotherapist Rosalie Brown formed a bibliotherapy group of seven institutionalized men confined to wheelchairs and with varying capacities to speak. The group met for 21 months. Poetry presented included "The Pasture" by Robert Frost, "People" by Lois Lenski, "The Flag Goes By" by Henry Bennett, "Washington, D.C." by James Metcalfe, the slogan "Let's all pull together" adopted by citizens of Kenya, and excerpts from the preamble to the "Declaration of Independence." Each one caught the men's imagination. They expressed how it felt to be a patient in a mental hospital, their attitudes toward family and neighbors, their awareness of their restricted freedom, and their desire to go home. Learning that Clara Barton was once afraid of people and that she experienced recurrent difficulty in speaking gave members courage to share their fear of doctors and of hearing voices as well as the incentive to encourage each other to make appropriate sounds. Communication, verbal and nonverbal, is a group venture rather than an individual struggle (Brown, 1977, p. 347).

Developmental bibliotherapy, on the other hand, is provided by educators, librarians, and health care workers to healthy individuals. Participants can be recommended books and/or utilize support/intervention/therapy. The goals are to facilitate normal development and self-actualization or to maintain mental health (Rubin, 1978, 1979). An abundance of resources are available to help people understand changes in family structure; death and grieving; disability and physical limitations; obesity; learning differences; emotional conflict or suffering; and family, work, or community social issues, to name a few.

Nurses in Canada provide an example of developmental bibliotherapy. Nurses who care for the elderly in their homes have successfully used American psychologist Peter Lewinsohn's *Control Your Depression* to assist their clients in dealing with their conditions (Sautter, 2010). Bibliotherapist Stefania Moro often suggests *The Twins* by Tessa De Loo (a fictional account of two sisters separated by World War II who meet again 40 years later) and J. R. Moehringer's memoir *Tender Bar* (in which he recounts his childhood experiences with quirky patrons of a New York pub, who become substitutes for his absent father) (Sautter, 2010).

While many prefer to read alone (i.e. without the input from others), book clubs and poetry groups have increased in popularity over the years for those who want to read and discuss literature in the company of others. For the blind, partially sighted, or dyslexic, audiobooks are available, allowing them to participate in such groups.

Last, *client-developed* bibliotherapy allows participants to be creative through writing. Riordan (1996) asked clients to create their own therapeutic writings, a practice he called *scriptotherapy*. Client-generated poetry, another category of imaginative literature, or writing in response to a poem or a passage read is an additional creative way to combine bibliotherapy with scriptotherapy.

Bibliotherapy may be conducted as self-help (stand-alone), one-on-one (supported and supplementary), or in a group setting. It can be complemented with discussion, play activity, or writing. Bibliotherapy is currently used within nearly every helping profession, with all age groups, in multicultural populations, with diverse diagnoses and treatment approaches, and with a wide variety of documented effectiveness (McMillen & Pehrsson, 2004; Pehrsson & McMillen, 2005). Among the problems and issues that have been addressed through bibliotherapy are: behavioral issues, adoption, addictions, family dissolution, cultural awareness and ethnic identity, grief and loss, physical abuse and domestic trauma, dispute resolution, clinical depression, homelessness, disability, night terrors, obsessive–compulsive disorder, AIDS, chronic illness, divorce, foster care, attention deficit hyperactivity disorder, pathological gambling, hypochondria, homosexuality, literacy, tolerance, pregnancy, postpartum depression, smoking cessation, rape, social alienation, suicide, violence, learning problems, and self-destructive behaviors (Pehrsson & McMillen, 2006). In addition, problems and issues that have been addressed through bibliotherapy in younger children have included: character building, suspension, bullying, social phobia, stuttering, excessive peer group pressure, resiliency, self-confidence, decision-making, problem-solving, and goal setting.

Bibliotherapy is more than recommending reading material. It includes assessment of the emotional, cognitive, physical, behavioral, and developmental factors of an individual. Careful consideration must be given to the recommended choice of material, including subject matter, appropriateness, reading level, and whether or not it will address therapeutic/patient goals. Quality is necessary to elicit a response. The client may need varying degrees of assistance from a facilitator, depending on their age and ability to assimilate the information (McMillen & Pehrsson, 2004).

Michael Duda, quoted in Sautter (2010, pp. 2–3), believes that "when we immerse ourselves in a text, the words stimulate the production of mental images. We imagine what characters look and sound like; we visualize the places they live and work; we act out the words on the page in our minds .... Stimulating the feelings and experiences of the literary figures allows readers to perceive and express their own emotions ... That's why it's crucial to recommend the right reading material."

Self-Help Books

Starker (1988) was one of the first to report on the use of self-help books in bibliotherapy. He described self-help books as providing a means of self-improvement by alleviating distress, facilitating problem-solving, changing behavior, or improving coping. Self-direction books include programmed writing or workbooks that "consist of a sequential series of programmed, written homework assignments involving questions, tasks, and exercises that systematically address specific topics" (L'Abate & Kern, 2002, p. 242). Self-help treatment may increase the accessibility and affordability of evidence-based psychological treatments (Cuijpers & Schuurmans, 2007; Den Boer, Wiersma, & Van den Bosch, 2004). Self-help treatments can take various forms with varying levels of therapist contact (Carlbring & Anderson, 2006). Therapist contact, if any, is usually administered via telephone or e-mail. In 2008, Amazon.com listed more than 151,000 self-help titles. Gaining popularity, this number reflected an increase of titles in that genre by 67% from listings posted in 2007 (American Writers and Artists Inc., 2011). *The Authoritative Guide to Self-Help Books* (1994) can help guide lay readers and librarians through today's proliferation of self-help literature. There also exists a wealth of online resources that explore bibliotherapy and list titles of books, according to topic such as the University of Wisconsin at Whitewater's "Official Bibliotherapy 2009 Class Resources."

L'Abate proposed the use of the traditional dictionary to define terms, items, and adjectives (L'Abate, 2007). As covered in Chapter 8 of this volume, he uses this technique in treating dysfunctional patterns in couples (L'Abate, 2008b), and individuals with psychiatric symptoms. Patient experiences can also be reflected upon through comics. HIV and hospice care nurse M. K. Czerwiec encouraged medical students to reflect on their experiences through comics. She asked students to draw a diagnosis as if they were a patient receiving it and then asked them to draw a different diagnosis as if they were a doctor giving it. Czerwiec says, "When they drew diagnoses as a doctor, they drew disembodied body parts, but when they drew as a patient, they drew embodied experiences of illness, with reference to an emotional reaction and to their whole families and lives" (O'Luanaigh, 2010). The combination of text and image present in comics gives creators the opportunity to tap into both the right and left sides of their brains, for insight into an experience. "Words can access one thing, but when you challenge yourself to make images, you access more and possibly different information. It's very powerful to put those two things together" (O'Luanaigh, 2010). A few examples of works in the growing subgenre of comics, now called graphic narrative, include: *Stitches* by David Small (growing up with illness), *Binky Brown* by Justin Green (obsessive–compulsive disorder), *Swallow Me Whole* by Nate Powell (depression, bipolar disorder, and dissociative disorder), and *Psychiatric Tales* by Darryl Cunningham.

Programmed Writing

Bibliotherapy has expanded to also include writing. Programmed writing can range from open-ended journal writing to specific writing assignments related to treatment goals (King, Engi, & Poulos, 1998). Writing assignments offer clients tangible evidence of their improvement. The client has the opportunity to remain actively engaged in the therapeutic process. Therapists can point to issues that need to be addressed such as emotional avoidance or readiness to change. Assignments can be used for further discussion, looking at generalizations, distortions, contradictions, and omissions (L'Abate & Platzman, 1991) (see Chapter 7 in this volume).

Traditional psychotherapy and programmed writing complement each other. Programmed writing as a weekly assignment helps patients keep centered between sessions, assume personal responsibility for change, and experience self-knowledge and self-mastery (Jordan & L'Abate, 1995). Writing exercises can further discussion, exploration, and evaluation, and can set the stage for providing corrective feedback (Jordan and L'Abate, 1995; L'Abate, 1991). Programmed writing in conjunction with traditional psychotherapy may not be suited for certain therapists' styles or for certain patients. It has, however, been reported to be successful in increasing communication by couples, encouraging change, intensifying short-term therapy effects, enhancing cost-effectiveness, aiding in dealing with forgotten traumas, and guiding therapy progression (Jordan & L'Abate, 1995). Programmed writing with interactive practice exercises or workbooks is one technique that can be used by counselors to elicit and facilitate feelings or help clients translate experience into language (De Giacomo et al., 2010).

Creative/Expressive Writing

Bibliocounseling is a method that uses literature and/or creative writing, including journal writing to achieve emotional, behavioral, cognitive, and/or social life changes. Emphasis is placed on the individual's emotional and cognitive response to the reading first, in order to evoke transfer to the individual's own life situation (Gladding, 2005). The emotional response to the chosen text is the most elementary response, since it is what contributes to the interpretation of the read text originating from one's own inner and also the objective world. Bibliocounseling is based on subjectivity, since it originates within the individual (Hynes & Hynes-Berry, 1986).

The main goal of bibliocounseling is the introduction of knowledge and skills that an individual can use in the future in dealing with life. The experiential process of bibliocounseling begins with recognition, the written work having drawn the reader's attention and interest, and stimulated his or her imagination. Examination, the next phase, engages the reader more deeply. This phase explores what the feeling-response means to the reader (Hynes & Hynes-Berry, 1986). Distinguishing the reader from the literary subject, and the reader's experience from the fictional experience, happens by juxtaposing images, subjects, situations, problem approaches, and feelings. Last, after evaluating new viewpoints and behavior introspectively, the reader applies his or her own life insights learned from the process (Ličen & Furland, 2006).

Therapists can meet a range of client needs by assigning readings and engaging clients in discussion on assigned literature based on quality and relevance. Clients can then be asked to write, for example, to resolve the story in a different way, analyze decisions of characters, or reflect on the story's outcome in their journal. Problem-solving through writing can be an effective intervention.

For patients writing about their life and concerned about their writing competence, Gladding (2005) suggests the following ideas to overcome initial difficulties: write down the mistakes (unpleasant experiences) and delusions, and write down the good (the same situation as it was pleasant/satisfying). The goal is to find out what was learned and gained from past events.

For some, writing experiences down can provide a positive way to externalize pain, fear, confusion, embarrassment, and vulnerability that otherwise would be carried inside. Staying with the flow, taking thoughts as they come — just as one would do if he or she were sitting opposite someone face-to-face — can promote moving eventually away from the confusion and on to what the conflicts are really about (Turner, 1992, p. 8). As varying levels of awareness are revealed, internal feelings can be explored.

In reviewing evidence to support expressive writing in its many applications and implications, as well as evidence to support Pennebaker's original model of writing about past traumatic events for 15–20 minutes a day for four consecutive days (see Chapter 5 in this volume), Pennebaker and Chung (2007) concluded that

> Although experiencing emotions while writing is clearly a necessary component of the expressive writing effects, cognitive work is required as well … . The mere emotional experience of a trauma is not sufficient. Health gains appear to require translating experience into language (p. 275) … . Verbally labeling an emotion may itself influence the emotional experience. Indeed changing any sensory experience into language affects the experience … .

Pennebaker's model may explain the process and outcome of distance and expressive writing in health promotion, prevention, and psychotherapy. This process may put greater reliance on the left hemisphere rather than the right hemisphere, as when a participant is talking emotionally in therapy. Therefore the process, when it occurs in writing, may equalize the contribution of both hemispheres, requiring essentially the coordinated usage of both (L'Abate & Hecker, 2004).

Two Danish authors (Rasmussen & Tomm, 1992) have suggested that clients start therapy with writing a letter to their therapist about what they see as their main problem, what they would like to change, and what they have tried before to overcome their difficulties. In a second letter, patients are encouraged to write down their personal history, giving information about important others who have been good and bad influences in their life, and about important feelings and events in their past history, including their ideas about the origin and meaning of their own symptoms and their goals for the therapy. Their guiding principle, similar to that in the Pennebaker paradigm, is that writing should be "unrestrained, uncensored, ...[and] express spontaneous and intuitive feelings, even irrational thoughts ... ."

The authors point out that they do not see writing as the essence of the therapeutic work but as "only a pathway, a channel, or a means towards the therapeutic end of self-discovery and self-healing." Further writing assignments are given to the patient or are jointly negotiated. Other examples of writing assignments include writing about the three most disappointing events in their life and then the three most gratifying or affirming events in their life. They may be asked to give an account of three situations in which they felt most loved, followed by three situations in which they felt most rejected (Schmidt, Bone, Hems, Lessem, & Treasure, 2002, p. 307).

Biblionarrative

Biblionarrative is a child-focused narrative therapy technique that combines oral and written stories about life events in order to facilitate conversation and to gather a child's life story for clinical and research purposes (Eppler & Carolan, 2005). When writing and talking are used in tandem, this technique may allow clinicians to access information that otherwise may not be discovered when relying on either talk or writing therapy alone and further facilitate the process of change (Eppler & Carolan, 2005).

The process begins with conducting an interview where life story information is gathered. The role of the interviewer is to ask perceptions, to clarify the sequence of events, relationships and feelings, and then to focus on adaption and mastery of the events (p. 35). The story develops when the therapist asks direct and indirect questions, places the story in context, and provides a safe atmosphere where the story can be told (Zimmerman & Dickerson, 1994).

Once the verbal story information is obtained, the clinician aids the child in writing his or her story as text. A modified version of Harold, Palmiter, Lynch, and Freedman-Doan's (1995) storyboard serves as an open-ended template to gather information for the written story. Templates include areas such as: the family and individual dynamics before and during the problem, the current situation, their thoughts and feelings, and their perceptions and expectations regarding the future.

Medical Narrative

Since the 1990s, a number of medical students have been taught the skills of close reading, self-expression, and reflective capacity, in addition to compassionate presence, mindful listening, practicing empathy, and exercising moral imagination.

Narrative medicine makes the case that narrative training in these skills contributes to clinical effectiveness and may help students too in their search for meaning (Charon, 2006).

Fictional characters can provide medical students insights that facilitate learning about medical diagnoses, especially from characters with psychological issues. They may also help students learn about topics they have not experienced or might never know or help a student come to terms with his or her own feelings from a safe distance. The "reading" of nontextual sources, films, images, or material objects also carries layers of meaning, each open to discernment and interpretation. *On Doctoring: Stories, Poems, Essays* is a collection that represents the issues, concerns, and challenges of doctors and patients. Literature is often used as a springboard to create writing prompts. Expressive writing and journal writing can facilitate venting of fears, self-awareness, creativity, and clarity. Writing can lead to productive discussions between faculty and students. Some clinicians and patients review their writings with one another. Outside of medical school, journal writing plays a role in inpatient or outpatient settings, group or individual therapy, and 12-step programs.

Interactive Multimedia Scriptwriting Therapy

With the advent of interactive multimedia, entertainment can be "learning," and learning can be "therapy." Inner personal journaling has become popular as a means of self-growth and self-expression in a therapeutic setting. Creative writing therapy may use interactive multimedia emotive writing from the inner self, where the writer must think in three dimensions to create interactive multimedia and use it therapeutically.

Writing scripts for interactive multimedia helps clients examine how writing expresses their feelings. Poems, stories, scripts, and games are analyzed, discussed, and examined for personal influence on feelings. Options for scriptwriting therapy include choosing alternative branch endings or central narratives or creating a computer game, novel, story, teleplay, video, radio play, or graphic novel–comic book out of a finished script. Alternative branching pathways allow the writer to make choices, to grow, and to measure the range of change or growth (Hart, 2010).

Therapeutic Application

It is important to note that therapeutic applications offered through the Internet do not attempt to replace traditional therapy. Rather, Internet-supported interventions allow a broadening of the scope and diversity of ways of approaching and reaching out to different clientele, as well as opportunities for providing different methods of interventions (Barak, Klein, & Proudfoot, 2009). Typed text communication necessitates using words, skills in verbal expression, and emotions to clarify messages and have them understood correctly. Voice tones, body language, and physical appearance are absent in text communication. However, writing gives the client a high degree of freedom to define his or her own experiences, explore whatever feels most relevant, and work at a comfortable rate (Bolton, 1999a; Cohen & Kerr, 1998; Collie, Mitchell, & Murphy, 2000; Rasmussen & Tomm, 1992).

Some researchers have even proposed that the lack of physical presence of a therapist or reader may not lessen the therapeutic value of the writing process (Pennebaker, 1990). Rather, the effort required to "reconstruct a story of psychological debilitation could offer potential for mental healing and begin to alleviate persistent symptoms of numbing, dysphoria, and uncontrollable flashbacks" (Henke, 2000, p. xii).

No two individuals will react in the same fashion to a given piece of literature or writing assignment. In the process, children and adolescents can be expected to go through similar stages as adults.

Research on Writing in Bibliotherapy

Studies have been conducted to evaluate the effectiveness of bibliotherapy. These studies vary in the type of bibliotherapy used and the types of problems studied (see appendix). To follow are some examples of studies in the use of bibliotherapy. A number of randomized control trials have found self-help bibliotherapy, either alone or in combination with other therapies, to be an effective treatment for a variety of conditions (Mead et al., 2005). Kraaj et al. (2009) conducted a randomized controlled trial that suggested that a cognitive-behavioral self-help program, along with a computerized structured writing intervention, was effective in reducing depressed mood in HIV-positive individuals.

Bibliotherapy using recommended self-help books has also been found to be effective. For example, the self-help book *Coping with Panic* (Clum, 1989), delivered without therapist input, was found to be effective with people suffering from panic disorders with or without agoraphobia (Nordin, Carlbring, Cuijpers, & Andersson, 2010). Women with personality disorders who had been given a problem-solving workbook cut their hospital stay in half compared to women who received medication (L'Abate & Goldstein, 2007). Bibliotherapy has been shown to be an effective treatment for anxiety and depression in non-Caucasian or culturally different individuals. For example, a study with Chinese patients with depression showed that bibliotherapy improved the status of social support in these patients. The bibliotherapy component was found to relieve anxiety and helped patients obtain support, restore confidence in the future, and eliminate discrimination of their own diseases (Wang, 2011).

Bibliotherapy has also been used to treat common issues encountered in everyday life. For example, university undergraduate students who had a problem with academic worrying were instructed to write for 20 minutes in as much detail and exploration as possible about their worry. Besides encouraging findings in improving their worrying, the authors found expressive writing lends itself to self-administration (Goldman, Dugas, Sexton, & Gervais, 2007). Colon (1996) studied therap-e-mail. Two therapy groups were contacted via e-mail through a commercial online service. Participants were required to post messages to the group at least three times a week. The researcher commented:

> Most posted an email every day and noted that even though online group therapy is labor intensive, and members had to connect through a medium that diminishes the sense of personal interaction, I sensed fewer emotional distractions in the online group than exist in off-line therapies. Group conference members learned to trust each other and were willing to disclose more, making the therapy more in-depth. (Colon, 1996, p. 215)

This process of writing has been described as externalizing and reframing the clients' problems, in a manner that is more empowering to its resolution, therefore promoting therapeutic change (Colon, 1996). Perhaps with this form of therapy, it is less likely that clients will contradict themselves in the body of a therap-e-mail than they would in a face-to-face session.

Although findings in a study on therapeutic writing as an intervention for symptoms of bulimia nervosa (BN) suggested that therapeutic writing tasks are of limited benefit to individuals experiencing symptoms of BN, it did find that individuals high in body shame may benefit most from e-mail–based writing tasks that may be less anxiety provoking, shaming, and embarrassing than face-to-face discussion (Johnston, Startup, Lavender, Godfrey, & Schmidt, 2010). In another study, letter writing is used to encourage patients to express the pros and cons of change and to envisage a future with or without eating disorders. One of the structured exercises instructs patients to write a letter to their eating disorder as a friend and to write another letter to their eating disorder as an enemy. These letters have been examined by Serpell, Treasure, Teasdale, and Sullivan (1999) in a qualitative study, and are described as often revealing important emotional themes (Schmidt, Bone, Hems, Lessem & Treasure, 2002).

An Internet-administered self-help program with minimal therapist contact has been used to treat social phobias (Carlbring et al., 2007). In further work with social phobias, weekly phone calls were added to the intervention, resulting in increased adherence to treatment (Andersson et al., 2006). The treated participants achieved significant improvement in measures that included social anxiety, fear, and depression, compared to those in the control group (from the wait list). At 12-month follow-up, measures of quality of life were significantly higher for both groups. Carlbring, Ekselius, and Andersson (2003) found the use of e-mail in therapy to be effective in treating panic disorders.

The Amsterdam Writing Group set up *Interapy*, a Web site to provide Internet-mediated communication between research participants and therapists. They reported encouraging findings from controlled trials (Lange et al., 2000, 2002; Lange, van de Ven, Schrieken, & Emmelkamp, 2001).

Parsons (2008) presents a literature review that includes a general overview of online counseling practices and evidence-based research on various writing therapy techniques and Web site evaluations in her master's project, *Finding Reliable On-Line Therapeutic Writing Sources: A Manual for Counseling Professionals.*

Suggestions for Future Research

To meet the challenge of providing effective mental health services, there is a need for the scientific study of the costs and efficacy of treatments offered outside of face-to-face settings. *State of the Field Report: Arts in Healthcare* (State of the Field Committee, 2009) found a growing body of research linking the arts to improved quality of care, although much of the research on the economic benefits of arts in health care is anecdotal. Almlöv, Carlbring, Berger, Cuijpers, and Andersson (2009) suggest that future studies focus on what online therapists write to their clients. Others suggest that studies are needed comparing Internet to face-to-face therapy and larger studies to examine the individual responses of patients to treatment (Carlbring et al., 2007).

Wright proposes that future studies focus on the following:

- How are forms of therapeutic writing explained by and linked to the various theoretical approaches in counseling and psychotherapy?
- How are practices of journal writing, (auto) biographical writing, and autoethnography developing in different disciplines and in different parts of the world?
- How can we connect across the divide between the "evidence base" for writing developed by the empirical scientist and those more inclined toward narrative- and arts-based research? (2009, p. 239).

Summary

Bibliotherapy has long been used to benefit mental health consumers. Bibliotherapy is a practical treatment alternative for people with limited access to psychological services. Many psychologists now recommend self-help books for advice on problem-solving, coping, or for changing behavior. The self-paced format of bibliotherapy appeals to individuals who are reluctant to utilize traditional therapy or pharmacological treatments. Internet-supported interventions offer a variety of alternatives to traditional face-to-face therapeutic sessions. Writing assignments or text messaging offers clients the opportunity to actively engage in the therapeutic process.

The field of bibliotherapy is ever-evolving. Accessible in many forms, bibliotherapy is currently used to some degree by nearly every helping profession, with a variety of age groups, in multicultural populations, and dealing with diverse diagnoses and treatment approaches. Proposed benefits are many, including enhanced self-concept, increased self-expression, increased understanding of personal or generic human behavior or motivation, realization of the variety of potential solutions, and exploring a workable solution to identified problems.

Appendix: Selected Research on Bibliotherapy

Research has increased since the 1990s on bibliotherapy's use in a variety of client groups. The majority of research reports have been published on the use of bibliotherapy in depression and anxiety. Other problems addressed include: hair pulling, problem drinking, eating, panic disorders, and insomnia. Below is an alphabetized list of studies adapted from Chamberlain, Heaps, and Robert (2008) on the types of bibliotherapy indicating either the group studied or the focus area.

Study, *Type of Bibliotherapy*
Client Group or Problem Area(s)

Ackerson et al. (1998)
RCT, Cognitive therapy, Adolescents suffering from depression

Almlöv et al. (2009)
Internet-delivered CBT, Depression

Anderson et al. (2005)
Review, Self-help books based on CBT approach, Depression

Andersson and Cuijpers (2009)
Meta-analysis, Computerized psychological treatments, Depression

Apodaca and Miller (2003)
Meta-analysis, Self-help materials, Problem drinking

Bogels (2007)
RCTs, Bibliotherapy, Children suffering from anxiety disorders

Bower et al. (2001)
Systematic review, Self-help treatments, Anxiety and depression

Bruwer and Stein (2005)
Survey, Internet support groups, Hair pulling

Campbell and Smith (2003)
Review and study, Self-help books, Psychotherapy intervention

Carlbring et al. (2005)
RCT, CBT with Internet program, Panic disorders

Carlbring et al. (2006)
RCT, Internet-based CBT supplemented with telephone calls, Panic disorders

Carrard et al. (2006)
Study, Online help program, Bulimia nervosa

Christensen et al. (2002)
A study, Web-based CBT intervention, Depression and anxiety

Cuijpers (1997)
Meta-analysis, Book is taken home to be worked through independently, Unipolar depression

Cuijpers (1998)
Meta-analysis, Bibliotherapy in the community, Depression in older adults

Cuijpers et al. (2006)
Meta-analysis of RCT, Psychological interventions including bibliotherapy, Late-life depression

D'Alessandro et al. (2004)
RCTs, Internet health information, Children

den Boer et al. (2004)
Systematic review, Written materials based mainly on behavioral principles, Depression/anxiety

Du Plock (2005)
Discussion paper with case studies, Bibliotherapy, Two case studies

Ehlers et al. (2003)
RCT, Self-help booklet, Posttraumatic stress

Evans et al. (1999)
RCT, Manual-assisted cognitive behavior, Self-harm

Eysenbach (2005)
Electronic health initiatives, ——

Eysenbach et al. (2004)
Systematic review, Online peer-to-peer interactions, Online community

Farrand (2005)
Case study, Self-help book, Primary care

Febbraro (2005)
RCTs, Bibliotherapy alone (BT), bibliotherapy with phone contact (BT + PC), and phone contact alone (PC), Panic attacks

Fingeld (2000)
Study, Self-help manuals, Problem drinking

Floyd (2003)
Discussion paper with two clinical case studies, Reading a self-help book, Depression in older adults

Floyd et al. (2004)
Compared individual psychotherapy and bibliotherapy, Depression

Forest (1998)
Study, Self-help psychology books, ——

Frazer et al. (2005)
Systematic review, Self-help books, Mild to moderate depression

Frude (2004a) study
Bibliotherapy, Psychological therapy

Frude (2004b)
Case study, Books on prescription, Primary care

Gould (1995)
Meta-analysis, Cognitive-behavioral treatments, Panic disorders

Hooper (2003)
Cochrane review, Self-help resources, Advice to reduce dietary salt

Jamison and Scogin (1995)
Minimal-contact CBT bibliotherapy utilizing the self-help book Feeling Good, Depression

Jones (2002)
Study, Cognitive-behavioral self-help treatment, Health anxiety

Jorm et al. (2004)
Meta-analysis, Use of written materials or computer programs or audio and video tapes, Anxiety

Kaltenthaler et al. (2006)
Systematic review, CCBT, Depression and anxiety

Landreville and Bissonnette (1997)
Minimal-contact cognitive bibliotherapy, Depressed older adults with a physical disability

Latner (2001)
Literature review, Self-help treatments, Obesity

Mains and Scogin (2003)
Literature review, Self-administered treatment, —

Marrs (1995)
Meta-analysis, Use of written materials or computer programs or audio and video, Sexual dysfunction, assertion, anxiety, and depression in adults

McKendree-Smith et al. (2003)
Review, Cognitive and/or behavioral bibliotherapy, Depression

Mead et al. (2005)
RCT, Guided self-help, Anxiety

Mettler and Kemper (2003)
Discussion paper, IPs, Content of IPs

Mettler and Kemper (2005)
Discussion paper, IPs, Content of IPs

Mimeault and Morin (1999)
Study, Bibliotherapy, Insomnia

Montgomery et al. (2001)
Cochrane review, Media-based cognitive-behavioral therapies, Children with behavioral disorders

Newman et al. (2003)
Literature review, Self-help and minimal, Contact therapies, Anxiety disorders

NICE Guidance (2004)
Guided self-help program based on CBT, Depression in primary and secondary care

NICE Guidance (2004)
Bibliotherapy based on CBT principles, Anxiety in adults in primary, secondary, and community care

NICE Guidance (CCBT) February (2006a)
CCBT, Mild/moderate, Depression/anxiety

NICE Guidance February (2006b)
CCBT for depression (and anxiety) (CCBT), Panic and phobia

Rapee et al. (2006)
RCT, Bibliotherapy, written materials for parents, Children suffering from anxiety disorders

Reeves and Stace (2005)
Trial, Self-help treatments, Mild to moderate stress/anxiety in adults

Ruskin et al. (2004)
RCT, Face-to-face psychiatric treatment vs. videolink treatment, Depressed veterans

Ruwaard et al. (2009)
RCT, Therapist-guided Web-based CBT, Depression

Salkovskis et al. (2006)
Individual self-help package vs. standard primary care treatment, Depression

Scogin et al. (1989)
Cognitive and behavioral bibliotherapy in older adults, Depression

Scogin et al. (1996)
Meta-analysis, Self-administered treatment, Depression

Semple et al. (2006)
Study, CBT, bibliotherapy, and group therapy, Head and neck cancer

Thompson et al. (2001)
Cochrane review, Self-help resources, Dietary advice to lower blood cholesterol

Liu et al. (2009)
Cognitive bibliotherapy among Chinese individuals in Taiwan, Depression

Van Kesteren et al. (2006)
Intervention mapping using bibliotherapy, Promoting sexual health in HIV-positive men who have sex with men

Van Lankveld (1998)
Meta-analysis, Self-help books, Sexual dysfunction

van't Veer-Tazelaar et al. (2010)
Stepped care prevention intervention, Depression and anxiety
Vos et al. (2005a)
Study, Bibliotherapy, Cost-effectiveness in mental health

Vos et al. (2005b)
Study, CBT delivered via therapist, Cost-effectiveness

Wollersheim and Wilson (1991)
Supportive group treatment vs. bibliotherapy, Depression

Yeater et al. (2004)
Bibliotherapy, Sexual assault prevention with college-aged women

Notes: CBT, cognitive-behavioral therapy; CCBT, computerized cognitive-behavioral therapy; GP, general practitioner; IP, information prescription; RCT, randomized control trial.

Chapter 6

The Expressive Writing Method

Jenna L. Baddeley and James W. Pennebaker

> "*Throughout history, writing has had a profound influence on the feelings, thoughts, and behaviors of individuals and societies ... whether, when, for whom, and how writing can be used as a therapeutic tool to reduce the harmful effects of stress and trauma on health and well-being.*" (Lepore & Smyth, 2002, p. 3).

Psychotherapy's roots lie in the observation that when patients talk about traumatic events from the past, their current distressing symptoms abate (Freud, 1920). Talk-based psychotherapy continues to be an effective method of treatment for numerous mental health concerns. However, research over the last 25 years has shown that expressive writing — simply writing about one's deepest thoughts and feelings about an emotional event — can alleviate both physical and psychological symptoms.

Expressive writing is built on a set of relatively open-ended instructions that encourage letting go and opening up about emotional events and exploring their meanings. In the first studies, people wrote for 15–20 minutes at a time over several days (e.g., Pennebaker & Beall, 1986), though more recent work has shown that writing can be massed over just 1 day (Chung & Pennebaker, 2008). Relative to writing about trivial topics, expressive writing results in a range of benefits including improved physical health and immune functioning (Pennebaker, Kiecolt-Glaser, & Glaser, 1988), well-being (Barclay & Skarlicki, 2009), cognitive functioning (Klein & Boals, 2001), social integration (Kim, 2008), and relationship satisfaction (Baddeley & Pennebaker, 2011; Snyder, Gordon, & Baucom, 2004). The method is effective across a range of populations, from college students (Pennebaker & Beall, 1986) to maximum-security prisoners (Richards, Beal, Seagal, & Pennebaker, 2000).

Research on Writing Approaches in Mental Health
Studies in Writing, Volume 23, 85–92

ISSN: 1572-6304/doi: 10.1108/S1572-6304(2011)0000023010

Expressive writing's effectiveness and the low cost of its delivery (only a pen and paper are necessary) make it an especially valuable intervention in an era of rising health care costs and managed care.

This chapter will describe the main features of the expressive writing method in terms of Sweeney and L'Abate's (2011, this volume) dimensions of writing and will review the literature on expressive writing with an emphasis on recent studies investigating novel applications of the paradigm.

The Pennebaker Paradigm

The core of the expressive writing method is putting into words one's deepest feelings. Typical instructions are shown below:

> "I would like for you to write about your very deepest thoughts and feelings about the most traumatic experience of your entire life. In your writing, I'd like you to really let go and explore your very deepest emotions and thoughts. You might tie this trauma to your childhood or to your relationships with others, including parents, lovers, friends, or relatives. You may also link this event to your past, your present, or your future, or to who you have been, who you would like to be, or who you are now. All of your writing will be completely confidential. Don't worry about spelling, sentence structure, or grammar. The only rule is that once you begin writing, continue to do so until your time is up."

Sweeney and L'Abate (see Chapter 1 in this volume) have described seven dimensions of writing, which can classify and describe various writing methods. We discuss where expressive writing fits on each of the five dimensions which we view as the most relevant to expressive writing. These five dimensions are: expressive–instructive, structured–unstructured, cathartic–prescriptive, content, and face-to-face–at a distance. The first two are structural aspects of writing. The expressive–instructive dimension describes a continuum from writing that is creative, spontaneous, and free-flowing on one end, and on the other end, writing that is concerned with a logical ordering of ideas and/or with precise use of grammar, spelling, and vocabulary. The structured–unstructured dimension describes how much scope the writer has to choose writing topics. It ranges from writing that is structured in the sense that it answers specific questions to writing that is unstructured in the sense that it is entirely open-ended. The cathartic–prescriptive dimension addresses the goals of writing. It addresses whether the goal is to enable the writer to express emotions (cathartic) or to move the writer toward specific outcomes (prescriptive). The content dimension broadly describes what the writing is about, whether it is about emotional or neutral topics, personal or relational issues, or other topics. Finally, the face-to-face–at a distance dimension describes the context in which the writing occurs, specifically, whether the writing occurs near (face-to-face with) or at a distance from a mental health professional.

Structural Aspects of Expressive Writing

Expressive writing, as the name suggests, falls near the "expressive" end of the expressive–instructive continuum. Its instructions are designed to promote the uninhibited articulation of thoughts and feelings. As the expressive writing instructions above show, expressive writing instructions typically encourage people not to worry about spelling and grammar. These instructions reflect the method's emphasis on writing as an expressive process rather than as a means to a final, structured product.

As the expressive writing instructions above show, the typical expressive writing instructions pull for the articulation of thoughts and feelings related to a single, specified event. In this sense, expressive writing is a structured/closed method. Yet expressive writing is unstructured/open-ended in the sense that although the instructions direct the writer to focus on a particular event, they then encourage the writer to connect it to a relatively open-ended range of issues that are important in his or her life. Across the various expressive writing studies, instructions have varied in terms of the degree of direction they provide. Frattaroli's (2006) meta-analysis suggested that studies with more detailed instructions or examples of what to disclose provided greater benefits to psychological health.

Goals of Expressive Writing

The original expressive writing instructions encourage people to let go and express whatever they are feeling about a traumatic event in their lives. In that sense, expressive writing falls toward the cathartic end of the cathartic–prescriptive continuum. However, the processes by which expressive writing works are complex and multifaceted and do not fit neatly into either a cathartic or prescriptive model. The original explanation for the health benefits of expressive writing was that when individuals gave up the physiologically taxing effort of inhibiting troubling thoughts and feelings, the reduction in stress gave rise to physical healing (Pennebaker & Beall, 1986). However, later studies found that writing about previously disclosed traumatic events is as beneficial as writing about previously undisclosed traumatic events, suggesting that the release of inhibition is unlikely to fully explain the benefits of writing (e.g., Pennebaker et al., 1988).

There are now a number of other compelling explanations for the benefits of expressive writing. One explanation for the benefits of expressive writing is that it changes emotional experience by providing opportunities for habituation in individuals with significant traumatic experiences (Sloan & Marx, 2004). Expressive writing may also change emotional experience by promoting the cognitive labeling and representation of previously amorphously experienced emotions, as well as the integration of those emotions into the broader context of one's life (De Giacomo et al., 2010).

Still other work suggests that expressive writing (and an offshoot of expressive writing, benefit-finding writing) may work not through helping individuals habituate to process their negative emotions, but through enhancing positive emotions and facilitating social integration. Some of the evidence for this viewpoint comes from a study of expressive writing in breast cancer survivors. The authors found that self-affirmation statements, in which the writer articulates positive experience in a valued domain of life, explained the benefits of expressive writing and benefit-finding writing for physical health (Creswell et al., 2007a). Finally, evidence suggests that writing may change how people interact with their social worlds; after writing, individuals talk more with others than they did before writing (Kim, 2008; Pennebaker & Graybeal, 2001).

Content of Expressive Writing

At its core, expressive writing is emotional writing. Typically, expressive writing instructions have asked people to write about their deepest thoughts and feelings about a traumatic event or personal upheaval. Recent studies have extended this basic paradigm to investigate the results of expressive writing focused on a range of stressful or traumatic events, from the personal to the relational, as well as positive events and positive feelings.

Expressive writing has been applied to help people cope effectively with a variety of stressful personal experiences, including stressful transitions or circumstances in professional or academic settings; coping with physical or psychological illness; and coping with stressful personal relationships.

In the professional arena, when laid-off engineers were assigned to write about their deepest thoughts and feelings about their job loss, they found new jobs more quickly than controls who wrote about trivial topics (Spera, Buhrfeind, & Pennebaker, 1994). In the academic arena, studies have assessed the effects of doing expressive writing about upcoming graduate school entrance exams on exam performance and psychological health. Students assigned to write about their deepest thoughts and feelings about their upcoming exam reported better mood prior to their exams and performed better on the exams than did controls who wrote about trivial topics (Dalton & Glenwick, 2009; Frattaroli, Thomas, & Lyubomirsky, 2011).

For individuals with serious medical illnesses, expressive writing about their illness may result in improvements in disease symptoms. Among women with breast cancer, those assigned to write about either their deepest thoughts and feelings (expressive writing) or their positive thoughts and feelings (benefit finding) about their cancer diagnosis showed lower cancer-related medical visits and lower somatic symptoms than those assigned to a neutral-writing control group (Stanton et al., 2002). In a similar study with arthritis and lupus patients, individuals who did expressive writing or benefit-finding writing reported reduced fatigue 3 months after writing (Danoff-Burg, Agee, Romanoff, Kremer, & Strosberg, 2006).

Aside from effects on physical health, expressive writing can aid psychological and social adjustment in individuals with serious health problems. For individuals who had undergone kidney transplants, writing about their thoughts and feelings related to their experience of kidney failure and transplant resulted in somewhat fewer PTSD symptoms relative to controls who wrote about only the facts of their experience (Possemato, Ouimette, & Geller, 2010). In another study, women who had survived breast cancer who were assigned to do expressive writing about their illness reported higher perceived social support than those who did not write (Gellaitry et al., 2010).

Evidence from two expressive writing studies involving gay men points to the benefits of expressive writing for helping individuals manage stigma. In both studies, the men were assigned to write about their most stressful experience related to their sexual orientation, or to a nonemotional writing condition. In one study, those who did expressive writing reported being more open about their sexual orientation months later, and those with relatively low levels of social support also experienced reductions in physical symptoms (Pachankis & Goldfried, 2010). In the other study, those who did expressive writing reported lower avoidance of thoughts, feelings, and situations related to their sexual orientation 1 month after writing (Swanbon, Boyce, & Greenberg, 2008).

In the past decade, expressive writing interventions have been successfully used to help couples weather stressful experiences in their relationships. When soldiers did expressive writing about being reunited with a spouse after a military deployment, their marital satisfaction increased (Baddeley & Pennebaker, 2011). When both spouses did expressive writing as part of psychotherapy after an extramarital affair, they experienced reduced anger, depression, and PTSD symptoms subsequent to treatment (Snyder et al., 2004). Thus, writing about one's thoughts and feelings about a wide variety of stressful or traumatic experiences can facilitate emotional, social, and behavioral adjustment and can improve task-related performance.

Although much of the expressive literature has documented the effectiveness of writing about personal traumas and upheavals, there is now evidence that writing about positive feelings and experiences yields similar benefits to writing about negative ones. Writing about the perceived benefits of a traumatic event (King & Miner, 2000) or about intensely positive experiences (Burton & King, 2009) promotes better physical health in the months following writing.

Context of Expressive Writing: Distance from a Professional

One of expressive writing's major benefits is that it can be performed at distance from a professional helper. In the original expressive writing study, participants wrote in a room alone and turned in their writing under an anonymous code number; no professional helpers were involved at any point (Pennebaker & Beall, 1986). Many expressive writing studies follow Pennebaker and Beall's (1986) procedure and are set up as stand-alone interventions in which individuals come to a laboratory and write in private rooms.

Studies have since established the effectiveness of expressive writing conducted in other settings, such as group settings (Baddeley & Pennebaker, 2011; Chung & Pennebaker, 2008); and in the home (e.g., Henry et al., 2010). Both of these settings offer benefits for certain applications of expressive writing. Group administration of expressive writing has the potential to allow organizations to provide the intervention to large numbers of employees or clients at once. Home-based administration of expressive writing opens up the benefits of the intervention to individuals for whom access to a clinic or research facility is inconvenient, such as individuals living in rural areas (Henry et al., 2010).

The Internet can make expressive writing interventions even more accessible. Recent work has begun to show that conducting expressive writing interventions over the Internet is both feasible and beneficial for participants (e.g., Possemato et al., 2010). In addition to the traditional benefits of expressive writing, Internet-based interventions offer the possibility for tailored feedback and instruction based on a text analysis of individuals' writings. One example is a recent study (Owen, Hanson, Preddy, Bantum, & O'Carroll, 2011) which tested the effects of feedback encouraging emotional processing on participants' written emotional expression and negative mood. The study involved three separate writing sessions and participants were assigned to one of three conditions. In the control condition, no feedback was offered; in a "simple feedback" condition, participants were told whether they were low, medium, or high in negative and positive emotion word use; and in a "directive feedback" condition, participants were provided with feedback regarding their level of emotion word use, and in addition, participants low or moderate in positive or negative emotion words were asked to discuss emotions more in future writing. Although receiving feedback did not reduce self-reported negative mood, individuals in the two feedback conditions increased in their use of positive emotion language (but not negative emotion language) over the three writing sessions. The provision of feedback is a promising direction for future research.

Expressive writing may be used effectively as an adjunct to psychotherapeutic treatment. Snyder and colleagues (2004) reported on their use of expressive writing as an intervention to help couples recover from an extramarital affair. In their intervention, the writing was a multistep process designed to help the partners both come to terms with their own feelings and to share their feelings with each other. The treatment involved coming to terms with feelings about the affair, exploring factors contributing to the affair, and deciding how to move forward with the relationship. Expressive writing was involved at each stage of this process. Each partner wrote in private about his or her deepest thoughts and feelings about the perpetrating partner's affair. Next, the therapist worked with the injured partner to write a letter to the perpetrating partner conveying his or her feelings in a way that was designed to elicit empathy and support rather than defensiveness and anger. Finally, the injured partner shared the letter with the perpetrating partner. The perpetrating partner went through a similar writing and sharing process of his or her responses to the injured partner's letter. The intervention resulted in decreased anger, PTSD-related symptoms, and depression at posttreatment in both partners.

Frattaroli's (2006) meta-analysis suggested that the more distance between the writer and any potential observers, the better. The studies in which expressive writing resulted in better psychological outcomes were those in which participants wrote in a private room rather than a public room; at home rather than in the lab; and were instructed to keep their writing rather than turning it in. Broadly speaking, distance from a professional helper does not pose a problem to the effectiveness of the intervention and may even have benefit.

Conclusions

At least 200 research studies have been conducted on the expressive writing paradigm, and expressive writing interventions are now widely used as an adjunct to professional treatment for a variety of psychiatric and medical conditions. This review has highlighted examples of the expressive writing method being tailored and applied to meet the needs of a variety of populations facing a variety of specific stressors, from disease to academic- or work-related problems to challenges related to sexual orientation. We expect that expressive writing will prove beneficial for problems and in populations as yet unresearched.

Expressive writing can be effectively used alone or as an adjunct to traditional therapy (Baddeley & Pennebaker, 2009). Because it can be conducted at a distance with no therapist involvement, it is a flexible, cost-effective approach for addressing a variety of physical and mental health needs for a large number of people.

Editorial Addendum

There is nowadays a real interest for assessing in a scientific manner the effect of writing on health. In this respect, we consider that James Pennebaker's paradigm, the expressive writing (EW) task, conceived for the study of emotional disclosure, represents a useful framework in which to study the effects of confronting with distressing (traumatic) events on physical and psychological health. Using Pennebaker's paradigm, in the present study Opre, Coman, Kallay, Rotaru, and Manier (2005) aimed at assessing the impact of EW on both physical and psychological health. Actually, we were focusing our attention on emotional distress (trauma) related to students' college life. Based on the outcomes of similar experimental studies, we have assumed that following the EW task, psychological distress, physical and mental health problems, the level of negative emotions of the college students would decrease, and their level of positive emotions would increase. Our results have shown that the participants benefit from the EW task by reducing their psychological distress and by improving their physical and mental health. The results confirm the utility of the EW paradigm for health improvement in a Romanian student population.

A meta-analysis was conducted to examine the effects of the written emotional disclosure paradigm on health outcomes of people with physical or psychiatric disorders (Frisina, Borod, & Lepore, 2004). After nine studies were meta-analyzed, it was determined that expressive writing significantly improved health ($d = .19$; $p < .05$). However, this positive relationship ($r = .10$) was not moderated by any systemic variables because of the nonsignificant test of homogeneity ($Qw = 5.27$; $p = .73$). Nonetheless, a planned contrast illustrated that expressive writing is more effective on physical ($d = .21$; $p = .01$) than on psychological ($d = .07$; $p = .17$) health outcomes ($Qb > 10.83$; $p < .001$). One explanation for the small effect size (ES) results and the nonsignificant test of homogeneity may be the small and heterogeneous samples used in some of the studies within this research synthesis. Future research with expressive writing should be tested with randomized controlled trials (RCTs) to increase the likelihood of detecting a larger treatment effect.

Meads and Sheffield (2005) comment on the article by Frisina et al. (2004) which examined the effects of the written emotional disclosure paradigm on health outcomes of people with physical or psychiatric disorders. A number of methodological points are worth commenting on since we believe that they have the potential to alter the conclusions drawn by the authors. First, the combination of search terms is not given, and they do not appear to have included the term disclosure. They also did not include the dates of their searches, but we surmise from the other references they included that it was probably early in 2003. Second, there is clinical heterogeneity in the populations of the RCTs and in the outcomes assessed. The authors have combined the results from cancer patients with those with psychiatric problems (prison inmates, severely depressed, and PTSD). Given this clinical heterogeneity, it is questionable whether the populations should be combined into one ES. Third, the authors combine physical and psychological outcomes into one ES for four of the included RCTs. Composite outcomes can give greater precision but at a cost of the greater difficulty in interpretation of the results. Taking all these factors into account, we consider that this meta-analysis is flawed. This means that the overall ES may not represent the true effect of emotional disclosure on clinical populations. Because of this, we believe that the conclusions the authors reach should be viewed with considerable caution.

Frisina, Lepore, and Borod (2005) responded to comments made by Meads and Sheffield (2005) on the original report by Frisina et al. (2004) which examined the effects of the written emotional disclosure paradigm on health outcomes of people with physical or psychiatric disorders. The current authors address the criticisms of Meads and Sheffield that pertained to the search strategy used, as well as defend their use of aggregate analyses. Additionally, the current authors disagree with Meads and Sheffield's contention that they should have used a random effects model.

Chapter 7

Poetry Therapy

Debbie McCulliss

Midway along the journey of our life
I woke to find myself in a dark wood
for I had wandered off from the straight path.
(Dante, trans. 1954, canto 1, lines 1–3)

This chapter explores poetry as a form of therapy. Poetry therapy, its history, and research efforts are reviewed. Words cannot always convey an experience as remote and profoundly personal as, for example, emotion. Yet words are powerful tools. With the language of poetry, one *can* utter the unutterable, say the unsayable, sense the insensible, and explore those far distant dark woods that many never hear expressed otherwise (Jeffs & Pepper, 2005, p. 90). Jones suggests that poetry is in a way analogous to psychoanalysis. Poetry provides an approach to the unsayable, allowing one "to come as close as possible to the edge of what cannot be said" (Jones, 1997, p. 684).

Poetry emphasizes each person's uniqueness and offers a format in which one's "soul" can communicate with another (Bell, 1982, p. 30). In *The Poetic Mind* (Prescott, 1922), the therapeutic value of poetry was described. The "creation of a poem is a result of an unconscious act — the poetic imagination based on the fact that poetry is an expression of repressed and unconscious desires, and that the function of poetry, like dreams, is to enhance mental health" (Prescott, 1922).

The Early History of Poetry Therapy

Poetry is the oldest form of literature (Kreuter, 2009). Aristotle discovered that through the process of creating poetry, people were able to transform their problems

Research on Writing Approaches in Mental Health
Studies in Writing, Volume 23, 93–114

ISSN: 1572-6304/doi: 10.1108/S1572-6304(2011)0000023011

into power and their sadness into strength (Furman, Pepi-Downey, Jackson, & Bender, 2002, p. 147). The first poetry therapist on record was Soranus, a Roman physician. In the first century AD, Soranus prescribed the reading of tragedy for his manic patients and comedy for those who were depressed (NAPT, 2004). American counter-culture poet Bukowski (1991) referred to writing as the "ultimate psychiatrist" (1991, n.p., lines 22–23).

Today, a growing number of physicians and therapists use poetry therapy to help their patients cope with the emotional aspects of their illness. Gorelick explained the therapeutic power of poetry as a way for patients to "find the truth of their own experience reflected back in a way they can recognize" (Milk, 2009). Gorelick died of brain cancer in June 2009, but used his knowledge of poetry therapy in dealing candidly with his brain cancer. In an interview in the May 2009 *Washingtonian Magazine*, he wrote as "doctor as patient":

> Looking back I feel my life has been right
> No second-guessing that this or that might have been better,
> No ache that I might have climbed higher mountains.
> I am in a generous leisurely mood with myself
> Filled with gratitude and awe for what has been,
> The gifts, the luck, the love.
>
> (Malchiodi, 2009)

Poetry has long been used as a means of understanding mental illness and the experiences of the mentally ill, as an important tool in rehabilitation, growth, and healing. Laing explored the dynamics of mental illness through poetic language in *Knots* (1970). His collection uses "the knot" as a metaphor to illustrate a variety of self-reflections and interpersonal interactions common to most people (Furman, Collins, Langer, & Bruce, 2006, p. 333). Poetry can capitalize on the ability to contain self-expression. Feelings and perceptions may deepen into greater understanding or may be transformed, resulting in emotional reparation, resolution of conflicts, and a sense of well-being (Malchiodi, 2005, p. 9).

Evolution of Poetry Therapy

Poetry therapy is the intentional use of poetry and related forms of literature and creative writing for personal growth and healing. It has been used in a variety of settings throughout its history. Poetry therapy uses language arts in therapeutic and community building capacities.

Pennsylvania Hospital in Philadelphia, PA, was the first hospital in the United States to use adjunct treatments for the mentally ill. Rush, the father of American psychiatry, was the first American physician to prescribe poetry as an adjunct to mental health care at the Pennsylvania Hospital (NAPT, 2004; Weimerskirch, 1965). In 1810, Rush asked his patients go to the hospital library to read, write, or publish poetry to gain insight into their personal issues. Many of the poems were published in the patients' newspaper, *The Illuminator*.

Beginning in the 1920s, some hospital librarians selected patient reading materials specifically for their potential to help patients understand themselves and their conditions. Prescott believed that poetry should be recognized as hygienic, and that it could clean and cure a sick soul (1922). Schauffler's (1927[1925]) *The Poetry Cure: A Pocket Medicine Chest of Verse* contained poems described as "prescriptive" (i.e., ones he thought would have the ability to help the mentally ill).

In the 1950s, Greifer and Blanton proposed that poetry be used as a tool in an interactive process between therapist and client (NAPT, 2004). Poetry was found to be an effective vehicle of expression, allowing clients a safe mode to voice their personal experiences and emotions. Greifer, Leedy, and Spector established the first formal American "poemtherapy" group at the Mental Hygiene Clinic of Cumberland Hospital in Brooklyn, NY, in 1959. Leedy persuaded Greifer to rename *poemtherapy* as *poetry therapy* (Lerner, 1997, p. 83). Guided reading was used to help patients learn about and develop insight into illness, stimulate catharsis, and aid in the healing process at Cumberland Hospital and the Poetry Therapy Center in New York. Blanton, in *The Healing Power of Poetry* (1958), documented poetry's therapeutic value.

In 1969, Leedy, White, and Schloss founded The Association for Poetry Therapy. Leedy compiled and edited two major works in the field of poetry therapy, *Poetry Therapy: The Use of Poetry in the Treatment of Emotional Disorders* (1969) and *Poetry as Healer: Mending the Troubled Mind* (1985).

Edgar and Hazley (1969) proposed an undergraduate curriculum and a series of graduate courses for training poetry therapists. Jaskoski (1984) later proposed adding substantive areas that certified poetry therapists should be competent in. Edgar, Hazley, and Levit (1969) did some of the first empirical studies of poetry therapy focusing on group modalities. Leedy (1969, 1973) used poetry therapy to clarify the intrapsychic self, facilitate self-affirmation and integration, build up self-esteem, and aid in the development of more rewarding interpersonal relationships (Antebi, 1986). Kobak used poetry therapy with four socially and emotionally maladjusted boys enrolled in a special school in New York City. She described poetry as therapeutic in that the boys "re-created" themselves and "rebuilt" their mental health (1969, pp. 180–187).

Poetry therapy was further described in the treatment of emotionally vulnerable persons. Kramer reported they were more apt to "record their emotional upheavals and imaginative wanderings" (1969, p. 210) through poetry than another other artistic venue. Poetry may even help the writer problem-solve, as giving form to thought takes effort and may be considered "a growth-producing experience" (Robinson & Mowbray, 1969, p. 192).

In 1971, Schecher became the first official poetry therapist at Odyssey House in New York City. She worked with addiction clients and victims of rape and incest. Lerner was appointed Poet-in-Residence and poetry therapist at the Calabasas Neuropsychiatric Center in California. In 1974, Richardson convinced the Governor of Maryland to hold a Poetry Therapy Day.

Bell developed the "feedback" poem, a writing tool used by counselors to assess their listening skills while empowering their clients (Bell, 2005). During this decade, Buck and Kramer (1973) used poetry therapy with patients who were "deaf or disturbed." Bosveld created the Ohio Poetry Therapy Center and Library in Columbus, OH. Librarians continued to play an important role in poetry therapy. For example, in 1974, McCarty-Hynes created the first comprehensive hospital-based bibliotherapy training program (Lamb, 2006). A librarian at St. Elizabeths Hospital in Washington, DC, Hynes' work was encouraged and supported by Gorelick. Hynes and her daughter wrote an authoritative book on the use of poetry in healing, *Biblio/Poetry Therapy: The Interactive Process: A Handbook* (Hynes & Hynes-Berry, 1994). St. Elizabeths was one of the few institutions in the country that offered biblio/poetry training.

The use of poetry was described in training nurses at St. Elizabeths Hospital by Anderson (1975) "the flexibility of poetry therapy makes it highly advantageous as a treatment modality in psychiatric nursing" (p. 133). She also commented on the interest patients had in the lives of poets, and how reassured many were that writers often suffered from mental illnesses (Fanner & Urquhartt, 2008). Another advantage of this therapy was described as revitalizing the self by integrating emotion, cognition, and imagery (Stainbrook, 1978).

Several groups were formalized to meet the needs of those interested in poetry therapy. Morrison published *Poetry as Therapy* (1987), and founded the Association for Poetry Therapy in Austin, TX. The National Federation of Biblio/Poetry Therapy was created in 1980, spearheaded by Hynes. Incorporated in Minnesota in 1983, it focused on qualifications and requirements for acceptable professional performance. In 1981, The Association for Poetry Therapy became the National Association for Poetry Therapy (NAPT), a nonprofit membership organization. NAPT sponsors both Certified Poetry Therapist (CPT) and Registered Poetry Therapist (RPT) degrees. The purpose of NAPT was described as promoting growth and healing through language, symbol, and story.

Poetry therapy is currently widely practiced in a one-to-one relationship, group, or both, and is found in diverse settings. It is used with developmental (healthy) or clinical (mental health problems), male and female populations, and is practiced among all races and all ages, including the chronically mentally ill, the elderly, troubled children and adolescents, veterans, the terminally ill, substance abusers, and families. Poetry therapy has been utilized by practitioners working in diverse settings, including women's shelters, nursing homes, and elementary schools. In addition, poetry has been incorporated into family work, diversity work, community work consciousness-raising, and research (Furman et al., 2002, p. 147).

In recent years, many articles detailing poetry therapy interventions in a variety of populations have been published in scholarly literature, including The National Association of Poetry Therapy's *Journal of Poetry Therapy*, founded by Nicholas Mazza. The *Journal of Poetry Therapy* published its first issue as the quarterly publication of NAPT in fall 1987. The Journal describes its aims in its subtitle as "The Interdisciplinary Journal of Practice, Theory, Research and Education." It serves the profession as a disseminator of knowledge and information (Lerner, 1997). The intended audience for the *Journal* includes those in the allied helping professions and education, as well as those in literary/artistic fields with a concern for the healing/therapeutic aspects of the language arts. The essence of the *Journal* is "writing from the heart with scientific discipline" (Mazza, 2008). The Journal publishes case studies, practice reports, and research conducted in the area of poetry therapy. Between 1987 and 2007, approximately 200 articles were published that dealt with poetry and poetry writing (Kidd, p. 39).

Combining Poetry with Other Forms of Healing Arts

Berger proposed poetry as a vehicle for self-discovery for both teachers and children. He used rock, blues lyrics, and "jazz cinquains" to elicit writing from children. Opportunities for creativity in poetry therapy were further expanded when Schloss combined poetry with drama, coining the term *psychopoetry*. Schloss authored *Psychopoetry: A New Approach to Self-Awareness through Poetry Therapy* (1976). Reiter (registered poetry and drama therapist and Director of the Creative "Righting" Center), taught poetry therapy with Leedy at the New School of Social Research in New York City. She combined poetry therapy with drama therapy and as today, continues to teach poetry therapy and drama therapy at Hofstra University.

Adams, founder of the Center for Journal Therapy, combined poetry therapy with journal writing (Lerner, 1997). According to Adams "Poetry and journals enhance each other. A poem's nature is to reveal and conceal — showing and hiding at exactly the same moment. Therefore, writing a journal poem can be a very effective way to express the inexpressible. Another point of compatibility is the contemporary or classic poet's capacity to evoke a large feeling or capture a huge emotional experience in just a few words or lines. That articulation can be a godsend to those who struggle to find language to express overwhelming thoughts, feelings and experiences. Writing down key lines or images from a poem, and using them as springboards into a journal entry can bring useful structure to internal chaos" (Adams, personal communication, December 31, 2010).

School programs for children were also explored. For example, Fox and Longo were very active in the California-Poets-in-the-Schools program. Mirriam-Goldberg facilitated "Poetry Camp" for low-income children. She developed and administered the "Midnight Poetry League," which helped teens write, perform, and play poetry. She is founder and director of the Transformative Language Arts (TLA) graduate program (at the time of this writing), at Goddard College, Plainfield, VT.

Theoretical Basis for Poetry Therapy

The theoretical basis of poetry therapy is not yet fully explained, but theories explaining its therapeutic utility are numerous (Abell, 1998; Coulter, 2000; Hynes & Hynes-Berry, 1994; Lauer & Goldfield, 1970; Lerner, 1978; Mazza, 1999; Smith 2000). These include theories that poetry therapy enhances self-understanding; overcomes "repressive mechanisms"; offers a "reality-correcting experience";

improves group cohesion; offers personal consensual validation; redefines situations; "improves the capacity to respond by stimulating and enriching mental images"; and "organizes experience" (Olson-McBride, 2009, p. 14).

It has been suggested that the poem chosen for use in therapy must reflect a universal experience or emotion, and must be powerful, positive, and easy to understand (Hynes & Hynes-Berry, 1994). In addition, the poem's emotional tone should match the clinical situation or mood of the group or individual client (Adams & Rojcewicz, 2003). The more pertinent aspects of the healing experience in poetry therapy are proposed as follows (Lerner, 1991):

- "Individuals invariably reveal a good deal about themselves through reading and/or writing of poems that articulate their feelings.
- The use of a poem in therapy may enable the person to facilitate his or her own understanding of feelings and lifestyle.
- Reading and writing poetry can be a creative experience as well as an organizing process for gaining self-esteem.
- The poem may act as a catalyst through which emotions are filtered, as an interpretation, as a projective instrument, and even as a dream.
- In general, there is usually a good deal of emotional safety when the patient is exposed to poetry in psychotherapy." (pp. 213–214)

Choosing the "right" poem to use for poetry therapy is critical. The following guidelines are suggested for clinicians selecting poems for use in poetry therapy groups (Rolfs & Super, 1988):

- Identify current group and individual themes.
- Choose the therapeutic goal or goals for the next session.
- Begin to think about categories of poems that address these issues.
- Begin to think about specific poems within these categories.
- Do a careful reading of poems, trying to imagine all possible meanings.
- Reject poems that (a) are not clear, (b) have messages that conflict with the goal, (c) are premature in the life of the group, (d) are clinically contraindicated for any individual patient, and (e) are problematic for the therapists.
- Select a poem that meets the goal.
- Select a complementary poem.

Poetry Therapy and Cognitive Theory

Stainbrook (1994) captured the philosophy and the meaning of the merger of two separate fields, implying a special expertise in *Poetry in the Therapeutic Experience* (Lerner, 1994):

> "Finally, and perhaps most important, there exists the possibility that in its optimum potential the merger of poetry with therapy may result in

> the revitalizing and re-moralizing of the self by providing a wholeness of consciousness — an integration of emotion, cognition, and imagery — with which to create and maintain personal meaning." (p. 11)

Hirshfield (1997) stated that the goal of poetry is the "magnification and clarification of being" (p. 5). This is the goal not only of cognitive therapy but most types of psychotherapy concerned with human potential. By helping clients use poetry and written exercises to explore and resolve distorted and maladaptive thoughts, therapists empower clients with tools to improve health and well-being.

In her 1997 report, "Poetry Therapy: Testimony on Capitol Hill," Reiter wrote that the basic goal of poetry therapy is to promote change. Although there are threads of connection and application between psychology and poetry therapy, specific goals of poetry therapy are therapeutic, not diagnostic like those of psychiatry or psychological counseling, and include:

- "To improve the capacity to respond to vivid images and concepts, and the feelings aroused by them;
- To enhance self-understanding and accuracy in self-perception;
- To increase awareness of interpersonal relationships;
- To heighten reality orientation;
- To develop creativity, self-expression, and greater self-esteem;
- To encourage positive thinking and creative problem-solving;
- To strengthen communication, particularly listening and speaking skills;
- To integrate the different aspects of the self for psychological wholeness;
- To ventilate overpowering emotions and release tension;
- To find new meaning through new ideas, insights, and/or information; and
- To help participants experience the liberating and nourishing qualities of beauty." (pp. 169–178)

Training and Workshops

Information on professional and credentialing matters including a listing of mentor supervisors can be found on the websites of The National Association for Poetry Therapy (www.poetrytherapy.org), National Federation for Biblio/Poetry Therapy (www.nfbpt.com), and Lapidus: Creative Words for Health and Wellbeing (www.lapidus.org.uk).

The Wordsworth Center, established in 1993, provides comprehensive training programs to prepare students for credentials in poetry therapy and to enhance skills in the creative arts therapies for mental health professionals and writers. The International Academy of Poetry Therapy (iaPOETRY.org) offers the opportunity to train in poetry therapy with an emphasis on creative arts.

Bell published an article on themes of past NAPT conferences in the *Journal of Poetry Therapy* (1992). Poetry therapy workshops were presented in St. Petersburg, Russia, in the 1990s as part of the International Conference on Creativity and the

Arts in Psychotherapy and Education. In 1995, the Italian poetry therapy association, LAUBEA, was founded. It launched in Rome with a workshop led by U.S. poetry therapists. The poetry therapy movement in Germany began to grow when von Werder began to research "the effects of poetry therapy" (Lerner, 1997).

There are now poetry therapists practicing around the world. Some of the countries represented are Ireland, Lithuania, New Zealand, Switzerland, England, Canada, Germany, Republic of South Korea, Israel, and Japan.

Categories of Poetry Therapy Methods

Worldwide, credentialed poetry therapists, a community of psychiatrists, psychologists, social workers, family therapists, substance abuse specialists, teachers and educators, nurses, and poets recognize three uses of poetry in healing: receptive-prescriptive, expressive-creative, and symbolic-ceremonial. The first category, receptive-prescriptive, is described as using existing poetry to draw forth responses from students or patients. Receptive methods of poetry therapy are those that rely on the utilization of preexisting poems, that is, poems that have been published in collections, anthologies, literary journals, or that are circulated among individuals or on the Internet (Mazza, 1999). Receptive methods of poetry therapy can be employed in two ways: self-directed (for those who are not in a formal clinical setting) and client-directed (for those who engage in this effort as part of their work in counseling or psychotherapy). Facilitated or therapist-guided methods occur when a therapist or group facilitator carefully chooses a poem that s/he feels will be in the best interest of the client. The latter is described in detail in *Biblio/Poetry Therapy: The Interactive Process* (Hynes & Hynes-Berry, 1994). Universality (realizing that other individuals outside of the immediate group have experienced situations, thoughts, and feelings similar to those experienced by the group members) in poetry therapy groups occurs when explored through this receptive-prescriptive component.

The expressive-creative category encourages people to write. It "provides a vehicle for the client to express emotions and gain a sense of order and concreteness" (Mazza, 1999, p. 20). Mazza (1999) has identified three types of writing in the expressive/creative model: creative writing (which includes poetry and stories), journal writing, and letter writing. In a meta-analysis of effect sizes in studies involving written expression, Smyth (1998) states that "historically and recently, psychologists have cited the expression of emotions as vital for good mental and physical health" and that "expressive writing ... has been used to promote good health in a number of controlled studies" (p. 174).

The symbolic-ceremonial category connects people to the emotional power of metaphors, rituals, and storytelling. In poetry therapy, the metaphor is defined as "something that stands for something else ... . Metaphors ... are symbols or images for emotions, actions, or beliefs" (Mazza, 1999, p. 21). He adds that metaphors provide a "connection between internal and external reality" and "reframe problems, break resistance, and enhance the therapeutic relationship" (p. 22).

Overview of Research in Poetry Therapy

The term poetry therapy has largely come into usage in the last half of the twentieth century. For years, the existing body of literature on the use of poetry therapy as a therapeutic device with clinical populations primarily consisted of descriptive and exploratory studies (Olson-McBride & Page, 2006, p. 167). The first empirical studies focused on group therapies and used inpatient and other institutional settings as test sites. Edgar et al. (1969) compared a poetry therapy group to a conventional therapy group in a hospital for schizophrenic patients. The study showed improvement in attitudes, more patients were discharged home and more home visits were made by those in the experimental poetry group (Mazza, 1993, p. 53). From early studies such as this one, directions for future research about poetry therapy emerged.

Berry (1978) concluded that it may be possible to objectify "the process of poem-prescription based on feelings evoked by the poems" (p. 141). Roosevelt (1982) used a semantic differential instrument to validate his finding that subjects reacted more emotionally to "good" poetry than to "popular" poetry and suggest that good poetry elicits a higher level of participation. Mazza (1981a) found that group poetry therapy advances group cohesion and self-discovery.

A need for analytical research on criteria and evaluation of the creative process still existed (Hynes, 1988). There were as many ways of evaluating what makes appropriate and effective therapy as there are ways of judging what constitutes a good poem (Jaskoski, 1987).

In 1987, recommendations (Mazza, Magaz, & Scaturro, 1987, pp. 90–91) for research in the area of poetry therapy and child abuse included:

- Poetry as a medium in providing consultation, training, and education in the dynamics of child abuse to helping professions.
- Development of poetic resources that can be utilized in the prevention and treatment of all forms of child abuse. This includes ethnic and gender-sensitive material. There is also the issue of accessibility. Perhaps in the tradition of Meals on Wheels and Stember's (1977) Artmobile, Poetry on Wheels could be added.
- Systematic qualitative and quantitative evaluation of poetic approaches with abused children and their families.
- Further investigation of the complementary use of poetry with other art forms (e.g., art, music, and dance) in the assessment and treatment process.
- Examination of literary influences on child abuse (including research on children's reading experiences).
- Examination of literary influences (including lyrics of pop music) used as coping mechanisms.
- Precise reports dealing with the use of poetry with specific types of abuse (e.g., incest).

By the end of the 1980s, practitioners had been building their skills, theorizing, writing articles about their experiences, and doing research to evaluate outcomes.

Hynes (1988) noted that it was now time to move into developing unique qualitative and quantitative instruments for assessment and evaluation of poetry therapy. Mazza reported that art-based therapies such as poetry therapy were "past the stage of good intentions and anecdotal reports" (Mazza, 1999, p. 115). Yet, there were still few controlled studies to demonstrate the connection between the use of a poetry therapy intervention and the outcome of that intervention (Olson-McBride & Page, 2006, p. 167; Rosen, Proctor, & Staudt, 1999).

A study on 25 interactive poetry therapy groups led by 17 different facilitators over a 10-year period in an inpatient mental health facility was conducted (Rossiter & Brown 1988). Findings indicated positive results with regard to the quality of interaction among patients. It was noted that poetry therapy was particularly beneficial to withdrawn patients and least helpful to those with limitations in cognitive functioning.

In 2002, existing poetry therapy research tended to focus on process issues, such as group cohesion and positive interactions, and not client outcomes (Mazza, 1999; Rossiter & Brown, 1988). Hartman (1990) states that "there are many truths and there are many ways of knowing. Each discovery contributes to our knowledge, and each way of knowing deepens our understanding and adds more dimension to our view of the world" (p. 3). Because poetry therapy is interdisciplinary and concerned with language and communication, the heuristic paradigm was recommended as a research strategy. Hartman believed that the heuristic paradigm also "draws upon the strengths of cultural diversity and is gender sensitive" (Tyson, 1992, p. 52).

Kissman (1989) discussed the role of poetry and feminist social work practice. Recognizing social, economic, and political factors, she notes that evaluation of outcomes should consider "the extent to which the uses of poetry and other literary forms were effective in promoting empowerment, connectedness, and consciousness-raising" (p. 229). Through this research, poetry therapy can meet demands for accountability and social responsibility.

Mazza (1993) presented several models of poetry therapy that could be tested and further developed, including:

- Leedy's (1969) prescriptive model using the isoprinciple of choosing a poem that is similar to the client's mood but includes elements of hope.
- Lerner's (1976, 1978) interpersonal model of utilizing poetry as a pathway for expressing feelings and becoming more enlightened to internal processes.
- Schloss's (1976) psychopoetry model, evolved from psychodramatic theory and practice.
- Hynes and Hynes-Berry's (1986) interactive bibliotherapy model, focusing on the relationship "of the triad of participant-literature-facilitator as well as the use of creative writing as material" (Mazza, 1993, p. 12).
- Mazza's (1981b) poetry group therapy model using a "pre-existing poem at the beginning of each session and a collaborative poem at the end of each session." (Mazza, 1993, p. 53)

Some of the major directions identified by Mazza in 1993 for future research in poetry therapy included:

- "Formulation of research questions that address process and outcome in poetry therapy.
- Development of poetry therapy practice models that can be replicated and subjected to empirical evaluation.
- Use of a cross-sectional survey method to examine the use of literature and creative writing by selected helping professions in clinical practice.
- Partnerships between researchers in the creative arts therapies should be encouraged.
- Further development of new instruments and/or the adaptation of existing instruments for assessment and evaluation purposes in poetry therapy. For existing instruments, see, for example, Corcoran and Fisher's (1987) *Measures for Clinical Practice* and Bellack and Hersen's (1988) *Dictionary of Behavioral Assessment Techniques.*
- Promotion of both experimental and qualitative/heuristic research.
- Investigation of patient/client characteristics with different forms of poetry therapy for patients/clients suffering from a specific disorder (adjustment disorder with depressed mood).
- Exploration of the variability between different forms of poetry therapy and between particular stages of the specific treatment process.
- Research on the classification of poetry and other forms of literature for therapeutic purposes.
- Integrate a research approach with the practice of poetry therapy through case studies and single system research designs.
- Develop research on the therapeutic aspects of reading.
- Promotion of literary analysis relating to poetry therapy.
- Promotion of cultural linguistic studies related to poetry therapy.
- Develop research-funding priorities. Explore public and private sources of support. Special attention to socially responsive programs (at-risk children, AIDS, family violence) is strongly encouraged.
- A consideration of epistemological and value questions relating to poetry therapy. This has particular significance for women and minorities in that their experience has often been omitted or distorted in the clinical research literature.
- Research to explore the specific experiences and perceptions of those who engage in creative writing for therapeutic purposes.
- Drawing from Turner's (1986) framework, engage in theory building through research activities and an integration of thought systems related to poetry therapy. This includes an integration of appropriate existing theories (social, psychological, literary) that can further solidify the base of poetry therapy practice." (Mazza, 1993, p. 57)

The lack of empirical research on poetry therapy intervention was not, however, indicative of a lack of published information about poetry therapy interventions in general (Boone, 2006, p. 3; Olson-McBride, 2009, p. 34). Between 1996 and 2006,

Box 7.1. Controlled studies of poetry therapy research 1996–2006

Study
Poetry Therapy
Client Group
Findings

Blake and Cashwell (2004)
Focused on utilizing poetry therapy to facilitate communication about ethnic diversity and women's issues.
Nonclinical population of college students.
Authors did not provide statistical analyses, or any other related information, to indicate the degree to which change occurred.

Golden (2000)
Explored group poetry therapy sessions with a variety of poems that weren't focused on a predetermined theme.
Following group discussion of each poem, subjects were provided with a structured poetry writing exercise and encouraged to share their writing with the group. Only in the treatment group was the structured poetry writing exercise followed by the creation of a group collaborative poem.
Nonclinical population of college students.
A significant difference was found between the treatment and control group.

Howard (1997)
Compared the effects of a music therapy-based intervention and a poetry therapy-based intervention.
Individuals with substance abuse-related issues.
No statistical difference was found between the groups on the measures utilized in this project or between groups related to on-task versus off-task behaviors.

Meunier (1999)
Explored the impact of group poetry therapy and writing in an effort to provide additional supportive programming to clients.
Adults in a vocational department at a community mental health center.
Participants felt that the program was flexible, improved current skills in addition to providing new skills, and improved quality of life and self-esteem.

Papadopoulos et al. (1999)
Explored the effectiveness of group poetry therapy as an intervention.
Older adults with mental-health related issues.
Participants experienced varying degrees of hopelessness, therapeutic efficacy, and respite.

Shechtman (1999)
Explored group poetry therapy (utilizing poems, stories, pictures, and films), role-playing and drawing, focused on the theme of aggression.

Highly aggressive eight-year-old boys.
Transcript analyses indicated that there was a decrease in within-group aggressive behaviors and an increase in within-group constructive behaviors throughout the course of the group.

Tyson (2002)
Hip Hop Therapy, defined as "an innovative synergy of rap music, bibliotherapy, and music therapy," was used to address issues related to "self-identity, peace, unity, cooperation, and individual and (ethnic) group progress."
At-risk youth.
Findings revealed no statistically significant difference between the treatment and control group.

Box 7.1, seven controlled studies of poetry therapy research were published in scholarly literature (Blake & Cashwell, 2004; Golden, 2000; Howard, 1997; Meunier, 1999; Papadopoulos, Wright, & Harding, 1999; Shechtman, 1999; Tyson, 2002); however, a statistically significant difference in outcomes between the treatment and control group was only found in the Golden study (Olson-McBride, 2009, p. 167). In addition, some of the research designs were less rigorous than expected of empirical research.

In a review of the state of poetry therapy research (Heimes, 2011), a basis for designing and carrying out study projects was described. Using a systematic review using AMED, Cochrane Collaboration, Embase, MEDLINE, PsychINFO and PSYINDEX, studies were classified according to country, subject, publication date, and the level of evidence-based medicine. Of 1129 entries found, 203 were used. The majority of the studies were conducted in the United States in the fields of psychiatry and psychology. Investigative activities reached the highest levels in the period from 1999 to 2010. Most of the studies correspond to level 5 on the scale of evidence-based medicine.

The findings showed that poetry therapy is better established (in a scientific sense) in the United States than in other countries (e.g., Germany and England). Studies in areas other than psychiatry and psychology, such as oncology, point to future ranges of application. Heimes (2010) concludes that the rising levels of interest over the past 10 years in poetry therapy and its scientific establishment have encouraged additional research projects for which appropriate evaluation methods need to be developed (p. 7).

Quantitative Studies in Poetry Therapy

The following studies have taken place over the last five years and have strengthened poetry therapy's preexisting knowledge base. Olson-McBride and Page (2006) used poetry therapy as a group intervention with physically, mentally, or cognitively disabled children. The Poetry Club met twice weekly over the six-week course of the southern Mississippi summer day camp group. Session activities included icebreaker activities, writing "getting to know you" poems based on their observations of another club member, creating a poem based on some or all of the comments generated during the activity, writing a modified version of an "Autobio" poem (Korb-Khalsa & Leutenberg, 2000, p. 11), writing a friendship poem, writing a poem about right and wrong, creating a "story poem" about a person, imaginary or real, and an emotion this person may be experiencing, and writing an acrostic poem utilizing the word "goodbye." Discussion was sparked with poems such as "Slammed/Crammed/Jammed" (Harrington, n.d.) and "The Voice" (Silverstein, 1996).

While formal measures were not used to monitor the outcomes of the intervention, group interaction and self-confidence were reported as changed for the positive. The investigators noted less verbal and physical aggressive behaviors. There was an observable increase in members' ability to interact with one another and each member was described as becoming more confident in their skills as writers over the course of the Poetry Club.

Domestic violence counselors have an increased likelihood of developing symptoms of secondary posttraumatic stress due to working in an underfunded agency, the nature of the work, or having to remain secretive about the location of their workplace. Outside large cities, they may be the only mental health professional on site. In all circumstances, the characteristics of the client population may include extreme vulnerability, dependency, distrust, learned helplessness, or lack of initiative to get out of an abusive relationship. Boone and Castillo (2008) explored variables that predict secondary posttraumatic stress disorder (SPTSD), Gender, agreeableness, and openness to experience were significantly related to SPTSD symptoms. The authors discussed whether poetry therapy had an impact on SPTSD in domestic violence counselors. In addition, Boone and Costillo recommended that part of the counselors' professional education on SPTSD should include information on writing as a technique for self-care.

The study used structured poetry therapy activities, with the time and spacing of activities similar to that used in Pennebaker's basic expressive writing paradigm (Pennebaker, 1997). Poetry therapy was used in accordance with the Hynes and Hynes-Berry model (1994) in order to promote deeper levels of emotional disclosure about personal emotions in participants in response to literature. Findings suggest that practitioners can benefit from writing and poetry therapy to relieve stress associated with SPTSD. Support groups that utilize writing and poetry therapy may be an especially effective means of helping counselors cope with stress. For counselors working in isolation at satellite or smaller sites, Internet writing may provide a way to engage in self-care or to connect with others and in this way increase their resiliency to the demands of their work. The need for additional support by less experienced counselors was also suggested by the study's findings (Boone, 2006, pp. 79, 80). This offers empirical support for practice recommendations by Courtois (2000) for providing support for newer staff.

Olson-McBride combined music (primarily the genres of hip-hop and rap) and poetry to form a client-centered therapeutic approach to group psychotherapy with urban at-risk youth that encouraged connection, communication, and self-expression. This research was guided by two questions (2009, p. 7): "What therapeutic factors occur during these poetry therapy groups? What group processes and characteristics contribute to the development of the therapeutic factor of self-disclosure during these poetry therapy groups?"

The most meaningful finding of Olson-McBride's research was that poetry therapy intervention was found to have a "remarkable impact on engagement, honesty, and bold self-disclosure among three-groups of at-risk youth" (Olson-McBride, 2009, p. 123). A client-centered poetry therapy intervention such as Olson-McBride's is especially appropriate for providers who provide services that are culturally competent and strengths-based.

The issue of quantifying the more intangible aspects of poetry therapy intervention seems to be key in the development of a strong poetry therapy research base. For example, the purpose of the intervention described in Papadopoulos et al. (1999) is fourfold: (a) build bridges of understanding (via learning from own and other's experiences), (b) encourage a sense of community by providing a supportive environment, (c) increase members' well-being and self-esteem, and (d) encourage members' personal empowerment (p. 30).

In the present form, these four outcomes are difficult to measure; however, these outcomes can be transformed into variables that are more easily measured. For example, encouraging a sense of community could easily be transformed into a variable related to group cohesion and measured via the Cohesion subscale on the Group Environment Scale (Moos & Hanson, 1974) or the Therapeutic Factors Inventory-S (Lese & MacNair-Semands, 2000); while item (a) fits the definition of vicarious learning from the Classification of Therapeutic Factors Manual (Block, Reibstein, Crouch, Holroyd, & Themen, 1979) and the frequency of its occurrence during a session could be measured via content analysis. An additional systematic measure, Hynes and Hynes-Berry's (1994) *Responsive Patterns in Bibliotherapy* record has already been tailored for use with poetry therapy; however, no accounts of research employing this measure have been published to date. Finally, Blake's (2003) use of qualitative matrices and Tyson's (2006) *Rap-music Attitude and Perception Scale* could prove valuable in future poetry therapy research (Olson-McBride, 2009, pp. 34–35).

A poetry therapy group intervention with a small number of cancer patients offers encouraging statistical results. The six-week intervention was found to improve emotional resilience, represented by reduced emotional control (Courtauld Emotional Control Scale). It was hypothesized that the intervention would result in improved adjustment to having cancer, measured by the mini-MAC; and increased psychological growth (Post-Traumatic Growth Inventory), but the statistics measuring these results were inconclusive (Tegnér, Fox, Philipp, & Thorne, 2009). Poetry therapy sessions were led by an experienced certified poetry therapist who was familiar with group work in clinical settings.

In a crossover experimental design, half of the participants experienced a series of six weekly poetry sessions, while the rest acted as controls in a "waiting" period before experiencing the same intervention. After discussion of each poem, participants were invited to write, using a given prompt that arose from the discussion or from the poem itself. An increase in emotional resilience was noted in the significant drop in total CECS scores and Anger subscale scores seen after the series of workshops, as well as a significant reduction in the experience of anxiety (HADS-A). Little change was seen in the control group after the no-intervention period.

Poetry therapy has been used with individuals with developmental disabilities as a therapy uniquely suited to understanding and expressing ones' thoughts and feelings. Individuals with developmental disabilities may have little or no say in where they live, with whom they live, or where they work; therapies for this population should encourage client voice. Therefore, Campbell (2007) designed a double-blind experiment to examine the effectiveness of poetry therapy (reading poetry and writing individual and collaborative poems) with 24 adults (8 males, 16 females) with intellectual disabilities (mild or moderate retardation) in a supervised environment at a support agency in the northeastern United States.

The purpose of the study was to determine if poetry therapy was an effective therapeutic strategy for improving self-esteem, decreasing severity and distress associated with psychopathology, and decreasing interpersonal difficulties. Four groups of six were randomly assigned as two treatment groups and two wait-listed control groups. All four groups completed assessment measures before the two treatment groups began therapy. After 12 weekly one-hour sessions of poetry therapy, all four groups again completed assessment measures, followed by 12 weeks of poetry therapy for the two wait-listed groups. A third phase of assessment followed the final poetry therapy groups. Each participant received copies of each poem they wrote and of the poems that were read at the beginning of each session. A few of the introductory poems included Wordsworth's "I Wandered Lonely as a Cloud"; Carlos-Williams' "This is Just to Say"; and Lawrence's "Butterfly" (Campbell, 2007).

Individual comments on the evaluation tool were examined for positive versus negative responses. Using a Likert-type scale, participants were asked questions about the poetry group. A score of one indicated the most negative response and five was the most positive response, for a possible score of 4–20. Scores ranged from 17 to 20, with a mean of 19.8. Participants indicated they liked the poetry group, would keep writing poetry, and wanted to do it again (Campbell, 2007). Many themes emerged from the large volume of poems produced including universal feelings, personal things they wanted others to know about, friendship, gratitude, appreciation for staff, and importance of writing poetry. Findings showed a significant decrease in distress associated with psychopathology, a significant decrease in interpersonal problems, and a significant increase in self-esteem, indicating that poetry therapy may be an alternative therapy for working with adults with developmental disabilities (Campbell, 2007). Campbell suggests poetry therapy as an adjunct or alternative therapy with individuals with intellectual disabilities, with individuals experiencing a lack of client voice, or those interested in pursuing a creative arts therapy.

Mulji-Dutt applied poetry therapy to find a healing tool that would give voice to the lived experience of refugees in Canada. Eleven sessions of poetry therapy were conducted with refugees who had lived in Canada for less than two years in transitional housing in Sojourn House, Toronto. The quantitative questions emerged from the general hypothesis that opening up about their lived experience as refugees would assist in building an identity in a new situation in their new home country. The high attrition rate created too small a sample size and the quantitative study was inconclusive.

Hence, a qualitative approach, specifically the hermeneutic phenomenological method, was most suitable in interpreting the data, while looking for overarching themes within the writings of these refugees. A comparison with her own poetry helped Mulji-Dutt see where the study participants' themes overlapped with the themes within her own immigrant story. As a result, she could separate the themes for refugees and for immigrants, and understand more deeply their experience of being a refugee. In what Gadamer (1960/2000) refers to as "fusion of horizons," the study author as the facilitator could ask questions of the transcripts/text and, through interpretation, broaden understanding and find meaning in the experience of refugees.

Mulji-Dutt (2010) conducted facilitating sessions using published poetry and prompts for discussion; subjects were guided to write about their lived experience. Home and language were the two themes that wove through their 11 writing sessions. It was as if the participants were learning to see again — a new view was emerging. Writing in fragments reduced the burden of grammar, style, and usage. Language played a key role in each participant finding the right words with which to articulate a changing identity and to find positive meaning in it. One client (AM) wrote about the community and giving, while also creating images of growth in her own life:

> Who I am
> I am growing flower
> Helping another growing
> With me like a green plant
> Like a seed and fruit
>
> (Mulji-Dutt, personal communication, December 5, 2010)

Through writing, the study participants learned to organize a new narrative, using language and poetic forms to shape their experiences, thoughts, and emotions.

Studies so far cannot prove that writing helps alleviate illness linked to trauma, even though research shows that both mental and physical health can improve with disclosure about extreme experiences (Pennebaker & Chung, 2007). However, Pennebaker's research (2007) tells us that the health benefit is dependent on how the writing is done and on the necessity of human intervention. More research needs to be conducted with a larger population sample in order to determine significant impact on health.

Mohammadian et al. (2011) studied the use of poetry therapy to reduce depression, stress, and anxiety in Iranian female college students. In this small group, poetry therapy had a significant effect on reduction in reported stress, anxiety, and depression.

Poetry and Writing

Creative/expressive writing, including writing poetry, is fast emerging as an invaluable tool to assist professionals in addressing the needs of a variety of individuals and groups. It is affordable for couples and families, professionals, caregivers, youths, and the elderly. It is accessible to those who are dealing with grief, abuse, or disability. It seems particularly appropriate for those who are at risk from illness or social status (Bolton, 1999). It is a "way of grasping life, nurturing every bit of good, connecting up severed bits of ourselves … . Poetry, even when it concerns death, pain, disfigurement, despair, is vibrant, alive, a way of life" (Bolton, 1999, p. 130).

Kobak (1969) described poetry therapy and creative writing as a "therapeutic vehicle" and as an "effective tool for uncommunicative and constricted clients impotent to express their feelings" (p. 180). Mazza and Prescott (1981) used the dyadic poem in couple's therapy. The couple is asked to create a two-line poem addressing a theme or issue, with each person writing one line. This type of poem has been found to be helpful in assessing couple needs and areas of strength. For example, were the lines contrasting or complimentary? Who went first? How did the couple approach the task? Families can also use dyadic poems to express feelings. Family members contribute one or more lines to a family collaborative poem on a theme or mood of the counseling session (Mazza, 1996). Similarly, a group collective poem allows group members to contribute one or more lines to a collective poem based on a predominant theme or mood (Baker & Mazza, 2004).

Philipp, Coppell, and Freeman (1994) sought responses to important questions via the *British Medical Journal*. Could or does reading or writing poetry benefit health? Do we or should we encourage patients, or try ourselves, to express poetry? This national call raised interest in poetry as a therapeutic tool among health care professionals and the public (Philipp, 1999; Philipp & Robertson 1996). A summary of the 196 responses received from the United Kingdom public indicated benefits related to reading and writing poetry (Hilse, Griffiths, & Corr, 2007).

Despite the evidence of the healing power of poetry, poets generally do not experience the same health benefits as others. Poets are more likely to suffer higher rates of mental illness, suicide, and mortality more than any other writers or the population at large (Kaufman & Sexton, 2006). Some argue that the reason is because poets are more depressed to begin with and depressive personalities appear to be drawn to the art of expression. Recently, an alternative answer may give insight into why writing poetry may not benefit the health of poets. Kaufman and Sexton suggest that the formation of a narrative is a necessary precondition for writers seeking improvements in their health. Expressive writing with a narrative format is coherent and linear and allows for exploration of thoughts and feelings or a shift in perspective and meaning. Because poetry tends to be shorter than prose, it may lack narrative. Poets seeking improvements in their health through writing are encouraged to write expressively with a narrative-based theme, whether in diaries, journals, or emails (Kaufman & Sexton, 2006).

Kidd (2010) explored the effect of a poetry writing intervention on self-transcendence, resilience, depressive symptoms, and subjective burden in family caregivers of older adults with dementia in the Midwest. The theoretical framework she employed synthesized theories of Adler and Frankl, and Reed's Theory of Self-Transcendence. She posed the following questions:

- Are there differences over time on self-transcendence, resilience, depressive symptoms, and caregiver burden between family caregivers of older adults with dementia who write poetry (Group A) and those not writing poetry (Group B)?
- Are higher positive psychological resources (self-transcendence and resilience) associated with lower negative psychological outcomes (depressive symptoms and caregiver burden) over time with continued poetry writing?
- Will psychological resources and negative outcomes in both groups improve over time?
- What common themes emerge from the poetry written by family caregivers?
- Will caregivers who write poetry (Group A) continue to write or verbalize intent to write poetry after no longer being required to do so?
- What is the feasibility of conducting a larger clinical trial?

Reiter offered 12 poetry therapists-in-training the opportunity to work with 12 poets-behind-bars in collaboration with the Creative Righting Center and the Indiana State Prison in the "Poets-Behind-Bars: A Creative 'Righting' Program for Prisoners and Poetry Therapists-in-Training" project (Reiter, 2010). Through monthly email exchanges, personal details of the prisoner-poet's writing, including his responses to poetic prompts and his descriptions of prison life, as well as the trainee's suggestions and reactions, were recorded. As one trainee wrote, "All this was written down, written down, indelibly, in words — words to be read, pondered, processed, re-read, and potentially saved forever" (Reiter, 2010, p. 224). Fourteen trainees and credentialed poetry therapists continued this work in 2010.

Longo once asked a mentally ill patient how it felt to hold a published copy of a poem he'd written. The man simply replied, "I feel like I am somebody, finally ..." (Longo, 2004). Publication is validation of the patient's voice because someone valued his words enough to type them up (Longo, personal communication, January 10, 2011).

Poetry therapy and music therapy have reportedly been used with women and adolescents with chemical addictions (Freed, 1988, 1989; Gladding & Mazza, 1983). Poetry is mentioned as a tool for spontaneous intervention within the context of various case studies in music therapy (Boone, 1991; Perilli, 1991). The use of poetry therapy and music therapy in a substance abuse setting has been described (Kaufman & Goodman 2010). *Cracking Up and Back Again: Transformation through Poetry* (Kaufman, 2007) is a workbook reflecting themes in suffering and healing as well as suggestions for reflections on these themes for recovery in substance abuse outpatient programs. The group of women in substance abuse recovery read two or three poems in sequential order from the text at each session, with different clients volunteering to read aloud. The women became motivated to write their own personal poems, infusing their poetry with their spirits as the group dynamics changed. At the end of the eight sessions, each client was given her own copy of the *Cracking Up and Back Again* book to encourage the group to travel together from poem to poem in order to reach the final ending of poetry and transformation. A collaborative group poem entitled "Expressive Arts for Recovery Group Poem" was created from lines taken from the client's own poetry during the fifth session (Kaufman & Goodman, 2010).

Music therapy was offered as a means of deepening the emotional exploration of the poetry. Each poem improvised and directed by each woman in the group. The group participated also in creating the group poem, first as a ballad and then as a scat. The authors suggest further exploration of the process of a poetry therapist and music therapist working together (Kaufman & Goodman, 2010, p. 10): "What comes first, the poem or the music? Who handles the verbal processing of the poetry? Of the music? What transferences and counter-transferences may interface between the clients and the therapists? Between the therapist and therapist? What devices exist in structuring both the poem and the song? How might additional understanding of each other's craft expedite the process further?"

Most people affected by a traumatic event do not seek therapy, but continue to cope with the aftermath of the event as best as they can. Findings of an 18-month qualitative poetry therapy study with Vietnam War era veterans demonstrated that poetry and writing were invaluable tools in assisting a community of soldiers who felt like "broken toy soldiers, now left to gather dust" (Deshpande, 2010, p. 241) in their recovery from trauma. Project Recon Mission introduced participating veterans — suffering posttraumatic stress disorder, mood disorders, substance abuse, and other Axis I diagnoses — to the concept of using writing and poetry for healing. None of the selected poems were war poems. The poems chosen were reflective of the veterans' state of mind at the time and progressively went on to nudge the men into thinking about the future, in a positive way, thus fulfilling the criteria outlined by Hynes and Hynes-Berry (1994). Project Recon Mission used military metaphors, where applicable, and created an atmosphere conducive to taking action. Tackling issues as a group gave the veterans a renewed sense of camaraderie and purpose.

"At the US National Monument along the Canadian Border" (Stafford, 1997), "Directions to the Armorer" (Olson, 1959), and "Tree House" (Silverstein, 1974) were among the many poems presented. The men also wrote a personal alpha poem (Adams, 1993) using the words, "Always Remember."

Other writing exercises included:

- *A thank you and goodbye letter.* Write a letter to something painful in your life and acknowledge it as a teacher. The men were then asked to thank this teacher, acknowledge what they had learned, and say goodbye to it. Through this exercise, participants were then able to accomplish what Morgan (2000) calls "creat[ing] a space for change."

- *Army of emotions.* Write down all the emotions you experience and wish to experience. Give the emotions a Military Rank. Write a letter of recommendation for the lowest-ranked emotion on the list.
- *Operation Salvage.* Fill in a chart that had ages birth to 85 years, in blocks of five years each. In each block, write down what was good or worth salvaging from this period. Pennebaker (2004) states, "The tricky aspects of negative emotions are that they need to be acknowledged, but not dwelt upon" (p. 55). Pennebaker also states that writing loses its therapeutic value if it is used to reiterate the negative aspects of life. Through *Operation Salvage*, the group learned that they could choose to look at the destruction that the trauma had wrecked on the landscape of their lives, or focus on what was still intact and could be used for rebuilding. Operation Salvage was adapted from "Loss Lifeline" (Adams, 2000, pp. 120–121).
- *Re-story.* Create a fictional account of an unpleasant experience in your life. They had to write for 15 minutes, condense it to a one sentence declaration, and create a fictitious character with the same strengths but not necessarily the same weaknesses as themselves (Adams, 2004, pp. 95–96). The exercise was modified for the veterans who now had to pick another group member's story, and complete it. While the members may not have agreed with the outcome that the others chose for them, the exercise sowed the seeds of an alternative possibility. It also expanded their creativity and helped them to reach out to fellow group members. They could also express their own experiences more safely by identifying vicariously with another's.

Poetry is becoming more useful in hospice work as an opportunity for reflection, self-expression and life review with hospice patients and bereaved family members (Howard, 1997; Mazza, 2001; Nelson, 2006; Weishaar, 1999). The therapist can select a poem that fits the patient's situation or expresses how the patient seems to be feeling. The poem is read and the patient is invited to react that can lead into reminiscence and analysis of past life events. Patients can share their feelings and reconcile and find peace with past life events through writing about them. Writing an acrostic poem (the first letter in each line vertically spells out a different word) with the words "My Life" or using the name of each family member, incorporating special memories with each individual into each poem may be preserved as a keepsake for the family or read at a family ceremony or celebration (Wlodarczyk, 2009).

Diary-writing and poetry are two writing forms that have been found to be especially helpful in seeking to understand the progression of Alzheimer's disease. The diary is an especially helpful tool because it is geared most naturally to the fragmented life. Helfgott writes about the benefits of writing in her diary as a means of confronting the challenges of dealing with her husband's diagnosis of Alzheimer's disease in "Witnessing Alzheimer's through diary and poem: Dear Alzheimer's why did you pick our sheltered lives to visit?" (2009).

Poetry is used in hospice work as an opportunity for reflection, self-expression, and life review with hospice patients and bereaved family members (Howard, 1997; Mazza, 2001; Nelson, 2006; Weishaar, 1999). The therapist can select a poem that fits the patient's situation or expresses how the patient seems to be feeling. The poem is read and the patient is invited to react, which can lead into reminiscence and analysis of past life events. Patients can share their feelings and reconcile or find peace with past life events through writing about them. Writing an acrostic poem (the first letter in each line vertically spells out a different word) with the words "My Life" or using the name of each family member, incorporating special memories with each individual into each poem may be preserved as a keepsake for the family or read at a family ceremony or celebration (Wlodarczyk, 2009).

Caregivers of veterans can write poems to navigate the complexities of daily life, explore emotions, and ease stress. Survivors of suicide will sometimes write poems in which they directly address their loved ones. People who are grieving or are members of an online support group may write letters or a series of letters containing poems over the course of several years as a way of coping and preserving relationships.

Summary

Poetry therapy has a long history, but it wasn't until the 1960s did it become introduced less randomly as a method of therapy. It was generally applied in the "mentally ill," but new applications have now been tried. Historically, there is a rich history of professionals applying poetry therapy and suggesting direction in its evaluation. The existing body of literature on research in poetry therapy continues to consist primarily of descriptive and exploratory studies. There remains a great need for rigorous, larger, longer, randomized controlled studies, definitive conclusions, and statistical results to determine therapeutic outcome measures of poetry therapy as an intervention and to evaluate the benefits and who does not benefit from poetry therapy intervention. Suggested areas for research include the therapeutic benefits of writing in poetry therapy and the impact of poetry therapy on group cohesion, cultural interpretation, personal growth, health, and the lived experience of illness.

Dante finished his epic journey through *The Inferno* with the words:

> We climbed, he first and I behind, until,
> through a small round opening ahead of us
> I saw the lovely things the heavens hold,
> and we came out to see once more the stars.
>
> (Dante, trans. 1970, canto 34, lines 136–139)

Chapter 8

Programmed Writing

Luciano L'Abate

> *"Today's mental health professional faces an onslaught of couples and families that present with arduous challenges that require good skills, as well as evidenced-based tools for facili'tating change. Hence, a clinician's "tool box" has become more vital than ever, preparing for a broad range of clinical and non-clinical conditions that are likely to be encountered during the course of one's practice."* (Dattilio, 2011, pp. 1–2)

The purpose of this chapter is to summarize research about written, interactive practice exercises (PEs), or workbooks (sometimes called protocols at the request of an editor) administered as homework assignments. The phenomenal growth of handouts, worksheets, programmed materials, take-home, between-sessions exercises by many American publishers tends to support the position that most mental health services in this century will be structured and programmed to match one particular condition with one specific symptom, syndrome, or reason for referral (L'Abate, 2011b, in press-b).

Recent advances in homework assignments (Katzantizis & L'Abate, 2007), low-cost approaches to promote physical and mental health (L'Abate, 2007), and self-help in mental health (Harwood & L'Abate, 2010) include also distance writing with single, married, and family participants (L'Abate, 2008a, 2008b). These advances should make it easier for mental health professionals to choose among many modalities of treatment in addition to or not requiring face-to-face talk-based psychotherapy.

One of the major advances in mental health has been the publication of interactive PEs, also called workbooks, derived from a variety of theoretical and practical sources (L'Abate & De Giacomo, 2003; L'Abate & Goldstein, 2007). These sources include symptoms and syndromes from the DSM-IV (American Psychiatric Association, 1994), factor analyses, and single-and multiple-score tests, such as,

Research on Writing Approaches in Mental Health
Studies in Writing, Volume 23, 115–122

ISSN: 1572-6304/doi: 10.1108/S1572-6304(2011)0000023012

respectively among others, the Beck Depression Inventory and the Minnesota Multiphasic Personality Inventory (L'Abate, 2011b).

There are interactive PEs for most psychiatric categories or dimensions for individuals (children, youth, and adults), conflictful couples, and families. There are also interactive PEs for lifelong learning for individuals, couples, and families without a diagnosed illness (L'Abate & Goldstein, 2007).

This advance, linking evaluation with distance writing treatment, is due to a simple procedure: asking participants to answer regularly to items or dimensions on a test. Once this task is completed, participants are asked to define the items, using even a dictionary if necessary (L'Abate, 2007a, 2011c). After defining the items, participants are ask to give two examples for each items. This nomothetic task is to make sure that participants know exactly and concretely the meaning and nature of each item or dimension. A second step is to ask participants to rank-order items according to how they apply to themselves in importance or concern, This is an idiographic task that determines the order of administration of the following homework assignments, as described below.

Early Beginnings: Structured Enrichment Programs

Interactive PEs found their early beginnings in structured enrichment programs for couples and families described and evaluated in several publications (L'Abate & Kern, 2002; L'Abate & Rupp, 1981; L'Abate & Weinstein, 1987; L'Abate & Young, 1987). Early studies about the long-term outcomes of workbooks measured with pre–post evaluation and follow-up were published by L'Abate, Boyce, Fraizer, and Russ (1992). The results of these studies demonstrated a sufficient reliability and validity to continue production and publication of workbooks.

Additionally, for interventions in the fields of self-help, promotion, prevention, and psychotherapy, quite a few structured enrichment programs with verbatim instructions to trainers for couples and families are entirely reproducible for computer administration (L'Abate & Weinstein, 1987; L'Abate & Young, 1987). Some of these programs follow the same sequence outlined above about evidence. Some are independent from any theory. Some are dependent on some theory. Some are related to some theory. Some are derived from theory.

Research on Interactive Practice Exercises

Results from those early studies were summarized and reanalyzed for their effect sizes and published in L'Abate (2004a, pp. 75–93). A meta-analysis of 18 mental health and 12 physical health workbooks (Smyth & L'Abate, 2001) produced effect sizes of $d = .44$ and .25, respectively. Unfortunately, these research studies were conducted by graduate students mentored by this author's laboratory for their research and doctoral dissertations. We have yet to find external evidence from sources other than those generated by this author to support the validity and reliability as well as the clinical, preventive, and psychotherapeutic usefulness for workbooks.

Classification of Workbooks

Workbooks can be classified around various variable characteristics included in Box 8.1. These characteristics are concrete and specific enough to be self-explanatory without the need for further explication.

Relationship Between Theory and Workbooks

However, two characteristics of interactive PEs included in Box 8.1 need highlighting and further expansion. Those two characteristics are (1) levels and types of functionality and (2) relationships between theory and a classification of PEs. To link a classification of PEs with theory, we shall use one specific Model[11] of Relational Competence Theory (Cusinato & L'Abate, in press; L'Abate, Cusinato, Maino, Colesso, & Scilletta, 2010). This Model[11] deals with Selfhood, how we bestow a sense of importance to ourselves and to intimate others. When importance is bestowed positively toward self and intimate others, we obtain a high level of functionality. When importance is bestowed positively to self and negatively to others, we obtain most Axis II Cluster B personality disorders from the SMD-IV. When importance is bestowed negatively to self and positively to others, we obtain most Axis Cluster C personality disorders. When importance is bestowed negatively to self and others, we obtain Cluster A of Axis II and most disorders of Axis I.

Box 8.1. Classification of interactive practice exercises (workbooks)

Composition of Participants: singles (adults, children, youth), couples, families, groups,
Reason for Referral: that is, concern(s), diagnosis(es), single versus dual or multiple, problem (s), symptom(s),
Level and Type of Functionality: DSM-IV or Reason for Referral,
  Functional; No diagnosis
  externalizations; Axis II. Cluster B
  internalization: Axis II. Cluster C
  borderline: Axis II. Cluster A
  severe: Axis I.
Specific Symptoms versus General Condition, Symptom-free versus symptom-related & diagnosis-linked,
Theory-derived, theory-related, theory-independent,
Format: (1) fixed (nomothetic); (2) flexible (idiographic); & (3) mixed (nomothic and idiographic)
Style: Linear versus circular (paradoxical), dictionary-driven versus no-dictionary,
Derivation: Research from factor analyses, single versus multiple-score tests, that is, BDI versus MMPI-2, DSM-IV, clinical experience, and selected literature,
Content: clinical versus nonclinical conditions.

Box 8.2. Relationships among selfhood propensities, functionality, psychopathology (DSM-IV), and sample interactive practice exercises

		Self-Importance	
		High	*Low*
Importance of Others	*High*	*Functionality* Life-long learning exercises	*Cluster C Disorders* Depression Anxiety
	Low	*Cluster B Disorders* Acting-out Psychopathy Impulsivity	*Severe Axis I* Cluster A Disorders Mood Swings Schizophrenia

From this Model[11], it is possible to link functional conditions and psychiatric disorders according to the DSM-IV Classification (American Psychiatric Association, 1994), as shown in Box 8.2.

Consequently, most PEs published by L'Abate (2011c) can be classified according to this model. With functional, diagnosis- and symptom-free participants (children, youth, single adults, couples, and families), they can be administered PEs constructed for lifelong learning in educational and nonclinical settings (churches, schools, community centers). With Cluster B personality disorders, there are PEs for disruptive, impulsive acting out and antisocial personality disorders. With Cluster C personality disorders, there are multiple PEs for anxiety and depression, as well as also for psychosomatic conditions.

With Cluster A in Axis II borderline personality disorders and most severe disorders of Axis I, there are PEs about mood swings, thought disorders, and severe psychopathology, as well as unexpressed hurt feelings (L'Abate, 2011a) and expressed feelings (L'Abate, 2011c).

However, there are some workbooks that include either some, that is, Negotiation, or most of the 16 models of Relational Competence Theory, such as Planned Parenting. One recent workbook has been developed for this chapter as an example of how to convert an inert and from the Brief Psychiatric Rating Scale (BPRS). Included below is a specific example of how a well-known, widely validated, but inherently inert test instrument, such as the BPRS, as in the case of most psychological tests, can be transformed into an interactive PE or workbook.

Matching Evaluation with Treatment: A Written Treatment Modality for the Brief Psychiatric Rating Scale

One important psychiatric rating scale that was not included among the many already published (L'Abate, 2011c) is the BPRS. This screening instrument has been subjected to a great deal of research demonstrating robust statistical features in its criterion and concurrent validities, summarized in a few, representative studies below. Copies of this test, in 18 or 24-item formats, scoring, and training instructions are all available on the Internet. This BPRS will be used as an example of how to convert an inert passive questionnaire or test into an interactive PE or workbook.

Selected Validation Studies About the BPRS

The BPRS has been the workhorse of psychopathology assessment in studies of schizophrenia and related psychotic disorders for over 40 years. Kopelowicz, Ventura, Liberman, and Mintz's (2008) goal was to evaluate the discriminant validity of the BPRS across the broad spectrum of persons with schizophrenia. The total sample of 565 participants with schizophrenia (84%) or schizoaffective disorder (16%) came from eight separate studies conducted under the aegis of the UCLA Clinical Research Center for Schizophrenia and Psychiatric Rehabilitation over a period of 15 years. The total sample could be divided into three subsamples based on illness chronicity and degree of refractoriness to treatment: Recent-onset patients had been ill for less than 2 years ($n = 178$), stable chronic patients between 2 and 19 years ($n = 243$), and treatment-refractory patients for more than 19 years ($n = 144$). Exploratory principal components analysis and varimax rotation were performed on the total sample. The results of each of the three subsamples were compared to the total sample using a correlation matrix and by calculating a coefficient of congruence. Results: A four-factor solution was considered the most interpretable for each subsample, reflecting the same four components identified in the total sample: positive symptoms, negative symptoms, agitation–mania, and depression–anxiety. Correlation coefficients and coefficient of congruence were very high, ranging from 0.91 to 0.98. Conclusions: The consistency of the four-factor solution of the 24-item BPRS across the range of subjects, from first psychotic episode to long-stay, institutionalized patients, supports the use of these factors and this instrument as a whole to track changes over time and with treatment in research and clinical samples.

Despite increasing interest in dimensional psychopathology and the use of symptom clusters in clinical research, factor analytic studies of mania are rare. Most studies included not only manic patients but also patients with a mixed episode or other severe mental disorders. Picardi et al. (2008) aimed at further elucidating the symptom structure of manic states. As part of a national survey of acute psychiatric inpatient care, all patients admitted to a random sample of Italian public and private facilities during an index period underwent a standardized assessment, including the 24-item BPRS. Eighty-eight patients (90% of all manic patients admitted) with an ICD-10 diagnosis of Bipolar Affective Disorder, Current Episode Manic with complete data were included in this study. Principal axis factor analysis with Varimax rotation was performed on BPRS-24 items. Four factors were extracted, explaining 51% of total variance. They were interpreted as Mania, Disorganization, Positive Symptoms, and Dysphoria. The distribution of the Disorganization factor was positively skewed, with most patients relatively free from disorganization symptoms and some patients showing varying degrees of severity. The sample size was relatively small; also, patients were not administered a structured diagnostic interview. However, reasonably large samples are usually sufficient when communalities are high. Also, the manic episode is a clear-cut diagnostic entity easily identified by experienced clinicians, and the independent BPRS-24 ratings corroborated the diagnosis.

The identification of a Mania, Positive Symptoms, and Dysphoria factor is consistent with most previous studies. The identification of a Disorganization factor in a sample including only manic patients is a new finding that may have clinical implications, as its distribution suggests the possibility of distinguishing two patient groups, which may require different interventions to achieve optimal therapeutic response. The factorially derived BPRS-24 subscales may be useful for evaluation of treatment effects in clinical trials of antimanic agents.

In clinical practice, patients with unipolar depression present with a variety of symptom clusters that may combine together in many different ways. However, only few factor analytic studies used general psychopathology scales to investigate the symptom structure of unipolar depression (Biancosino, Picardi, Marmai, Biondi, & Grassi, 2010). In this study, those investigators included 163 consecutive inpatients with an ICD-10 diagnosis of depressive disorder (ICD-10 codes F32 to F33). All patients were assessed with the 18-item version of the BPRS within 3 days from admission. Exploratory factor analysis with Varimax rotation was performed on BPRS items. Four factors were extracted, explaining 52% of total variance. They were interpreted as Apathy, Dysphoria, Depression, and Psychoticism. The distribution of factor scores was approximately normal for Apathy, while it displayed a slight negative skewness for Depression, a slight positive skewness for Dysphoria, and a marked positive skewness for Psychoticism. Patient sex, family history of depression, lifetime history of suicide attempt, and recent serious family conflict were not associated with any factor. Occupational status, age, and age at onset displayed a positive correlation with Apathy. Duration of illness and number of previous admissions were positively correlated with Dysphoria.

Patients were not administered a structured diagnostic interview, and no detailed assessment of personality disorders was performed; also, patients were recruited only at a single site, which reduces the generalizability of the results. These findings suggest that in depressive disorders there are psychopathological dimensions other than depressed mood that are worthy of greater clinical attention and research. Dimensions such as apathy and dysphoria may play an important part in the clinical phenomenology of unipolar depression and deserve systematic and careful assessment in order to provide patients with the best possible treatment and improve clinical outcomes.

Although the Clinical Global Impression (CGI) and the BPRS are both frequently used in drug trials for schizophrenia, their relative sensitivity in detecting differences between antipsychotics has not yet been examined. Leucht and Engel (2006), therefore, reanalyzed original patient data from all four pivotal, randomized controlled studies ($n = 1205$) that compared amisulpride with haloperidol in patients with schizophrenia. The sensitivity of the BPRS versus the CGI improvement and the CGI severity scales in detecting between drug differences was estimated by calculating effect sizes and their 95% confidence intervals for both continuous (standardized mean differences) and dichotomous outcomes (odds ratios). The primary end points were the last observation carried forward results at study end points pooling all studies, but the results of the observed cases at different study weeks and the results of the single studies were also examined. The effect sizes derived from the BPRS and from the CGI were similar. When the single studies were pooled, all outcomes analyzed showed a statistically significant superiority of amisulpride compared to haloperidol as early as two weeks after initiation of treatment. The CGI may be as sensitive as the BPRS in detecting efficacy differences between antipsychotic drugs, although specific studies with truly independent ratings would be needed for confirmation. The fact that it takes only 1–2 min to fill in the CGI justifies its use in addition to more specific scales in drug trials for schizophrenia. Further development and evaluation of the CGI is warranted.

Anderson, Crist, and Payne (2004) examined whether assessment data from administration of the extended version of the BPRS-E state hospital patients within 72 hours of their admission could be used to predict length of hospital stay. BPRS-E data for 222 first-admission patients, for whom the mean length of stay was 118.4 ± 88.6 days, were factor analyzed, yielding a model with four factors: patient's resistance to treatment, positive symptoms, mood, and negative symptoms. Discriminate analysis showed that the negative symptoms factor (blunted affect, emotional withdrawal, motor retardation, self-neglect, and disorientation) correctly predicted whether length of stay would exceed the mean in 94% of cases. These findings suggest that the severity of negative symptoms can be a useful predictor of length of stay among patients with severe and persistent mental illness.

The generalizability of previously isolated prototypical profiles of the BPRS was examined by Burger, Yonker, Calsyn, Morse, and Klinkenberg (2005) in a sample of homeless individuals with both severe mental illness and substance-use problems who were part of a 24-month study that evaluated the effectiveness of various treatment interventions. These prototypical profiles (depressed, actively psychotic, and withdrawn) did generalize to the new sample, with a 59.4% coverage rate. In addition, some of the participants' BPRS profiles (10%) were characterized by negative correlations with the withdrawn profile (termed agitated) and others (17%) by minimal within-profile variability (labelled flat). Overall, with these additions, the coverage of the prototypical profiles was 86.4%. These prototypical profiles were then used to evaluate changes in profile elevation and shape over the course of the study. Generally, changes in both profile elevation and shape were moderated by the particular prototypical profile that the participants resembled. The use of these prototypical profiles in evaluating change permits a more precise analysis of what kind of individuals manifest particular effects. The clinical meaning of the BPRS profile changes observed was also discussed.

Administration of BPRS in Office and Online

Instead of ratings based on an interview, this scale could be administered as a paper-and-pencil, self-report instrument for screening first as well as for specific treatment based on distance writing second. This procedure can occur face-to-face through talk as well as online through writing. Ideally, this scale should be answered by participants before they are scheduled to see a professional. It only takes a few minutes to complete and score it, either by an assistant or by professionals themselves. After establishing initially the reason for the referral, some history about the reason or symptom, an Informed Consent Form (ICF) should be given to participants to read before the end of the first session or seeing the professional for a second "evaluation" session. This ICF (L'Abate, 2011c) informs participants from the very beginning how treatment will occur through systematic written homework consisting of interactive PEs to be completed between sessions. Participants should also be encouraged to evaluate whether the professional is the right one for them, according to a principle of reciprocity exchange.

At the end of the first session, if and after participants have read and signed the ICF, they would receive as homework an assignment with the same list of 18 or 24 items (terms) to be rank-ordered according to how they apply to each participant. Rank-order would range from the item that is of greatest concern as No. 1, then to an item of second concern No. 2, and so on to no more than 6 items, with the other items ranked or answered as not applying (N/A) to the participant. Once participants bring their rank-ratings to the second session, they can administer a standard form with the title of the No. 1 concern written at the top of the page. That form asks participants about the developmental origins, frequency, intensity, and duration, including the personal and social consequences of their rank-ordered concern.

Standard, general purpose forms are available in L'Abate (2011c). After the No. 1 concerned is completed, shown to or shared with the professional, and discussed with feedback from the professional, the same general, standard form with the title of the No. 2 concern is administered. The same process of completion, presentation, discussion, and feedback is repeated with this concern as well with all the other remaining concerns, until all ranked concerns have been attended to.

If after retesting an area of concern still prominently exists, either another specialized workbook for that area could be administered, or referral for face-to-face, talk-based psychotherapy, or anti-psychotic medication may be necessary.

Conclusion

The basic issue with these PEs is evaluation because one cannot rely on an notoriously unreliable interview to reach a psychiatric diagnosis (L'Abate, 2012). Therefore, I have taken the (controversial) position that no PE should be administered without a small battery of validated instruments including the BPRS as well as tests derived from Relational Competence Theory (L'Abate et al., 2010). This battery should be administered before and after PE interventions and ideally at follow-up, as described in Chapters 1 and 10 of this volume. Of course, there is no way one can control or enforce such a standard. Nonetheless, I am personally and professionally convinced that in the future, with so many verbal, nonverbal, and writing alternatives available in the market of mental health service delivery, administration of an objective evaluation composed by a test battery on a pre–post intervention basis will allow us to separate artists/charlatans from professionals/scientists.

PART III

AN UNACCEPTABLE WRITING APPROACH

Chapter 9

Automatic Writing

Laura G. Sweeney

> "*All scams have one thing in common: they all serve to propagate the illusion of longer, richer, and better life, and, in some cases, even above and beyond the present life.*" (L'Abate & Sweeney, 2011)

The purpose of this chapter is to review research on automatic writing (AW). This review will follow studies in a descending order, moving first from a completely subjective experience based on personal impressions, anecdotal reminiscences, and mystical accounts as found in the popular literature, second to clinical case studies, third to eventually empirical evidence, and lastly to theory.

Popular Literature

Perhaps outlandish claims from just one representative source (Michele, 2006), among many others (Andrews, 2006; Conner, 2008; Couturier, 2005; Diehl, 2009; McCoy, 1994; Muhl, 1930; Richardson, 2007; Zerner & Farber, undated), may exemplify the flavor underlying this literature. Their titles and subtitles tell it all. These claims furnish the background that may establish AW more as a fashionable fad rather than as an established scientific approach to improve mental health. There is no way to document any of the incredible "mystical" claims that apparently are accepted at face value on faith, perhaps by individuals in need of mystical and semireligious experiences to fill and fulfill their lives.

Perhaps some readers or some investigators may adopt the criteria developed by L'Abate (2011d) to spot a phony huckster, a bogus con-person, and an unreliable cheat, who advertise without impunity nostrums for any imaginable and

Research on Writing Approaches in Mental Health
Studies in Writing, Volume 23, 125–129

ISSN: 1572-6304/doi: 10.1108/S1572-6304(2011)0000023013

unimaginable health condition and sexuality, including: (1) outlandish claims; (2) complete lack to evidence; (3) magical outcomes guaranteed; (4) use of personal testimonies from unknown individuals, including also (5) the authority of individual with the Doctor title, white coat, and a stethoscope draped over the neck.

The fact that at least three sources (McCoy, 1994; Richardson, 2007; Zerner & Farber, undated) give detailed instructions on how to do AW indicates that it can be performed at a distance, even though it is clear from these many sources that no professional or quasi/semi-professional helpers are included in the process.

Clinical Case Studies

Of the 49 studies published in peer-reviewed journals from 1950 to date, only three qualify as reliably documented clinical case studies. Joseph (1986), for instance, described two female patients (aged 17 and 45 years) who wrote complex textual material suddenly, automatically, and without volitional control. Each met Diagnostic and Statistical Manual of Mental Disorders (DSM-III) criteria for major affective disorder, had temporal lobe epilepsy, absence spells, episodic expressive aphasia, and a history of traumatic loss of consciousness. The episodes of AW met the criteria for ictal events; thus participants may have experienced an ictal analog of interictal hypergraphia. Behavioral neurologic features of this syndrome are discussed in relation to its clinical presentation and known disorders of writing.

van Vugt, Paquier, Kees, and Cras (1996) reported on the increased writing activity in a 70-year-old right-handed man with a history of alcohol misuse and maturity onset diabetes. Brain CT disclosed corticosubcortical atrophy and Tc-HMPAO single photon emission computerized tomography (SPECT) disclosed severe bilateral frontal hypoperfusion more prominent on the right. The patient's neuropsychological symptomatology consisted of severe (verbal) aspontaneity, intermittent utilization behavior, and pronounced increased writing activity, which mainly consisted of a perseverative, micrographic written reproduction of visually or verbally perceived language fragments. Several neurological causes of increased writing activity and the equivocal terminology met in the medical literature are reviewed. A distinction between hypergraphia and AW behavior is proposed. It is concluded that the patient's increased writing activity may be characterized as AW behavior.

Evyapan and Kumral (2001) reported on three cases (patients aged 48–68 years) of visuospatial stimulus-bound AW behavior which were identified among 80 patients with acute right cerebral hemispheric stroke. All cases had similar clinical characteristics and writing behavior, and visuospatial stimulus-bound AW was related to visually perceived letters. This syndrome might be specific for right hemispheric stroke and might be included among other hypergraphic syndromes attributable to right hemispheric damage.

Even though this case study did not deal directly with AW, it may be relevant to understanding some of the mechanisms possibly underlying it, such as the ability to concentrate and pay attention to self-directed cues (Spelke, Hirst, & Neisser, 1976).

Two subjects read short stories while writing lists of words at dictation. After some weeks of practice, they were able to write words, discover relations among dictated words, and categorize words for meaning, while reading for comprehension at normal speed. The performance of these subjects is not consistent with the notion that there are fixed limits to attentional capacity.

Experimental Studies

Koutstaal (1992) reviewed experimental investigations of AW beginning with those at the beginning of the last century, including luminaries such as F. Myers, E. Gurney, P. Janet, A. Binet, W. James, and M. Prince. Koutstaal focused at length on the research of L. M. Solomons and G. Stein (1896), who described AW as characterized by repetition, grammaticality, and alternation of unconsciousness with flashes of consciousness. More recently, AW has been subjected to increasingly stringent controls; researchers (e.g., E. Spelke et al., 1976; K. Bowers & H. Brenneman, 1981) have attempted to devise less fallible and more sensitive measures of the degree of a participant's awareness of automatically written material. Through demonstration of AW's occurrence in normal participants, and through a recognition of its similarities to automatic semantic activation, implicit memory, and divided controls and dissociations of awareness and intentionality, experimental psychology has "demystified" AW.

In an already outdated research, Hilgard (1973) reported that when cold pressor pain is reduced through hypnotically suggested analgesia, the concomitant changes in heart rate and blood pressure remain essentially what they were when the pain of the ice water was normally perceived. Investigation of this somewhat paradoxical finding by way of hypnotically induced AW (or its equivalent in automatic key pressing or automatic talking) reveals that at some cognitive level the subject has experienced the cold and can report its intensity, even though the suffering may be reduced. The theoretical problems posed by the experiment are presented according to a possible neodissociation interpretation, compared with interpretations according to psychoanalytic ego theory and role theory. The neodissociation theory is further explicated in relation to the gate theory of pain.

The possibility of a dissociative process hypothesized by Hilgard has led to studies evaluating its validity. Bowers and Brenneman (1981) described two experiments with 75 high and low hypnotically susceptible participants (Harvard Group Scale of Hypnotic Susceptibility). Detecting left-channel targets interfered less with the shadowing of right-channel prose when performance of the former task was posthypnotically dissociated from consciousness. However, this superiority over an ordinary divided-attention condition was not due to unconscious target detection by participants. Rather, the suggestions for posthypnotic responsiveness with amnesia apparently engendered a passive mode of attention to the left-channel task, such that participants did not actively listen for targets in order to hear them. In Exp II, explicit instructions to adopt a strategy of attentional passivity to the target-detection task proved to be far more effective in producing the reduced-interference effect than the posthypnotic suggestions had been. The posthypnotic suggestions seemed to induce attentional passivity as an indirect effect of amnesia for the posthypnotic suggestions and for previously detected targets. The findings of this study were interpreted in terms of Hilgard's (1973) neodissociation theory.

Green (1997), in another instance, examined whether 112 college students selected on the basis of high and low dissociative ability (Dissociative Experiences Scale [DES]), high and low/simulating hypnotizability (Harvard Group Scale of Hypnotic Susceptibility, Form A [HGSHS:A]), and past performance on the HGSHS:A amnesia item differentially passed an AW suggestion administered during a follow-up experiment. Results from a log-linear analysis supported a single main effect for hypnotizability. Low-hypnotizable, simulating participants were more than six times as likely to pass the AW suggestion as high-hypnotizable participants. Results found dissociation status and past performance on an ostensibly dissociative suggestion (i.e., amnesia) to be independent of passing the AW suggestion. Findings are discussed in light of other research regarding the relation between the DES and hypnotizability.

An additional study by Negro, Palladino-Negro, and Louzã (2002) noted that the religion Kardecism Spiritism accepts and fosters dissociative experiences such as spiritual incorporation, AW, and out-of-body experiences as part of its basic tenets. Mastery of these skills is valued and highly respected. Members underwent extensive formalized training under the guidance of experienced leaders who model socially appropriate religious behaviors. One hundred and ten participants at a prominent Kardecist Center in São Paulo, Brazil, were assessed with a variety of questionnaires and scales which addressed socialization, happiness, religiosity, mediumship, temperament (the Tridimensional Personality Questionnaire), and general dissociative experiences (the Dissociative Experiences Scale). Results show that the mediumship activity was associated with increased DES score in spite of good scores on socialization and adaptation. There was evidence for a positive association between mediumship training and the control of the religious-related dissociative experiences. Increased pathological dissociation was associated with younger age, less control of mediumship activity, poorer social support, and more antecedent psychiatric symptomatology.

Even though not directly associated to AW, Berninger et al. (2006) in three studies evaluated Tier 1 early intervention for handwriting at a critical period for literacy development in first grade and one study evaluated Tier 2 early intervention in the critical period between third and fourth grades for composing on high-stakes tests. The results contribute to knowledge of research-supported handwriting and composing instruction that informs practice as school psychologists are empowered to embrace the role of intervention specialist. The first study found that neurodevelopmental training (orthographic-free motor activities and motor-free orthographic activities) led to improved accuracy and legibility of letter formation, but that direct handwriting instruction with visual cues and verbal mediation led to improved automatic handwriting (rate of writing legible letters) and transfer to improved word reading. The second study found that neither motor training nor orthographic training alone added value to direct instruction in automatic letter writing and composing practice in developing handwriting skills, which transferred to improved word reading; but the added motor training did improve performance on a grapho-motor planning task for sequential finger movements that is relevant to composing. A related analysis showed that direct instruction with visual cues and memory delays may reduce reversals. A third study found that adding handwriting to reading instruction improved handwriting but did not add value to reading outcomes for at-risk readers; reading instruction alone was beneficial for word reading, decoding, and comprehension. The fourth study showed that comprehensive, explicit instruction in the processes of composition led to more significant improvement, based on group and individual data, than did the regular fourth grade program, on high-stakes writing assessment.

Burgess et al. (1998) investigated facilitated communication (FC) as automatism and studied the frequency with which it can be taught, the effect of its credibility on its production, and its relation to more simple automatisms. Forty college students were taught FC via a commercially available training videotape and were then asked to perform FC with a confederate, who was described as developmentally disabled and unable to speak. All 40 participants produced responses that they attributed at least partially to the confederate, and most attributed all of the communication entirely to her. Eighty nine percent produced responses corresponding to information they had received, most of which were unknown to the confederate. Responding was significantly correlated with simple ideomotor responses with a pendulum and was not affected by information about the controversy surrounding FC. These data support the hypothesis that FC is an instance of AW, and that the ability to produce AW is more common than previously thought.

Theory

Thus far, there is some evidence that a trance-like, possibly dissociative experience akin to hypnosis, and in some cases self-hypnosis, may be a process underlying AW. However, more evidence will be necessary to validate this possibility.

Conclusion

None of the studies reported here support the use of AW in general and in mental health in particular. There is no evidence from research that AW changes any behavior for the better and for an extensive period of time. The effects reported in subjective reports and clinical studies suggest that the possible, momentary high experienced by some participants may be due to a temporary state of self-induced dissociation, but nothing else. As in music (L'Abate, 2011d), one may enjoy the temporary, pleasant experience, but there is no concrete evidence that either AW or music will produce improvements in mental health.

Chapter 10

Epilogue: Distance Writing as the Preferred Medium of Help and Healing in the 21st Century

Luciano L'Abate and Laura G. Sweeney

> "... *we have a phenomenal variety of areas and contributions related to information processing and communication principles, theories and models, whose growth is now considered exponential.*" (De Giacomo, et al., 2011)
>
> "*Information processing links a vast and practically immense paradigm into unimaginable applications that pervade our lives to degrees never imagined a generation ago.*" (L'Abate & Sweeney, 2011)

The contents of most chapters in this volume have been written from a public rather than from a private practice mental health prospective. The aim of that *public prospective lies in providing the most cost-effective services for the most people in need of the most helpful interventions.* Distance writing is one of them. Giving up f2f, tb, one-on-one contacts is going to be difficult for the time being for many psychotherapists who are wedded to that model. For instance, the Italian Psychoanalytic Society has forbidden its members to rely on online therapy.

This change, however, is inevitable in the not too-distant future. Cost and inefficiency of 2f, tb, one-on-one approaches are slowly but inevitably giving way to one professional–many participants at a distance, online, and through a hierarchy of personnel, as discussed at great length by L'Abate (2012). This is the information-processing century. The far-reaching functions of information processing are contained in Table E.1 here.

Research on Writing Approaches in Mental Health
Studies in Writing, Volume 23, 131–134

ISSN: 1572-6304/doi: 10.1108/S1572-6304(2011)0000023014

Table E.1: Hierarchy in information processing.

	Information Processing			
Media:	Talk	Hybrid (Skype)	Writing	Nonverbal
Applications:				
Education		Internet		Play/Sports
Psychotherapy		Mil(itary)		Manual Labor
Preaching		Org(anizational)		Sex
		Com(mercial)		
		Individual (Net)		
Dimensions:		Billions	Billions	Billions

Source: From L'Abate and Sweeney (2011).

What about our children not having to learn cursive writing and instead learning to text on a keyboard? In addition to new, small, portable devices, such as smartphones, i-pads, and small computers mentioned in Chapter 1, there are at least three advances in the field of mental health that have serious implications on how mental health services will be delivered in this century. One advance lies in structured online interventions (Chapter 8 this volume; L'Abate, 2008a, 2008b, 2008c). The second advance lies in the advent of technology in psychology, psychiatry, and neurology (L'Abate & Kaiser, in press). The third advance will be specialization in evaluating which participant should receive which form of treatment, starting with the least expensive (physical exercise, vitamins, etc.) to the most expensive 1on1, f2f talk between a professional and a participant (L'Abate, 2011e, 2012).

There is no question in our minds that most mental health service deliveries will be performed online, with f2f tb contacts reserved for more severe disorders of Axis I in the DSM. However, instead of mimicking the unstructured nature of traditional talk-based psychotherapy, many online interventions very likely will be structured, that is, they will match a specific symptom, syndrome, or reason for referral (Abbott, Klein, & Ciechomski, 2008; L'Abate, 2008a, 2008b, 2008c). These interventions will be delivered on the basis of a prearranged number of sessions and price, as in the case of interactive practice exercises reviewed in Chapter 8 of this volume. Matching reason for referral with a specific treatment plan will bring much more emphasis on the importance of pre–posttreatment evaluation in the future (L'Abate, 2011b). However, what does writing and its phenomenal increase mean to how education will change, if any, in the future, near and distant?

Giving up 2f, tb, one-on-one contacts is going to be difficult for the time being for many psychotherapists who are wedded to that regressive model, but this change is inevitable in the not too-distant future. Cost and inefficiency of f2f tb, one-professional one-participant paradigms are slowly but inevitably giving way to one professional–many participants at a distance, online, and through a hierarchy of personnel.

The increasing use of writing in general and of distance writing in particular in this century is inevitable given the millions of troubled people who need professional help, not only in USA but around the world. The issue confronting most mental health disciplines will be evaluating and identifying who will be helped by which approaches that have emerged and developed during the last two generations. If this conclusion is valid, an important specialization that will be needed by most mental health disciplines will be evaluation and identification of who will be helped the most by which type of intervention at what cost.

However, this monograph cannot come to a close unless mental health professionals who want to practice online realize that they must become familiar with national and professional ethical and licensing laws, rules, and regulations governing clinical practices. While these practices are highly regulated in USA, surely there must be local and organizational rules and regulations in various European, Asiatic, and Middle East Countries. These rules need to be followed to make sure that the public is safeguarded from charlatans who will try to offer professional services illegally and unprofessionally.

At this point, we would like to close this Epilogue and this monograph with a quote from Dr. Marlene M. Maheu given with her expressed permission, and whom we consider the world expert on telemental health. If you plan to practice online, please refer to her for information and consultation:

From: Marlene Maheu <marlene.maheu@gmail.com>

Date: July 1, 2011 2:33:29 PM EDT

To: "Marlene M. Maheu" <marlene.maheu@gmail.com>

Bcc: llabate3@bellsouth.net

Subject: Cross-border Practice Online: Worth Re-considering?"

You may have heard colleagues and perhaps even "ethics" speakers condone the delivery of health care over state and national borders without first getting licensed in those foreign areas. The rationale? It boils down to "nobody is watching" or the belief that you won't "get caught." Our colleagues claim that licensing boards are not enforcing existing law or that it's highly unlikely that the consumer in other states or countries will come to your state to prosecute you. They are probably right on both counts, but is their stance practical, wise, or dare I say, "ethical?"
My thoughts:

1. From a purely practical point of view, the first issue to consider is that most malpractice insurance companies won't honor our policies if we are deemed to be practicing "illegally" as licensed professionals. Those policies usually contain a clause about being nullified when we engage in "illegal activity" as a professional. If we practice over state lines, either from one state to another, or from one country to another (international practice), by definition, according to most state law, we are practicing "illegally." Currently, chances are, we won't get caught. Nonetheless, our licensing board colleagues are working diligently to rectify

current problems with enforcement. They are focused on this issue, not only in the USA but also in many other countries, including the European Union and in Australia. Let's stop and think a bit further. When the authorities lower the boom on this illegal practice, who will get "caught?" Won't it be professionals who have world wide web pages that blatantly advertise their illegal, over-the-border practices? Beyond that, if any of us get into trouble for any other reason in our online practices, won't such a flagrant violation weigh against us in court? I'm not an attorney, but caution seems in order.

2. Aside from practicalities, the second issue to consider is that ethics are supposed to encourage us to think at a level above the law to help us think through potential conflicts. More basically, they demand that we adhere to the law. It is correct that many laws do not yet mention the word "Internet," but we are supposed to be educated enough to ask for help if we are struggling to think through all the issues ourselves.

For more information, see this blog post:
http://telehealth.net/blog/2011/06/ethics-code/

For further information on recommended online computer-assisted treatments please see L'Abate. L. (in press).

Potential mental health professionals who plan to practice online will not be able to say that they were not warned properly.

References

Abbott, J.-A. M., Klein, B., & Ciechomski, L. (2008). Best practices in online therapy. *Journal of Technology in Human Services, 26*, 360–375.

Abell, S. C. (1998). The use of poetry in play therapy: A logical integration. *The Arts in Psychotherapy, 25*(1), 45–49.

Ackerson, J., Scogin, F., McKendree-Smith, N., & Lyman, R. D. (1998). Cognitive bibliotherapy for mild and moderate adolescent depressive symptomatology. *Journal of Consulting and Clinical Psychology, 66*(4), 685–690.

Adams, K. (1993). *The way of the journal: A journal therapy workbook for healing*. Baltimore, MA: The Sidran Press.

Adams, K. (2000). Managing grief and loss. In: K. Adams (Ed.), *Write way to wellness: A workbook for healing and change* (pp. 118–125). Denver, CO: Center for Journal Therapy.

Adams, K. (2004). *Scribing the soul: Essays in journal therapy*. Denver, CO: Center for Journal Therapy.

Adams, K., & Rojcewicz, S. (2003). Mindfulness on the journey ahead. In: G. G. Chavis & L. L. Weisberger (Eds.), *The healing fountain: Poetry therapy for life's journey* (pp. 7–31). St. Cloud, MN: North Star Press.

Alaszewski, A. (2006). *Using diaries for social research*. London: Sage.

Alaszewski, A., & Alaszewski, H. (2005). Stroke and younger people: A longitudinal study of post-stroke normalisation and rehabilitation. Retrieved from http://www.kent.ac/chss/frames/index. Accessed on March 3, 2006.

Allen, J. L., Blatter-Meunier, J., Ursprung, A., & Schneider, S. (2010). Maternal daily diary report in the assessment of childhood separation anxiety. *Journal of Clinical Child & Adolescent Psychology, 39*, 252–259.

Allport, G. W. (1942). *The use of personal documents in psychological science*. New York, NY: Social Science Research Council.

Almlöv, J., Carlbring, P., Berger, T., Andersson, G., & Cuijpers, P. (2009). Therapist factors in inernet-delivered cognitive behavioral therapy for major depressive disorder. *Cognitive Behaviour Therapy, 38*(4), 247–254.

Alpers, G. W. (2009). Ambulatory assessment in panic disorder and specific phobia. *Psychological Assessment, 21*, 476–485.

American Psychiatric Association (1994). *Diagnostic Statistical Manual for Mental Disorders-IV*. Washington, DC: American Psychiatric Association.

American Writers and Artists Inc. (2011). *Industry spotlight: The self-help niche*. Retrieved from http://www.awaionline.com/2008/09/self-help-industry-spotlight/. Accessed on February 8, 2011.

Anderson, C. (1975). Bibliotherapy: Poetry therapy in psychiatric nursing. *Libri, 25*, 133–137.

Anderson, L., Lewis, G., & Araya, R. (2005). Self-help books for depression: How can practitioners and patients make the right choice? *British Journal of General Practice, 55*(514), 387–392.

Anderson, S. W., Crist, A. J., & Payne, N. (2004). Predicting inpatient length of stay with the expanded version of the brief psychiatric rating scale (Version 4.0). *Psychiatric Services, 55*, 77–79.

Andersson, G., Carlbring, P., Holström, A., Sparthan, E., Furmark, T., Nilsson-Ihrfelt, E., ... Ekselius, L. (2006). Internet-based self-help with therapist feedback and in-vivo group exposure for social phobia: A randomized controlled trial. *Journal Consulting in Clinical Psychology, 74*, 677–686.

Andersson, G., & Cuijpers, P. (2009). Internet-based and other computerized psychological treatments for adult depression: A meta-analysis. *Cognitive Behaviour Therapy, 38*(4), 196–205.

Andreasen, N. (1987). Creativity and mental illness: Prevalence rates in writers and their first degree relatives. *American Journal of Psychiatry, 144*, 1288–1292. http://findarticles.com/p/articles/mi_hb4345/is_1_36/ai_n29406570/.

Andrews, T. (2006). *How to meet & work with spirit guides*. Woodbury, MN: Llwellyn Publications.

Antebi, E. (1986). Poetry therapy: A means of increasing wholeness. *The Arts in Psychotherapy, 13*, 235–240.

Apodaca, T. R., & Miller, W. R. (2003). A meta-analysis of the effectiveness of bibliotherapy for alcohol problems. *Journal of Clinical Psychology, 59*(3), 289–304.

Armeli, S., Todd, M., & Mohr, C. A. (2005). Daily process approach to individual differences in stress-related alcohol use. *Journal of Personality, 73*, 1657–1686.

Armstader, A. B., Broman-Pulks, J., Zinzow, H., Ruggiero, K. J., & Cercone, J. (2009). Internet-based interventions for traumatic stress-related mental health problems: A review and suggestions for future research. *Clinical Psychology Review, 29*, 410–420.

Aspinwall, L., & Tedeschi, R. (2010). The value of positive psychology for health psychology: Progress and pitfalls in examining the relation of positive phenomena to health. *Annals of Behavioral Medicine, 39*, 43–47.

Asplund, J. (1985). *Tid, rum, individ och kollektiv*. Stockholm: Liber Förlag.

Baddeley, J. L., & Pennebaker, J. W. (2009). Expressive writing. In: W. T. O'Donohue & J. E. Fisher (Eds.), *Cognitive behavior therapy: Applying empirically supported techniques in your practice*). (2nd ed., pp. 197–201). New York, NY: Wiley.

Baddeley, J. L., & Pennebaker, J. W. (2011). A post deployment expressive writing intervention for military couples: A randomized controlled trial. *Journal of Traumatic Stress*. Published Online: 1 September 2011. doi:10.1002/jts.20679

Baikie, K., & Wilhelm, K. (2005). Emotional and physical health benefits of expressive writing. *Advances in Psychiatric Treatment, 11*, 338–346.

Baikie, K. A. (2003). *Rewriting trauma: How and for whom does the writing paradigm work?* Doctoral dissertation. Sydney: Macquarie University.

Bailey, S. L., Gao, W., & Clark, D. B. (2006). Diary study of substance use and unsafe sex among adolescents with substance use disorders. *Journal of Adolescent Health, 38*(297), e13–e20.

Baker, K. C., & Mazza, N. (2004). The healing power of writing: Applying the expressive/creative component of poetry therapy. *Journal of Poetry Therapy, 17*, 141–154.

Barak, A., Klein, B., & Proudfoot, J. G. (2009). Defining internet-supported therapeutic interventions. *Annals of Behavioral Medicine, 38*, 4–17.

Barclay, L. J., & Skarlicki, D. P. (2009). Healing the wounds of organizational injustice: Examining the benefits of expressive writing. *Journal of Applied Psychology, 94*, 511–523.

Barlow, D. H. (2010). Negative effects from psychological treatments. *American Psychologist, 65*, 13–20.

Barlow, D. H., Craske, M. G., Cerney, J. A., & Klosko, J. S. (1989). Behavioral treatment of panic disorder. *Behavior Therapy*, *20*, 261–262.

Barrett, M. (2006). 'Like dynamite going off in my ears': Using autobiographical accounts of autism with teaching professionals. *Educational Psychology in Practice*, *22*, 95–110.

Bell, G. L. (1982). Poetry therapy: Changing concepts and emerging questions. *The Arts in Psychotherapy*, *9*, 25–30.

Bell, G. L. (1992). NAPT: An overview through national conferences. *Journal of Poetry Therapy*, *6*, 101–105.

Bell, G. L. (2005). Narrative perspective: The use of the feedback poem as a tool for advancing interpersonal communication. *Journal of Poetry Therapy*, *18*, 283–291.

Bell, L. (1998). Public and private meanings in diaries, in researching family and childcare. In: J. Ribtens & R. Edwards (Eds.), *Feminist dilemmas in qualitative research: Public knowledge and private lives*. London: Sage.

Bellack, A. S., & Hersen, M. (1988). *Dictionary of behavioral assessment techniques*. New York, NY: Pergamon Press.

Bellizzi, K., Blank, T., & Oakes, C. (2006). Social comparison processes in autobiographies of adult cancer survivors. *Journal of Health Psychology*, *11*.

Bernard, M., Jackson, C., & Jones, C. (2006). Written emotional disclosure following first-episode psychosis: Effects on symptoms of post-traumatic stress disorder. *The British Journal of Clinical Psychology*, *45*, 403–415.

Berninger, V., Rutberg, J., Abbott, R., Garcia, N., Anderson-Youngstrom, M., Brooks, A., et al. (2006). Tier 1 and Tier 2 early intervention for handwriting and composing. *Journal of School Psychology*, *44*, 3–30.

Berry, F. M. (1978). Approaching poetry therapy from a scientific orientation. In: A. Lerner (Ed.), *Poetry in the therapeutic experience* (pp. 127–142). New York, NY: Pergamon.

Biancosino, B., Picardi, A., Marmai, L., Biondi, M., & Grassi, L. (2010). Factor structure of the Brief Psychiatric Rating Scale in unipolar depression. *Journal of Affective Disorders*, *124*, 329–334.

Blake, M. E. (2003). Use of matrices to facilitate qualitative analysis in poetry therapy. *Journal of Poetry Therapy*, *16*, 83–89.

Blake, M. E., & Cashwell, S. T. (2004). Use of poetry to facilitate communication about diversity. *Journal of Poetry Therapy*, *17*, 1–12.

Blanton, S. (1958). *The healing power of poetry*. Carmel, NY: Guide Posts Associates.

Block, S., Reibstein, J., Crouch, E., Holroyd, P., & Themen, J. (1979). A method for the study of therapeutic factors in group psychotherapy. *British Journal of Psychiatry*, *134*, 257–263.

Bloom, B. L. (1992). Computer-assisted psychological interventions: A review and commentary. *Clinical Psychology Review*, *12*, 169–197.

Bogels, S. M. (2007). Bibliotherapy is more effective than waiting list for reducing childhood anxiety disorder but not as effective as group cognitive behavioral therapy. *Evidence-Based Mental Health*, *10*(1), 22.

Bolger, N., Davis, A., & Rafaeli, E. (2003). Diary methods: Capturing life as it is lived. *Annual Review of Psychology*, *54*, 579–616.

Bolger, N., DeLongis, A., Kessler, R. C., & Schilling, E. A. (1989). Effects of daily stress on negative mood. *Journal of Personality and Social Psychology*, *57*, 808–818.

Bolton, G. (1999a). *The therapeutic potential of creative writing: Writing myself*. London: Jessica Kingsley.

Bolton, G. (1999b). 'Every poem breaks a silence that had to be overcome': The therapeutic power of poetry writing. *Feminist Review*, *62*(Summer), 118–133.

Boone, B. C. (2006). *The impact of poetry therapy on symptoms of Secondary Posttraumatic Stress Disorder in domestic violence counselors*. Unpublished doctoral dissertation, Texas A & M University, College Station, TX.

Boone, B. C., & Castillo, L. G. (2008). The use of poetry therapy with domestic violence counselors experiencing secondary posttraumatic stress disorder symptoms. *Journal of Poetry Therapy*, *32*(March), 3–14.

Boone, P. (1991). Composition, improvisation and poetry in the psychiatric treatment of a forensic patient. In: K. E. Bruscia (Ed.), *Case studies in music therapy* (pp. 433–450). Gilsum, NH: Barcelona Publishers.

Boscarino, J. (2004). Posttraumatic stress disorder and physical illness: Results from clinical and epidemiologic studies. *Annals of the New York Academy of Sciences*, *1032*, 141–153.

Bower, P., Richards, D., & Lovell, K. (2001). The clinical and cost effectiveness of self-help treatments for anxiety and depressive disorders in primary care: A systematic review. *British Journal of General Practice*, *51*(471), 838–845.

Bowers, K. S., & Brenneman, H. A. (1981). Hypnotic dissociation, dichotic listening and active versus passive modes of attention. *Journal of Abnormal Psychology*, *90*, 55–67.

Bowers, M., & Buchanan, M. (2007). A group-based program of emotional recovery for younger women following myocardial infarction. *Canadian Journal of Counselling*, *41*, 77–90.

Brown, D., Anda, R., Tiemeier, H., Felitti, V., Edwards, V., Croft, J., & Giles, W. (2009). Adverse childhood experiences and the risk of premature mortality. *American Journal of Preventive Medicine*, *37*, 389–396.

Brown, D. W., Anda, R. F., Felitti, V. J., Edwards, V. J., Malarcher, A. M., Croft, J. B., & Giles, W. H. (2010). Adverse childhood experiences and the risk of lung cancer. *BMC Public Health*, *10*, 20.

Brown, R. M. (1977). Bibliotherapy as a technique for increasing individuality among elderly patients. *Hospital Community Psychiatry*, *28*(5), 347.

Bruni, R., Serino, F., Galluzo, S., Coppolino, G., Cacciapaglia, F., Vadacca, M., … Afeltra, A. (2006). Alexithymia and neuroendocrine-immune response in patients with autoimmune diseases: Preliminary results on relationship between alexithymic construct and TNF-alpha levels. *Annals of the NY Academy of Sciences*, *1069*, 208–211.

Bruwer, B. R., & Stein, D. J. (2005). A survey of participants in two internet support groups for people with hair-pulling. *BioMed Central Psychiatry*, *5*(December), 37.

Buck, L., & Kramer, A. (1973). Opening new worlds to the deaf and the disturbed. In: J. J. Leedy (Ed.), *Poetry the healer* (pp. 142–174). New York, NY: Lippincott.

Bukowski, C. (1991). Writing. *Blank Gun Silencer*, (2)n.p.

Burger, G. K., Yonker, R. D., Calsyn, R. J., Morse, G. A., & Klinkenberg, W. D. (2005). Generalizability of brief psychiatric rating scale prototypical profiles and their use in evaluating treatment outcomes. *International Journal of Methods in Psychiatric Research*, *14*, 56–64.

Burgess, C., Kirsch, I., Shane, H., Niederauer, K., Graham, S., & Bacon, A. (1998). Facilitated communication as an ideomotor response. *Psychological Science*, *9*, 71–74.

Burton, C., Weller, D., & Sharpe, M. (2007). Are electronic diaries useful for symptoms research? A systematic review. *Journal of Psychosomatic Research*, *62*, 553–561.

Burton, C. M., & King, L. A. (2009). The health benefits of writing about intensely positive experiences: The role of broadened cognition. *Psychology and Health*, *24*, 867–879.

Cacioppo, J., Amaral, D., Blanchard, J., Cameron, J., Carter, S., Crews, D., … Quinn, K. (2007). Social neuroscience: Progress and implications for mental health. *Perspectives on Psychological Science*, *2*, 99–123.

Campbell, L. (2007). *Poetry therapy for adults with developmental disabilities*. Unpublished doctoral dissertation, University of Rochester, Rochester, NY.

Campbell, L. F., & Smith, T. P. (2003). Integrating self-help books into psychotherapy. *Journal of Clinical Psychology*, *59*(2), 177–186.

Carlbring, P., & Anderson, G. (2006). Internet and psychological treatment: How well can they be combined? *Computers in Human Behavior*, *22*, 545–553.

Carlbring, P., Bohman, S., Brunt, S., Buhrman, M., Westling, B., Ekselius, L., & Andersson, G. (2006). Remote treatment of panic disorder: A randomized trial of internet-based cognitive behavior therapy supplemented with telephone calls. *American Journal of Psychiatry*, *163*(12), 2119–2125.

Carlbring, P., Ekselius, L., & Andersson, G. (2003). Treatment of panic disorder via the internet: A randomized trial of CBT vs. applied relaxation. *Journal of Behavior Therapy and Experimental Psychiatry*, *34*(2), 129–140.

Carlbring, P., Gunnarsdóttir, M., Hedensjo, L., Andersson, G., Ekselius, L., & Furmark, T. (2007). Treatment of social phobia: Randomized trial of internet-delivered cognitive-behavioural therapy with telephone support. *British Journal of Psychiatry*, *190*, 123–128.

Carlbring, P., Nilsson-Ihrfelt, E., Waara, J., Kollenstam, C., Buhrman, M., Kaldo, V., … Andersson, G. (2005). Treatment of panic disorder: Live therapy vs. self-help via internet. *Behaviour Research and Therapy*, *43*(10), 1321–1333.

Carrard, I., Rouger, P., Fernandez-Arana, F., Volkart, A. C., Damoiseau, M., & Lam, T. (2006). Evaluation and deployment of evidence-based patient self-management support program for bulimia nervosa. *International Journal of Medical Informatics*, *75*(1), 101–109.

Carter, B. (2002). Chronic pain in childhood and the medical encounter: Professional ventriloquism and hidden voices. *Qualitative Health Research*, *12*, 28–41.

Castonguay, L. G., Boswell, J. F., Costantino, M. J., Goldfried, M. R., & Hill, C. E. (2010). Training implications of harmful effects of psychological treatments. *American Psychologist*, *65*, 34–49.

Causton-Theoharis, J., Ashby, C., & Cosier, M. (2009). Islands of loneliness: Exploring social interaction through the autobiographies of individuals with autism. *Intellectual and Developmental Disabilities*, *47*, 84–96.

Chamak, B., Bonniau, B., Jaunay, E., & Cohen, D. (2008). What can we learn about autism from autistic persons? *Psychotherapy and Psychosomatics*, *77*, 271–279.

Chamberlain, D., Heaps, D., & Robert, I. (2008). Bibliotherapy and information prescriptions: A summary of the published evidence-base and recommendations from past and ongoing books on prescription projects. *Journal of Psychiatric and Mental Health Nursing*, *15*, 24–36.

Charon, R. (2006). *Narrative medicine, honoring the stories of illness*. New York, NY: Oxford University Press.

Charon, R. (2008). The art of medicine: Narrative evidence based medicine. *Thelancet.com*, *371*(January), 296–297.

Cheng, J. (2011, June). The Gist: Students face withdrawal, distress, when cut off from the internet. *U.S. Airways: The Magazine that Connects You* (pp. 28–30). Phoenix, AZ: Pace Communications Inc.

Chepenik, L. G., Have, T. T., Oslin, D., Datto, C., Zubitsky, C., & Katz, I. R. (2006). A daily diary study of late-life depression. *American Journal of Geriatric Psychiatry*, *14*, 270–279.

Christensen, H., Griffiths, K. M., & Korten, A. (2002). Web-based cognitive behaviour therapy: analysis of site usage and changes in depression and anxiety scores. *Journal of Medical Internet Research*, *4*, e3.

Chung, C. K., & Pennebaker, J. W. (2008). Variations in the spacing of expressive writing sessions. *British Journal of Health Psychology*, *13*, 15–21.

Cisotti, E. (2011, June). Arrivano le tavolette al miele. *Android Magazine*, pp. 16–21, Italy.

Cleveland, J. N., & Fleishman, E. A. (2011). Series foreword. In: S. I. Donaldson, M. Csikszentmihalyi & J. Nakamura (Eds.), *Applied positive psychology: Improving everyday life, health, schools, work, and society* (pp. xiv–xxi). New York, NY: Routledge.

Clum, G. A. (1989). *Coping with panic: A drug-free approach to dealing with anxiety attacks*. Pacific Grove, CA: Thomson Brooks/Cole.

Cohen, G., & Kerr, B. (1998). Computer-mediated counseling: An empirical study of a new mental health treatment. *Computers in Human Services, 15*, 13–26.

Cohen, S., Janicki-Deverts, D., & Miller, G. E. (2007). Psychological stress and disease. *Journal of the American Medical Association, 298*, 1685–1687.

Collie, K. R., Mitchell, D., & Murphy, L. (2000). Skills for online counseling: Maximum impact at minimum bandwidth. In: J. W. Bloom & G. R. Walz (Eds.), *Cybercounseling and cyberlearning: Strategies and resources for the millennium*. Alexandria, VA: American Counseling Association.

Collins, R. L., Morsheimer, E. T., Shiffman, S., Paty J. A. Gnys, M., & Papandonatos, G. D. (1998). *Experimental and Clinical Psychopharmacology, 6*, 306–315.

Colon, Y. (1996). Chatter(ing) through the fingertips: Doing group therapy online. *Women and Performance: A Journal of Feminist Theory, 9*(1), 205–215.

Conner, J. (2008). *Writing down your soul: How to activate and listen to the extraordinary voice within*. San Francisco, CA: Conari Press.

Corcoran, K., & Fisher, J. (1987). *Measures for clinical practice: A source book*. New York, NY: Free Press.

Corcos, M., Guilbaud, O., Paterniti, S., Curt, F., Hjalmarsson, L., Moussa, M., … Jeammet, P. (2004). Correlation between serum levels of interleukin-4 and alexithymia scores in healthy female subjects: Preliminary findings. *Psychoneuroendocrinology, 29*, 686–691.

Coulter, S. J. (2000). Effect of song writing versus recreational music on post traumatic stress disorder (PTSD) symptoms and abuse attribution in abused children. *Journal of Poetry Therapy, 13*(3), 125–138.

Courtois, C. A. (2000). Treating the sexual intimacy concerns of sexual abuse survivors. *Sexual and Relationship Therapy, 17*, 321–327.

Couturier, A. (2005). *Writing opens the mind: Turning the subconscious to free the writing and the writer*. Berkeley, CA: Ulysses Press.

Creswell, J. D., Lam, S., Stanton, A. L., Taylor, S. E., Bower, J. E., & Sherman, D. K. (2007a). Does self-affirmation, cognitive processing, or discovery of meaning explain cancer-related health benefits of expressive writing? *Personality and Social Psychology Bulletin, 33*, 238–250.

Creswell, J., Way, B., Eisenberger, N., & Lieberman, M. (2007b). Neural correlates of dispositional mindfulness during affect labeling. *Psychosomatic Medicine, 69*, 560–565.

Csikszentmihalyi, M., & Larson, R. (1992). Validity and reliability of experience sampling method. In: M. W. de Vries (Ed.), *The experience of psychopathology. Investigating mental disorder in their natural settings* (pp. 43–57). New York, NY: Cambridge University Press.

Cuijpers, P. (1997). Bibliotherapy in unipolar depression: A meta-analysis. *Journal of Behavioral Therapy and Experimental Psychiatry, 28*(2), 139–147.

Cuijpers, P. (1998). Psychological outreach programmes for the depressed elderly: A meta-analysis of effects and dropouts. *International Journal of Geriatric Psychiatry, 13*(1), 41–48.

Cuijpers, P., & Schuurmans, J. (2007). Self-help interventions for anxiety disorders: An overview. *Current Psychiatry Reports, 9*, 284–290.

Cuijpers, P., van Straten, A., & Smit, F. (2006). Psychological treatment of late-life depression: A meta-analysis of randomized controlled trials. *International Journal of Geriatric Psychiatry, 21*(12), 1139–1149.

Cusinato, M., & L'Abate, L. (Eds.). (in press). *Advances in relational competence theory: With special attention to alexithymia*. New York, NY: Nova Science Publishers.

D'Alessandro, D. M., Kreiter, C. D., Kinzer, S. L., & Peterson, M. W. (2004). A randomized control trial of an information prescription for pediatric education on the internet. *Archives of Pediatric and Adolescent Medicine*, *158*(9), 857–862.

Dalton, J. J., & Glenwick, D. S. (2009). Effects of expressive writing on standardized graduate entrance exam performance and physical health functioning. *The Journal of Psychology*, *143*, 279–292.

Danoff-Burg, S., Agee, J. D., Romanoff, N. R., Kremer, J. M., & Strosberg, J. M. (2006). Benefit finding and expressive writing in adults with lupus or rheumatoid arthritis. *Psychology and Health*, *21*, 651–665.

Dante, A. (1954/1961/1970). *The divine comedy: The Inferno, the Purgatorio, the Paradiso*. (J. Ciardi, Trans.). New York, NY: New American Library.

Dattilio, F. (2011). Book review of L. L'Abate (2011). *Sourcebook of interactive practice exercises in mental health*. New York, NY: Springer-Science. *American Journal of Family Therapy*, Vol. 40, pp. 1–2.

Day, M., & Thatcher, J. (2009). "I'm really embarrassed that you're going to read this ...": Reflections on using diaries in qualitative research. *Qualitative Research in Psychology*, *6*, 249–259.

De Giacomo, P., L'Abate, L., Pennebaker, J. W., & Rumbaugh, D. M. (2010). Amplifications and applications of Pennebaker's analogic to digital model in health promotion, prevention, and psychotherapy. *Clinical Psychology and Psychotherapy*, *17*, 355–362.

De Giacomo, P., Mich, Santamaria, C., Sweeney, L. G., & De Giacomo, A. (2011). Information processing. In: L. L'Abate (Ed.), *Paradigm in theory construction*. New York, NY: Springer-Science.

Deane, F. P., Ronan, K. R., Kazantzis, N., & L'Abate, L. (Eds.). (2005). *Using homework assignments in cognitive behavior therapy*. New York, NY: Routledge.

DeGloma, T. (2010). Awakenings: Autobiography, memory, and the social logic of personal discovery. *Sociological Forum*, *25*, 519–540.

de Medeiros, K., Kennedy, Q., Cole, T., Lindley, R., & O' Hara, R. (2007). The impact of autobiographic writing on memory performance in older adults: A preliminary investigation. *American Journal of Geriatric Psychiatry*, *15*, 257–261.

De Moor, C., Sterner, J., Hall, M., Warneke, C., Gilani, Z., Amato, R., & Cohen, L. (2002). A pilot study of the effects of expressive writing on psychological and behavioral adjustment in patients enrolled in a Phase II trial of vaccine therapy for metastatic renal cell carcinoma. *Health Psychology*, *21*, 615–619.

De Moor, J. S., Moye, L., Low, M. D., Rivera, E., Singletary, S. E., Fouladi, R. T., & Cohen, L. (2008). Expressive writing as a presurgical stress management intervention for breast cancer patients. *Emotion*, *8*, 302–306.

DeMaria, R. (2003). Psychoeducation and enrichment: Clinical considerations for couple and family therapy. In: T. L. Sexton, G. R. Weeks & M. S. Robbins (Eds.), *Handbook of family therapy* (pp. 411–430). New York, NY: Brunner-Routledge.

Demetrio, D., & Borgonovi, C. (2007). Teaching to remember ourselves: The autobiographical methodology. In: L. L'Abate (Ed.), *Low-cost approaches to promote physical and mental health* (pp. 251–270). New York, NY: Springer-Science.

Den Boer, P. C. A. M., Wiersma, D., & Van den Bosch, R. J. (2004). Why is self-help neglected in the treatment of emotional disorders? A meta-analysis. *Psychological Medicine*, *34*(6), 959–971.

Deshpande, A. (2010). Recon Mission: Familiarizing veterans with their changed emotional landscape through poetry therapy. *Journal of Poetry Therapy*, *23*, 239–251.

Detweiler-Bedell, J. B., & Whisman, M. A. (2005). A lesson in assigning homework: Therapist, client, and task characteristics in cognitive therapy for depression. *Professional Psychology: Research and Practice*, *36*, 219–223.

Dewaraja, R., Tanigawa, T., Araki, S., Nakata, A., Kawamura, N., Ago, Y., & Sasaki, Y. (1997). Decreased cytotoxic lymphocyte counts in alexithymia. *Psychotherapy and Psychosomatics*, *66*, 83–86.

Diehl, K. M. (2009). *The collective awakening: Messages along the path of awareness*. Address not given: Gateway to Being.

Dimidjian, S., & Hollon, S. D. (2010). How would we know if psychotherapy were harmful? *American Psychologist*, *65*, 21–33.

Dreier, O. (2008). *Psychotherapy in everyday life*. New York, NY: Cambridge University Press.

Du Plock, S. (2005). "Silent therapists" and "the community of suffering": Some reflections on bibliotherapy from an existential-phenomenological perspective. *Existential Analysis*, *16*(2), 300–309.

Dube, S., Fairweather, D., Pearson, W. S., Felitti, V. J., Anda, R. F., & Croft, J. B. (2009). Cumulative childhood stress and autoimmune diseases in adults. *Psychosomatic Medicine*, *71*, 243–250.

Edgar, K. F., & Hazley, R. (1969). A curriculum proposal for training poetry therapists. In: J. J. Leedy (Ed.), *Poetry therapy* (pp. 260–268). Philadelphia, PA: Lippincott.

Edgar, K. F., Hazley, R., & Levit, H. L. (1969). Poetry therapy with hospitalized schizophrenics. In: J. J. Leedy (Ed.), *Poetry therapy* (pp. 29–37). Philadelphia, PA: Lippincott.

Edwards, V., Holden, G., & Felitti, V. (2003). Relationship between multiple forms of childhood maltreatment and adult mental health in community respondents: Results from the adverse childhood experiences study. *American Journal of Psychiatry*, *160*, 1453–1460.

Ehlers, A., Clark, D., Hackmann, A., McManus, F., Fennell, M., Herbert, C., & Mayou, R. (2003). A randomized control trial of cognitive therapy, a self-help booklet, and repeated assessments as early interventions for posttraumatic stress disorders. *Archives of General Psychiatry*, *60*(10), 1024–1032.

Elliott, H. (1997). The use of diaries in sociological research on health experience. *Sociological Research Online 2:2*. Retrieved from http://www.socresonline.org.uk/socresonline/2/2/7.html. Accessed on October 2, 2006.

Emmons, R., & McCullough, M. (2004). *The psychology of gratitude*. New York, NY: Oxford University Press.

Engels, R. C. M. E., Wiers, R., Lemmers, L., & Overbeek, G. (2005). Drinking motives, alcohol expectancies, self-efficacy and drinking patterns. *Journal of Drug Education*, *35*, 147–166.

Eppler, C., & Carolan, M. T. (2005). Biblionarrative: A narrative technique united oral and written life stories. *Journal of Family Psychotherapy*, *16*(4), 31–54.

Etherington, K. (2000). *Narrative approaches to working with adult male survivors of child sexual abuse: The clients', the counsellor's and the researcher's story*. London: Jessica Kingsley Publishers.

Evans, K., Tyrer, P., Catalan, J., Schmidt, U., Davidson, K., Dent, J., … Thompson, S. (1999). Manual-assisted cognitive-behaviour therapy (MACT): A randomized controlled trial of a brief intervention with bibliotherapy in the treatment of recurrent deliberate self-harm. *Psychological Medicine*, *29*(1), 19–25.

Evyapan, D., & Kumral, E. (2001). Visuospatial stimulus-bound automatic writing behavior: A right hemispheric stroke syndrome. *Neurology*, *56*(2), 245–247.

Eysenbach, G. (2005). The law of attrition (epub). *Journal of Medical Internet Research*, *7*, e11. Retrieved from http://www.jmir.org/2005/1/e11.

Eysenbach, G., Powell, J., Engelesakis, M., Rizo, C., & Stern, A. (2004). Health related virtual communities and electronic support groups: Systematic review of the effects of online peer to peer interactions. *British Medical Journal*, *328*, 1166.

Fanner, D., & Urquhartt, C. (2008). Bibliotherapy for mental health service users, Part 1: A systematic review. *Health Information and Libraries Journal*, *25*, 237–252.

Farrand, P. (2005). Development of a supported self-help book prescription scheme in primary care. *Primary Care Mental Health*, *3*(1), 61–66.

Febbraro, G. A. R. (2005). An investigation into the effectiveness of bibliotherapy and minimal interventions in the treatment of panic attacks. *Journal of Clinical Psychology*, *61*(6), 763–779.

Felitti, F., Anda, R., Nordenberg, D., Williamson, D., Spitz, A., Edwards, V., … Marks, J. (1998). Relationship of childhood abuse and household dysfunction to many of the leading causes of death in adults. The Adverse Child Experiences (ACE) Study. *American Journal of Preventive Medicine*, *14*, 245–258.

Fennel, J. (2008). A review of various medical illnesses and their relationship with PTSD. *Dissertation Abstract*. Retrieved from http://renewedserenity.com/yahoo Site_admin/assets/docs/A_Review_of_Various_Medical_Illnesses_and_Their_Relationship_with_PTSD.42140034.pdf.

Ferenc, P. (2006). Önéletrajzi emlékezet — önismeret — önéletírás. *Pszichológia: Az MTA Pszichológiai Intézéenek folyóirata*, *26*, 97–151.

Fingeld, D. I. (2000). Use of self-help manuals to treat problem drinkers. *Journal of Psychosocial Nursing and Mental Health Services*, *38*(4), 20–28.

Floyd, M. (2003). Bibliotherapy as an adjunct to psychotherapy for depression in older adults. *Journal of Clinical Psychology*, *59*(2), 187–195.

Floyd, M., Scogin, F., McKendree-Smith, N. L., Floyd, D. L., & Rokke, P. D. (2004). Cognitive therapy for depression: A comparison of individual psychotherapy and bibliotherapy for depressed older adults. *Behavior Modification*, *28*(2), 297–318.

Fonagy, P., Target, M., Cottrell, D., Phillips, J., & Kurtz, Z. (2002). *What works for whom? A critical review of treatments for children and adolescents*. New York, NY: Guilford.

Forest, J. J. (1998). Amount of information on case illustrations in self-help psychology books. *Psychological Reports*, *83*(3), 1147–1152.

Frattaroli, J. (2006). Experimental disclosure and its moderators: A meta-analysis. *Psychological Bulletin*, *132*, 823–865.

Frattaroli, J., Thomas, M., & Lyubomirsky, S. (2011, April 25). Opening up in the classroom: Effects of expressive writing on graduate school entrance exam performance. *Emotion*. Advance online publication. doi: 10.1037/a002294.

Frazer, C. J., Christensen, H., & Griffiths, K. M. (2005). Effectiveness of treatment for depression in older people. *The Medical Journal of Australia*, *182*(12), 627–632.

Freed, B. S. (1988). *Application of poetry in music therapy*. National Association of Music Therapy Conference, Atlanta, GA.

Freed, B. S. (1989). A sequential model for developing group cohesion in music therapy. *Music Therapy Perspectives*, *7*, 23–34.

Freedman, M. J., Lester, K. M., McNamara, C., Milby, J. B., & Schumacher, J. E. (2006). Cell phones for ecological momentary assessment with cocaine-addicted homeless patients in treatment. *Journal of Substance Abuse Treatment*, *30*, 105–111.

Freud, S. (1920). *A general introduction to psychoanalysis* (G. S. Hall, Trans.). New York, NY: Horace Liverlight.

Frisina, P., Borod, J., & Lepore, S. (2004). A meta-analysis of the effects of written emotional disclosure on the health outcomes of clinical populations. *The Journal of Nervous and Mental Disease*, *192*, 629–634.

Frisina, P. G., Lepore, S. J., & Borod, J. C. (2005). Written emotional disclosure and clinical populations: Confirming and updating our meta-analytic findings. *Journal of Nervous and Mental Disease*, *193*, 425–426.

Frude, N. (2004a). Bibliotherapy as a means of delivering psychological therapy. *Clinical Psychology*, *39*, 8–10.

Frude, N. (2004b). A book prescription scheme in primary care. *Clinical Psychology*, *39*, 11–14.

Furman, R., Collins, K., Langer, C., & Bruce, E. A. (2006). Inside a provider's perspective: Using practitioner poetry to explore the treatment of persons with mental illness. *The Arts in Psychotherapy*, *33*, 331–342.

Furman, R., Pepi-Downey, E., Jackson, R., & Bender, K. (2002). Poetry therapy as a tool for strengths-based practice. *Advances in Social Work*, *3*(Fall), 146–157.

Gadamer, H. G. (2000). *Truth and method* (2nd rev. ed.) (J. Weinsheimer & D. Marshall, Trans.). New York, NY: Continuum. (Original work published in 1960).

Gallego, M. J., & Emmelkamp, P. M. G. (2011). Effectiveness of internet psychological treatments in mental health disorders. In: L. L'Abate & D. A. Kaiser (Eds.), *Handbook of technology in psychology, psychiatry, and neurology: Theory, research and practice*. New York, NY: Nova Science Publishers.

Galvani, P. (Ed.). (2011). Facciamo spese sull android market. *Android Magazine*, Vol. 1, June, pp. 8–9.

Gellaitry, G., Peters, K., Bloomfield, D., & Horne, R. (2010). Narrowing the gap: The effects of an expressive writing intervention on perceptions of actual and ideal emotional support in women who have completed treatment for early stage breast cancer. *Psychooncology*, *6*, 59–66.

Germain, V., Marchard, A., Bouchard, S., Guay, S., & Drouin, M. S. (2010). Assessment of the therapeutic alliance in face-to-face or videoconference treatment for posttraumatic stress disorder. *Cyberpsychology, Behavior, and Social Networking*, *13*, 29–35.

Gladding, S., & Mazza, N. (1983, March). Uses of poetry and music in counseling. Paper presented at the Annual Convention of the American Personnel and Guidance Association, Washington, DC.

Gladding, S. T. (2005). *Counseling theories: Essential concepts and application*. Upper Saddle River, NJ: Prentice Hall.

Golden, K. (2000). The use of collaborative writing to enhance cohesion in poetry therapy groups. *Journal of Poetry Therapy*, *13*, 125–138.

Goldman, N., Dugas, M. J., Sexton, K. A., & Gervais, N. G. (2007). The impact of written exposure on worry: A preliminary investigation. *Behavior Modification*, *31*, 512–538.

Gonzales, V. M., Schmitz, J. M., & DeLaune, K. A. (2006). The role of homework in cognitive-behavioral therapy for cocaine dependence. *Journal of Consulting and Clinical Psychology*, *74*, 633–637.

Gould, R. A., Otto, M. W., & Pollack, M. H. (1995). A meta-analysis of treatment outcome for panic disorder. *Clinical Psychology Review*, *15*(8), 819–844.

Graham, J., Glaser, R., Loving, T., Malarkey, W., Stowell, J., & Keicolt-Glaser, J. (2009). Cognitive word use during marital conflict and increases in proinflammatory cytokines. *Health Psychology*, *28*, 621–630.

Grange, D., Gorin, A., Dymek, M., & Stone, A. (2002). Does ecological momentary assessment improve cognitive behavioural therapy for binge eating disorder? A pilot study. *European Eating Disorders Review*, *10*, 1–13.

Green, J. (1997). Hypnotizability, the dissociative experiences scale, HGSHS: An amnesia, and automatic writing: Is there an association? *International Journal of Clinical and Experimental Hypnosis*, *45*, 69–80.

Grossi, D., Postiglione, A., Schettini, B., Trojano, L., Barbarulo, A., Giugliano, V., ... Aiello, A. (2007). Autobiography recall training in elderly adults with subjective memory complaint: A pilot study. *Perceptual and Motor Skills, 104*, 621–628.

Grüter, T., & Grüter, M. (2007). Last but not least: Prosopagnosia in biographies and autobiographies. *Perception, 36*, 299–301.

Guilbaud, O., Corcos, M., Hjalmarsson, L., Loas, G., & Jeammet, P. (2003). Is there a psychoneuroimmunological pathway between alexithymia and immunity? Immune and physiological correlates of alexithymia. *Biomedicine & Pharmacotherapy, 57*, 292–295.

Gyllenhammer, L. (2010). A randomized controlled trial of emotionally expressive writing for women with metastatic breast cancer. *American Journal of Gastroenterology, 105*, 2440–2448.

Halpert, A., Rybin, D., & Doros, G. (2006). Expressive writing is a promising therapeutic modality for the management of IBS: A pilot study. *The American Journal of Gastroenterology, 105*, 2440–2448.

Hannigan, M. (1962). The librarian in bibliotherapy: Pharmacist or bibliotherapist? *Library Trends, 11*(2), 184–198.

Harold, R. D., Palmiter, M. L., Lynch, S. A., & Freedman-Doan, C. R. (1995). Life stories: A practice-based research technique. *Journal of Sociology & Social Welfare, 22*(2), 23.

Harrington, A. (n.d.) Slammed/Crammer/Jammed. Unknown: Unknown.

Harris, A. H. S. (2006). Does expressive writing reduce health care utilization? A meta-analysis of randomized trials. *Journal of Consulting and Clinical Psychology, 75*, 243–252.

Hart, A. (2010). *Should Sacramento women fear or embrace long-term side effects of cybertherapy?* Retrieved from http://www.examiner.com/women-s-issues-in-sacramento/should-sacramento-women-fear-or-embrace-long-term-side-effects-of-cybertherapy. Accessed on February 3, 2011.

Hartman, A. (Ed.) (1990). Editorial: Many ways of knowing. *Social Work, 35*, 3–4.

Harwood, T. M., & L'Abate, L. (2010). *Self-help in mental health: A critical review*. New York, NY: Springer.

Heimes, S. (2011). State of poetry therapy research (review). *The Arts in Psychology, 38*, 1–8

Helfgott, E. A. (2009). Witnessing Alzheimer's through diary and poem: Dear Alzheimer's why did you pick our sheltered lives to visit? *Journal of Poetry Therapy, 22*(December), 185–217.

Henke, S. A. (2000). *Shattered subjects: Trauma and testimony in women's life-writing* (p. xii). New York, NY: St. Martin's Press.

Henry, E. A., Schlegel, R. J., Talley, A. E., Molix, L. A., & Bettencourt, B. A. (2010). The feasibility and effectiveness of expressive writing for rural and urban breast cancer survivors. *Oncology Nursing Forum, 37*, 749–757.

Herndl, D. (2006). Our breasts, our selves: Identity, community, and ethics in cancer autobiographies. *Signs, 32*, 221–245.

Heron, K. E., & Smyth, J. M. (2010). Ecological momentary interventions: Incorporating mobile technology into psychosocial and health behaviour treatments. *British Journal of Health Psychology, 15*, 1–39.

Hilgard, E. (1973). A neodissociation interpretation of pain reduction in hypnosis. *Psychological Review, 80*, 396–411.

Hillix, W. A., Rumbaugh, D. M., & Savage-Rumbaugh, S. (in press). The emergence of reason, intelligence, and language in humans and animals. In: L. L'Abate (Ed.), *The role of paradigms in theory construction* (pp. 000–000). New York, NY: Springer.

Hilse, C., Griffiths, S., & Corr, S. (2007). The impact of participating in a poetry workshop. *British Journal of Occupational Therapy, 70*(October), 431–438.

Hirshfield, J. (1997). *Nine gates: Entering the mind of poetry*. New York, NY: Harper Collins.

Holliday, R. (1999). The comfort of identity. *Sexualities*, *2*.

Hölzel, B. K., Carmody, J., Evans, K. C., Hoge, E. A., Duse, J. A., Morgan, L., ... Lazar, S. W. (2010). Stress reduction correlates with structural changes in the amygdala. *Social Cognitive and Affective Neuroscience*, *5*, 11–17.

Honos-Webb, L., Harrick, E. A., Stiles, W. B., & Park, C. L. (2000). Assimilation of traumatic experiences and physical-health outcomes: Cautions for the Pennebaker paradigm. *Psychotherapy: Theory, Research, Practice, Training*, *37*, 307–314.

Hooper, L., Bartlett, C., Davey, S. G., Smith, G. D., & Ebrahim, S. (2003) Advice to reduce dietary salt for prevention of cardiovascular disease. [Cochrane Review]. In: *Cochrane Database Systematic Review*, Issue 1. No. CD 003656. Retrieved from Ovid Evidence Based Medicine Reviews: Cochrane Database of Systematic Reviews. doi: 10.1002/14651858.CD003656.pub2

Howard, A. A. (1997). The effects of music and poetry therapy on the treatment of women and adolescents with chemical addictions. *Journal of Poetry Therapy*, *11*, 81–102.

Hughes, G. (2009). Talking to oneself: Using autobiographical internal dialogue to critique everyday and professional practice. *Reflective Practice*, *10*, 451–463.

Husky, M. M., Mazure, C. M., & Carroll, K. M. (2008). Using the experience sampling method in the context of contingency management for substance abuse treatment. *Journal of Applied Behavioral Analysis*, *14*, 635–644.

Hynes, A. M. (1988). Some considerations concerning assessment in poetry therapy and interactive bibliotherapy. *The Arts in Psychotherapy*, *15*, 55–62.

Hynes, A. M., & Hynes-Berry, M. (1986). *Bibliotherapy — The interactive process: A handbook*. St. Cloud, MN: North Star Press.

Hynes, A. M., & Hynes-Berry, M. (1994). *Biblio/poetry therapy — The interactive process: A handbook*. St. Cloud, MN: North Star Press.

Jacelon, C. S., & Imperio, K. (2005). Participant diaries as a source of data in research with older adults. *Qualitative Health Research*, *15*, 991–997.

Jamison, C., & Scogin, F. (1995). The outcome of cognitive bibliotherapy with depressed adults. *Journal of Consulting and Clinical Psychology*, *63*(4), 644–650.

Jaskowski, H. (1984). Notes on a competency-based curriculum in poetry therapy. *The Arts in Psychotherapy*, *11*, 77–88.

Jaskoski, H. (1987). Artisan or genius: Two views of poetic process. *Journal of Poetry Therapy*, *1*, 5–13.

Jeffs, S., & Pepper, S. (2005). Healing words: A meditation on poetry and recovery from mental illness. *The Arts in Psychotherapy*, *32*, 87–94.

Johnson, E. I., Barrault, M., Nadeau, L., & Swendsen, J. (2009). Feasibility and validity of computerized ambulatory monitoring in drug-dependent women. *Drug and Alcohol Dependence*, *99*, 322–326.

Johnston, O., Startup, H., Lavendar, A., Godfrey, E., & Schmidt, U. (2010). Therapeutic writing as an intervention for symptoms of Bulimia Nervosa: Effects and mechanism of change. *International Journal of Eating Disorders*, *43*(5), 405–419.

Jones, A. A. (1997). Experiencing language: Some thoughts on poetry and psychoanalysis. *Psychoanalysis Quarterly*, *66*, 683–700.

Jones, E. K. (1939). *Hospital libraries*. Chicago, IL: American Library Association.

Jones, F. A. (2002). The role of bibliotherapy in health anxiety: An experimental study. *British Journal of Community Nursing*, *7*(10), 498–504.

Jones, R. K. (2000). The unsolicited diary as a qualitative research tool for advanced research capacity in the field of health and illness. *Qualitative Health Research*, *10*, 555–567.

Jordan, K. B., & L'Abate, L. (1995). Programmed writing and therapy with symbiotically enmeshed patients. *American Journal of Psychotherapy*, *49*(2), 225.

Jorm, A. F., Christensen, H., Griffiths, K. M., Parslow, R. A., Rodgers, B., & Blewitt, K. A. (2004). Effectiveness of complimentary and self-help treatments for anxiety disorders. *Medical Journal of Australia*, *181*(Suppl. 7), s29–s46.

Joseph, A. (1986). A hypergraphic syndrome of automatic writing, affective disorder, and temporal lobe epilepsy in two patients. *Journal of Clinical Psychiatry*, *47*, 255–257.

Kacewicz, E., Slatcher, R., & Pennebaker, J. (2007). In: L'Abate (Ed.), *Low-cost approaches to promote physical and mental health: Theory, research and practice* (pp. 271–284). New York, NY: Springer.

Kahneman, D., Krueger, A. B., Schkade, D., Schwarz, N., & Stone, A. A. (2004). A survey method for characterizing daily life experience — The day reconstruction method. *Science*, *306*, 1776–1780.

Kaltenthaler, E., Brazier, J., De Nigris, E., Tumur, I., Ferriter, M., Beverly, C., ... Sutcliffe, P. (2006). Computerised cognitive behavior therapy for depression and anxiety update: A systematic review and economic evaluation. *Health Technology Assessment*, *10*(33), iiixi–xiv, 1–168.

Kanfer, F. H. (1970). Self-monitoring: Methodological limitations and clinical applications. *Journal of Abnormal Psychology*, *35*, 148–152.

Katzantizis, N., & L'Abate, L. (Eds.). (2007). *Handbook of homework assignments in psychotherapy: Research, practice, and prevention*. New York, NY: Springer.

Kaufman, D. L. (2007). *Cracking up and back again: Transformation through poetry*. Calgary, Alberta, Canada: Palabras Press.

Kaufman, D. L., & Goodman, K. D. (2010). Cracking up and back again: Transformation through music and poetry. In: Z. Li & T. L. Long (Eds.), *The meaning management challenge: Making sense of health, illness and disease* (pp. 117–129). Oxford, UK: Inter-Disciplinary Press.

Kaufman, J. C., & Sexton, J. D. (2006). *Why doesn't the writing cure help poets? Review of General Psychology*, *10*(3), 268–282.

Kazantzis, N., & Dattilio, F. (2010). Definitions of homework, types of homework, and ratings of importance among psychologists with cognitive behavioral and psychoanalytic theoretical orientations. *Journal of Clinical Psychology*, *66*, 1–16.

Kazantzis, N., Deane, F. P., & Ronan, K. R. (2000). Homework assignments in cognitive and behavioral therapy: A meta-analysis. *Clinical Psychology: Science and Practice*, *7*, 189–202.

Kazantzis, N., & L'Abate, L. (2005). *Handbook of homework assignments in psychotherapy: Research, practice, and prevention*. New York, NY: Springer Science.

Kazantzis, N., & L'Abate, L. (Eds.). (2007). *Handbook of homework assignments in psychotherapy: Research, practice, and prevention*. New York, NY: Springer.

Kazantzis, N., Whittington, C., & Dattilio, F. (2010). *Meta-analysis of homework effects in cognitive and behavioral therapy: A replication and extension*. Manuscript submitted for publication.

Keleher, H. M., & Verrinder, G. K. (2003). Health diaries in a rural Australian study. *Journal of Qualitative Health Research*, *13*, 435–443.

Kennedy, M., & Franklin, J. (2002). Skills-based treatment for alexithymia: An exploratory case series. *Behaviour Change*, *19*, 158–171.

Kidd, L. I. (2010). *The effect of poetry writing intervention on self-transcendence, resilience, depressive symptoms, and subjective burden in family caregivers of older adults with dementia*. Doctoral dissertation, Case Western Reserve University.

Kim, Y. (2008). Effects of expressive writing among bilinguals: Exploring psychological well-being and social behaviour. *British Journal of Health Psychology*, *13*, 43–47.

King, L. A., & Miner, K. N. (2000). Writing about the perceived benefits of traumatic events: Implications for physical health. *Personality and Social Psychology Bulletin*, *26*, 220–230.

King, S., Engi, S., & Poulos, S. (1998). Using the internet to assist family therapy. *British Journal of Guidance & Counselling*, *26*(1), 43–52.

Kissman, K. (1989). Poetry and feminist social work. *Journal of Poetry Therapy*, *2*, 221–230.

Klein, K., & Boals, A. (2001). Expressive writing can increase working memory capacity. *Journal of Experimental Psychology: General*, *130*, 520–533.

Knoop, H. H. (2011). Education in 2025: How positive psychology can revitalize education. In: S. I. Donaldson, M. Csikszentmihalyi & J. Nakamura (Eds.), *Applied positive psychology: Improving everyday life, health, schools, work, and society* (pp. 97–115). New York, NY: Routledge.

Kobak, D. (1969). Poetry therapy in a '600' school and in a counselling center: Creative writing as a therapeutic instrument. In: J. J. Leedy (Ed.), *Poetry therapy: The use of poetry in the treatment of emotional disorders* (pp. 180–187). Philadelphia, PA: Lippincott.

Kohányi, A. (2005). Four factors that may predict the emergence of creative writing: A proposed model. *Creativity Research Journal*, *17*, 195–205.

Koocher, G. R. (2009). Any minute now but far far away: Electronically mediated mental health. *Clinical Psychology: Science and Practice*, *16*, 339–342.

Kopelowicz, A., Ventura, J., Liberman, R., & Mintz, J. (2008). Consistency of Brief Psychiatric Rating Scale factor structure across a broad spectrum of schizophrenia patients. *Psychopathology*, *41*, 77–84.

Korb-Khalsa, K. L., & Leutenberg, E. A. (2000). *SEALS II: Self-esteem and life skills* (Vol. III). Wilkes-Barre, PA: Wellness Reproductions and Publishing.

Koutstaal, W. (1992). Skirting the abyss: A history of experimental explorations of automatic writing in psychology. *Journal of the History of the Behavioral Sciences*, *28*, 5–27.

Kraaj, V., van Emmerick, A., Garnefski, N., Schroevers, M. J., Lo-Fo-Wong, D., van Empelen, P., … Maes, S. (2009). Effects of a cognitive behavioral self-help program and a computerized structured writing intervention on depressed mood for HIV-infected people: A pilot randomized controlled trial. *Patient Education and Counseling*, *80*, 200–204.

Kramer, A. (1969). The use of poetry in a private mental hospital. In: J. J. Leedy (Ed.), *Poetry therapy: The use of poetry in the treatment of emotional disorders* (pp. 200–211). Philadelphia, PA: Lippincott.

Kreuter, E. A. (2009). Catalyzing the inner spirit of the Type-A professional through poetic expression. *Journal of Poetry Therapy*, *22*(September), 165–171.

L'Abate, L. (2004). Systematically written homework assignment: The case for homework-based treatment. In: L. L'Abate (Ed.), *Using workbooks in mental health: Resources in prevention, psychotherapy, and rehabilitation for clinicians and researchers* (pp. 65–102). Binghamton, NY: Haworth.

L'Abate, L. (2007). A completely preposterous proposal: The dictionary as an initial vehicle of change in the family. *The Family Psychologist*, *23*(3), 39–42.

L'Abate, L. (2008a). Appendix. Proposed curriculum for a diploma or graduate degree in structured online mental health interventions. In: L. L'Abate (Ed.), *Toward a science of clinical psychology: Laboratory evaluations and interventions* (pp. 385–392). Hauppauge, NY: Nova Science Publishers.

L'Abate, L. (2008b). Proposal including distance writing in couple therapy. *Journal of Couple & Relationship Theory*, *7*, 337–362.

L'Abate, L. (2008c). Working at a distance from participants: Writing and nonverbal media. In: L. L'Abate (Ed.), *Toward a science of clinical psychology: Laboratory evaluations and interventions* (pp. 355–383). Hauppauge, NY: Nova Science Publishers.

L'Abate, L. (2011a). *Hurt feelings: Theory, research, and applications in intimate relationships.* New York, NY: Cambridge University Press.

L'Abate, L. (2011b). Psychotherapy consists of homework assignments: A radical iconoclastic conviction. In: H. Rosenthal (Ed.), *Favorite counseling and therapy homework techniques* (pp. 219–229). New York, NY: Routledge.

L'Abate, L. (2011c). *Sourcebook of interactive practice exercises in mental health.* New York, NY: Springer-Science.

L'Abate, L. (2011d). *The 7 sources of pleasure: Making way for the upside in the midst of modern demands.* Westport, CT: Praeger.

L'Abate, L. (2011e). Workbooks: Interactive practice exercises in mental health. In: L. L'Abate & D. A. Kaiser (Eds.), *Handbook of technology in psychology, psychiatry, and neurology: Theory, research, and practice.* New York, NY: Nova Science Publishers.

L'Abate, L. (2012). *Clinical psychology and psychotherapy as a science.* New York, NY: Springer-Science.

L'Abate, L. (in press). Recommended online computer-assisted treatments. In: G. P. Koocher, J. C. Norcross, & B. A. Greene (Eds.), *Psychologists' desk reference 3rd edition.* New York, NY: Oxford University Press.

L'Abate, L., Boyce, J., Fraizer, I., & Russ, D. A. (1992). Programmed writing: Research in progress. *Comprehensive Mental Health Care, 2*, 45–62.

L'Abate, L., Cusinato, M., Maino, E., Colesso, W., & Scilletta, C. (2010). *Relational competence theory: Research and mental health applications.* New York, NY: Springer-Science.

L'Abate, L., & De Giacomo, P. (2003). *Intimate relationships and how to improve them: Integrating theoretical models with preventive and psychotherapeutic approaches.* Westport, CT: Praeger.

L'Abate, L., & Goldstein, J. (2007). Workbooks to promote mental health and life-long learning. In: L. L'Abate (Ed.), *Low-cost approaches to promote physical and mental health: Theory, research, and practice* (pp. 285–303). New York, NY: Springer Science.

L'Abate, L., & Hecker, L. L. (2004). The status and future of workbooks in mental health: Concluding commentary. In: L. L'Abate (Ed.), *Using Workbooks in mental health: Resources in prevention, psychotherapy, and rehabilitation for clinicians and researchers* (pp. 351–373). Binghamton, NY: Haworth.

L'Abate, L., & Kaiser, D. A. (Eds.). (2012). *Handbook of technology in psychology, psychiatry, and neurology: Theory, research, and practice.* New York, NY: Nova Science Publishers.

L'Abate, L., & Kern, R. (2002). Workbooks: Tools for the expressive writing paradigm. In: S. J. Lepore & J. M. Smyth (Eds.), *The writing cure: How expressive writing promotes health and emotional well-being* (pp. 239–255). Washington, DC: American Psychological Association.

L'Abate, L., L'Abate, B. L., & Maino, E. (2005). A review of 25 years of part-time professional practice: Workbooks and length of psychotherapy. *American Journal of Family Therapy, 33*, 19–31.

L'Abate, L., & Platzman, K. (1991). The practice of programmed writing (PW) in therapy and prevention with families. *American Journal of Family Therapy, 19*(2), 99–109.

L'Abate, L., & Rupp, G. (1981). *Enrichment: Skill training for family life.* Washington, DC: University Press of America.

L'Abate, L., & Sweeney, G. L. (in press). Criteria and processes in paradigm selection. In: L. L'Abate (Ed.), *Paradigms in theory construction*. New York, NY: Springer-Science.

L'Abate, L., & Sweeney, L. G. (2011). *The book of scams*. Atlanta, GA: Avant Garde Books.

L'Abate, L., & Weinstein, S. E. (1987). *Structured enrichment programs for couples and families*. New York, NY: Brunner/Mazel.

L'Abate, L., & Young, L. (1987). *Casebook of structured enrichment programs for couples and families*. New York, NY: Brunner/Mazel.

Ladwig, K., Baumert, J., Marten-Mittag, B., Kolb, C., Zrenner, B., & Scmitt, C. (2008). Posttraumatic stress symptoms and predicted mortality in patients with implantable cardioverter-defibrillators: results from the prospective living with and implanted cardioverter-defibrillator study. *Archives of General Psychiatry*, *65*, 1324–1330.

Laing, R. D. (1970). *Knots*. London: Penguin.

Lamb, Y. S. (2006, September 15). Arlene Hynes, 90: Bibliotherapy pioneer. *The Washington Post*. Retrieved from http://www.washingtonpost.com/wp-dyn/content/article/2006/09/14/AR2006091401712.html. Accessed on October 8, 2010.

Landau, M., Greenberg, J., & Sullivan, D. (2009). Defending a coherent autobiography: When past events appear incoherent, mortality salience prompts compensatory bolstering of the past's significance and the future's orderliness. *Personality and Social Psychology Bulletin*, *35*, 1012–1020.

Landreville, P., & Bissonnette, L. (1997). Effects of cognitive bibliotherapy for depressed older adults with a disability. *Clinical Gerontologist*, *17*(4), 35–55.

Lange, A., Rietdijk, D., Hudcovicova, M., van den Ven, J-P., Schrieken, B., & Emmelkamp, P. (2003). Interplay: A controlled randomized trial of the standard treatment of posttraumatic stress through the internet. *Journal of Consulting and Clinical Psychology*, *71*, 901–909.

Lange, A., Schrieken, B., van de Ven, J. P., Bredeweg, B., Emmelkamp, P. M. G., van der Kolk, J., et al. (2000). "Interapy": The effects of a short protocol led treatment of posttraumatic stress and pathological grief through the internet. *Behavioural and Cognitive Psychotherapy*, *28*, 175–202.

Lange, A., van de Ven, J. P., Schrieken, B., & Emmelkamp, P. M. G. (2001). Interapy: Treatment of posttraumatic stress through the internet: A controlled trial. *Journal of Behavior Therapy and Experimental Psychiatry*, *32*(2), 73–90.

Lange, A., van de Ven, P., Schrieken, B., & Emmelkamp, M. (2002). Interapy: A model for therapeutic writing through the Internet. In: S. J. Lepore & J. M. Smyth (Eds.), *The writing cure: How expressive writing promotes health and emotional well-being* (pp. 99–117). Washington, DC: American Psychological Association.

Latner, J. D. (2001). Self-help in the long-term treatment of obesity. *Obesity Reviews*, *2*(2), 87–97.

Latner, J. D., & Wilson, G,T. (Eds.). (2007). *Self-help approaches for obesity and eating disorders: Research and practice*. New York, Ny: Guilford.

Lauer, R., & Goldfield, M. (1970). Creative writing in group therapy. *Psychotherapy: Theory, Research, and Practice*, *7*(4), 248–252.

Leedy, J. (1969). Principles of poetry therapy. In: J. J. Leedy (Ed.), *Poetry therapy: The use of poetry in the treatment of emotional disorders* (pp. 67–74). Philadelphia, PA: Lippincott.

Leedy, J. (Ed.) (1973). *Poetry the healer*. Philadelphia, PA: Lippincott.

Leedy, J. (1985). *Poetry as healer: Mending the troubled mind*. New York, NY: Vanguard.

Lepore, S. J., Greenberg, M. A., Bruno, M., & Smyth, J. (2002). Expressive writing and health: Self-regulation of emotion-related experience, physiology, and behavior. In: S. J. Lepore &

J. M. Smyth (Eds.), *The writing cure: How expressive writing promotes health and emotional well-being* (pp. 99–117). Washington, DC: American Psychological Association.

Lepore, S. J., & Smyth, J. M. (2002). The writing cure: An overview. In: S. J. Lepore & J. M. Smyth (Eds.), *The writing cure: How expressive writing promotes health and emotional well-being* (pp. 3–14). Washington, DC: American Psychological Association.

Lerner, A. (1976). Editorial: A look at poetry therapy. *Art Psychotherapy*, *3*, 1.

Lerner, A. (1978). *Poetry in the therapeutic experience*. New York, NY: Pergamon.

Lerner, A. (1991). Some semantic considerations in poetry therapy. *ECT: A Review of General Semantics*, *48*, 213–219.

Lerner, A. (1994). *Poetry in the therapeutic experience* (2nd ed.). St. Louis, MO: MMB Music, Inc.

Lerner, A. (1997). A look at poetry. *The Arts in Psychology*, *24*, 81–89, 106–108.

Lerner, R. M., & Steinberg, L. (2009). *Handbook of adolescent psychology*. Hoboken, NJ: Wiley.

Lese, K. R., & MacNair-Semands, R. R. (2000). The therapeutic factors inventory: Development of a scale. *Group*, *24*, 303–317.

Lester, D. (2004). *Katies diary. Unlocking the mystery of suicide*. New York, NY: Brunner-Routledge.

Leucht, S., & Engel, R. R. (2006). The relative sensitivity of the clinical global impressions scale and the brief psychiatric rating scale in antipsychotic drug trials. *Neuropsychopharmacology*, *31*, 406–412.

Leung, P. (2010). Autobiographical timeline: A narrative and life story approach in understanding meaning-making in cancer patients. *Illness, Crisis, & Loss*, *18*, 111–127.

Levine, M., & Calvanio, R. (2007). The recording of personal information as an intervention and as an electronic health report. In: L. L'Abate (Ed.), *Low-cost approaches to promote physical and mental health* (pp. 227–250). New York, NY: Springer.

Levitus, B. (2010). *iPad for dummies* (1 ed.). Hoboken, NJ: Wiley.

Ličen, N., & Furland, M. (2006). *Analysis of the family as a learning site: Expanding the discourse of lifelong learning to consider family learning and bibliotherapy as a method in family life education*. Retrieved from http://esrea2006.ece.uth.gr/downloads/nicenfurlan.doc. Accessed on February 10, 2011.

Lindenmeyer, A. (2006). 'Lesbian Appetites': Food, sexuality and community in feminist autobiography. *Sexualities*, *9*, 469–485.

Lipton, B. (2005). *The biology of belief: Unleashing the power of consciousness, Matter and Miracles*. New York, NY: Hay House.

Litt, M. D., Cooney, N. L., & Morse, P. (1998). Ecological momentary assessment (EMA) with treated alcoholics: Methodological problems and potential solutions. *Health Psychology*, *17*, 48–52.

Liu, T. H., Chen, W. L., Li, Y. H., Han Wang, C., Mok, T. J., & Huang, S. (2009). Exploring the efficacy of cognitive behavioral bibliotherapy and a potential mechanism of change in the treatment of depressive symptoms among the Chinese: A randomized controlled trial. *Cognitive Therapy Research*, *33*, 449–461.

Ljotsson, B., Lundin, C., Mitsell, K., Carlbring, P., Ramklint, M., & Ghaderi, A. (2007). Remote treatment of bulimia nervosa and binge eating disorder: A randomized trial of internet-assisted cognitive behavioural therapy. *Behaviour Research & Therapy*, *45*, 649–661.

Longo, P. J. (2004, February 18). Poetry as therapy. *Wings of Support*. Available at http://www.the-bright-side.org/site/thebrightside/content.php?type=1&section_id=884&id=1133. Retrieved on January 9, 2011.

Low, C., Stanton, A., & Danoff-Burg, S. (2006). Expressive disclosure and benefit finding among breast cancer patients: Mechanisms for positive health effects. *Health Psychology*, *25*, 181–189.

Low, C. A., Stanton, A. L., & Bower, J. E. (2008). Effects of acceptance-oriented versus evaluative emotional processing on heart rate recovery and habituation. *Emotion*, *8*, 419–424.

Low, C. A., Stanton, A. L., Bower, J. E., & Gyllenhammer, L. (2010). A randomized, controlled trial of expressive writing for women with metastatic breast cancer. *Health Psychology*, *29*, 460–466.

Ludwig, A. (1994). Mental illness and creative activity in female writers. *American Journal of Psychiatry*, *151*, 1650–1656.

Luminet, O., & Rime, B. (2004). A multimodal investigation of emotional responding in alexithymia. *Cognition and Emotion*, *18*, 741–766.

Lumley, M., Tojek, T., & Macklem, D. (2002). The effects of written emotional disclosure among repressive and alexithymic people. In: S. J. Lepore & J. M. Smyth (Eds.), *The writing cure: How expressive writing promotes health and emotional well-being* (p. 75). Washington, DC: American Psychological Association.

Mackrill, T. (2008a). Solicited diary studies of psychotherapeutic practice — pros and cons. *European Journal of Psychotherapy and Counselling*, *10*, 5–18.

Mackrill, T. (2008b). Exploring psychotherapy clients' independent strategies for change while in therapy. *The British Journal of Guidance & Counselling*, *36*, 441–453.

Mackrill, T. (2008c). Pre-treatment change in psychotherapy with adult children of problem drinkers — The significance of leaving home. *Counselling & Psychotherapy Research*, *8*, 160–165.

Mackrill, T. (2009). A cross-contextual construction of clients' therapeutic practice. *Journal of Constructivist Psychology*, *22*, 283–305.

Mackrill, T. (2011). A diary-based, cross-contextual case study methodology: Background for the case of "Jane and Joe". *Pragmatic Case Studies in Psychotherapy*.

Mains, J. A., & Scogin, R. F. (2003). The effectiveness of self-administered treatments: A practice-friendly review of the research. *Journal of Clinical Psychology*, *59*(2), 237–246.

Malchiodi, C. A. (2005). *Expressive therapies: History, theory, and practice*. New York, NY: Guilford Publications.

Malchiodi, C. A. (2009). Listen to presences inside poems: A tribute to poetry therapist Ken Gorelick. *Psychology Today*. Available at www.psychologytoday.com/blog/the-healing-arts/200906/listen-presences-inside-poems-tribute-poetry-therapist-ken-gorelick. Retrieved on October 25, 2010.

Maldonato, A., Piana, N., Bloise, D., & Baldelli, A. (2010). Optimizing patient education for people with obesity: Possible use of the autobiographical approach. *Patient Education and Counseling*, *79*, 287–290.

Malinowski, B. (1989). *A diary in the strict sense of the word*. London: Athlone.

Margola, D., Facchin, F., Molgora, S., & Revenson, T. (2010). Cognitive and emotional processing through writing among adolescents who experienced the death of a classmate. *Psychological Trauma: Theory, Research, Practice, and Policy*, *2*, 250–260. doi: 10.1037/a0019891.

Marks, I. M. (2007). *Hands-on help: Computer-aided psychotherapy*. New York, NY: Psychology Press.

Marks, I. M., & Cavanagh, K. (2009). Computer-aided psychological treatments: Evolving issues. *Annual Review of Clinical Psychology*, *5*, 121–141.

Marrs, R. W. (1995). A meta-analysis of bibliotherapy studies. *American Journal of Community Psychology*, *23*(6), 843–870.

Maruta T., Colligan, R., Malinchoc, M., & Offord, K. (2002). Optimism-pessimism assessed in the 1960s and self-reported health status 30 years later. *Mayo Clinic Proceedings*, *77*, 748–753.

Mazza, N. (1981a). Poetry and group counseling: An exploratory study. (Doctoral Dissertation. The Florida State University, 1981). *Dissertation Abstracts International*, *42*, 6.

Mazza, N. (1981b). The use of poetry in treating the troubled adolescent. *Adolescence*, *16*, 400–408.

Mazza, N. (1993). Poetry therapy: Toward a research agenda for the 1990s. *The Arts in Psychotherapy*, *20*, 51–59.

Mazza, N. (1996). Poetry therapy: A framework and synthesis of techniques for family social work. *Journal of Family Social Work*, *1*, 3–18.

Mazza, N. (1999). *Poetry therapy: Interface of the arts and psychology*. Boca Raton, FL: CRC Press.

Mazza, N. (2001). The place of the poetic in dealing with death and loss. *Journal of Poetry Therapy*, *15*, 29–35.

Mazza, N. (2008). Poetry and narrative: *JPT* as a home for language, symbol, and story in community practice, therapy, education and the arts. *Journal of Poetry Therapy*, *21*, 1–2.

Mazza, N., Magaz, C., & Scaturro, J. (1987). Poetry therapy with abused children. *Arts in Psychotherapy*, *14*, 90–91. The entire article appears on pp. 85–92.

Mazza, N., & Prescott, B. U. (1981). Poetry: An ancillary technique in couples group therapy. *American Journal of Family Therapy*, *9*, 53–57.

McCoy, E. (1994). *How to do automatic writing*. San Paul, MN: Llewellyn Publications.

McKendree-Smith, N. L, Floyd, M., & Scogin, F. R. (2003). Self-administered treatments for depression: a review. *Journal of Clinical Psychology*, *59*(3), 275–288.

McLeod, J. (2010). *Case study research in counselling and psychotherapy*. London: Sage.

McMillen, P. S., & Pehrsson, D. E. (2004). Specialty of the house: Bibliotherapy for hospital patients. *Journal of Hospital Librarianship*, *4*(1), 73–82.

Mead, N., MacDonald, W., Bower, P., Lovell, K., Richards, D., Roberts, C., & Bucknall, A. (2005). The clinical effectiveness of guided self-help versus waiting-list control in the management of anxiety and depression: A randomized controlled trial. *Psychological Medicine*, *35*(11), 1633–1643.

Meads, C., & Sheffield, D. (2005). Issues regarding systematic review reports and trial heterogeneity. *Journal of Nervous and Mental Disease*, *193*(6), 424–425.

Meth, P. (2003). Entries and omissions: Using solicited diaries in geographic research. *Area*, *35*, 195–205.

Mettler, M., & Kemper, D. W. (2003). Information therapy: Health education one person at a time. *Health Promotion Practice*, *4*(3), 214–217.

Mettler, M., & Kemper, D. W. (2005). Information therapy: The strategic role of prescribed information in disease self-management. *APLAR Journal of Rheumatology*, *8*(2), 69–76.

Meunier, A. (1999). Establishing a creative writing program as an adjunct to vocational therapy in a community setting. *Journal of Poetry Therapy*, *12*, 161–168.

Michele, D. (2006). *Enhance your psychic abilities through automatic writing*. Sedena, AZ: Infinity Books.

Milk, L. (2009). The doctor as patient. *Washingtonian*, *44*(8). Available at www.washingtonian.com/articles/people/12388. Retrieved on October 1, 2010.

Miller, A., Maletic, V., & Raison, C. L. (2009). Inflammation and its discontents: The role of cytokines in the pathophysiology of major depression. *Biological Psychiatry*, *65*, 732–741.

Milligan, C., Bingley, A., & Gatrell, A. (2005). Digging deep: Using diary techniques to explore the place of health and well-being amongst older people. *Social Science & Medicine*, *61*, 1882–1892.

Mimeault, V., & Morin, C. M. (1999). Self-help treatment for insomnia: Bibliotherapy with and without professional guidance. *Journal of Consulting and Clinical Psychology*, *67*(4), 511–519.

Mohammadian, Y., Shahidi, S., Mahaki, B., Mohamadi, A. Z., Baghaban, A. A, & Zayeri, F. (2011). Evaluating the use of poetry to reduce signs of depression: Anxiety and stress in Iranian female students. *The Arts in Psychotherapy*, *38*, 59–63.

Mohr, D. C. (2009). Telemental health: Reflections on how to move the field forward. *Clinical Psychology: Science and Practice*, *16*, 343–347.

Mondloch, M., Cole, D., & Frank, J. (2001). Does how you do depend on how you think you'll do? A systematic review of the evidence for a relation between patients' recovery expectations and health outcomes. *Canadian Medical Association Journal*, *165*, 174–179.

Monrouxe, L. V. (2009). Solicited audio diaries in longitudinal narrative research: A view from inside. *Qualitative Research*, *9*, 81–103.

Montgomery, P., Bjornstad, G., & Dennis, J. (2001). Media-based behavioural treatments for behavioural problems in children (Review). The Cochrane Library. In Cochrane Database Systematic Review, Issue 1. Retrieved from Ovid Evidence-Based Medicine Reviews: Cochrane Database of Systematic Reviews. Art. No CD002206. doi: 10.1002/14651858.CD002206.pub3

Moos, R., & Hanson, B. (1974). *Group environment scale: Form B*. Palo Alto, CA: Consulting Psychologist Press.

Moreira, S., França, C., Moreira, M., & Lana-Peixoto, M. (2009). Musical identity of patients with multiple sclerosis. *Arquivos de Neuro-Psiquiatria*, *67*, 46–49.

Morgan, A. (2000). *What is narrative therapy? An easy to read introduction*. Adelaide: Dulwich Centre.

Morgan, N., Graves, K., Poggi, E., & Cheson, B. (2008). Implementing an expressive writing study in a cancer clinic. *The Oncologist*, *13*, 85–93.

Morrison, M. R. (1987). *Poetry as therapy*. New York, NY: Human Sciences Press.

Muhl, A. M. (1930). *Automatic writing*. Dresden, GE: Theodor Steinkopff.

Mulji-Dutt, S. (2010). *Poetry therapy: A healing tool to voice the lived experience of refugees in Canada*. Unpublished Master of Arts thesis, York University, Toronto, Ontario, Canada.

Mumford, M. D. (2011). *Handbook of organizational creativity*. New York, NY: Elsevier.

Munsch, S., Meyer, A. H., Milenkovic, N., Schlup, B., Margraf, J., & Wilhelm, F. H. (2009). Ecological momentary assessment to evaluate cognitive-behavioral treatment for binge eating disorder. *International Journal of Eating Disorders*, *42*, 648–657.

Murphy, M. T., Michelson, L. K., Marchione, K., Marchione, N., & Testa, S. (1998). The role of self-directed in vivo exposure in combination with cognitive therapy, relaxation training, or therapist-assisted exposure in the treatment of panic disorder with agoraphobia. *Journal of Anxiety Disorders*, *12*, 117–138.

Murray, M. (2009). Health psychology and writing: An introduction. *Journal of Health Psychology*, *14*, 158–160.

Myin-Germeys, I., Oorschot, M., Collip, D., Lataster, J., Delespaul, P., & van Os, J. (2009). Experience sampling research in psychopathology: Opening the black box of daily life. *Psychological Medicine*, *39*, 1533–1547.

NAPT. (2004). *Revised December 2006*. Retrieved from http://www.poetrytherapy.org/history.html. Accessed on September 14, 2011.

National Institute for Health and Clinical Excellence (NICE) Guidance. (2004). *Computerised cognitive behaviour therapy for anxiety*. Retrieved from http://www.nice.org.uk/page.aspx?o = ourguidance

National Institute for Health and Clinical Excellence (NICE) Guidance. (2006a, February). *Computerised cognitive behaviour therapy for depression*. Retrieved from http://www.nice.org.uk/nicemedia/pdf/Depression_Update_FULL_GUIDELINE.pdf

National Institute for Health and Clinical Excellence (NICE) Guidance. (2006b, February). *Computerised cognitive behaviour therapy for panic and phobia*. Retrieved from http://guidance.nice.org.uk/TA97

Neff, L. A., & Karney, B. R. (2005). Gender differences in social support: A question of skill or responsiveness? *Journal of Personality and Social Psychology, 88*, 79–90.

Negro, P., Palladino-Negro, P., & Louzã, M. (2002). Do religious mediumship dissociative experiences conform to the sociocognitive theory of dissociation? *Journal of Trauma & Dissociation, 3*, 51–73.

Nelson, J. P. (2006). Being in tune with life: Complementary therapy use and well-being in residential hospice residents. *Journal of Holistic Nursing, 24*(3), 152–161.

Newman, M. G., Erickson, R., Przeworksi, A., & Dzus, E. (2003). Self-help and minimal contact therapies for anxiety disorders: Is human contact necessary for therapeutic efficacy? *Journal of Clinical Psychology, 59*(3), 251–274.

Nicholls, S. (2009). Beyond expressive writing: Evolving models of developmental creative writing. *Health Psychology, 14*, 171–180.

Nordin, S., Carlbring, P., Cuijpers, P., & Andersson, G. (2010). Expanding the limits of bibliotherapy for panic disorder: Randomized trial of self-help without support but with a clear deadline. *Behavior Therapy, 41*(3), 267.

Nuttman-Shwartz, O. (2008). Bridging the gap: The creation of continuity by men on the verge of retirement. *Ageing & Society, 28*, 185–202.

O'Donovan, A. , Epel, E., Lin, J., Wolkowitz, O., Cohen, B., Maguen, S., … Neylan, T. (2011). Childhood trauma associated with short leukocyte telomere length in posttraumatic stress disorder. *Biological Psychiatry*. doi: 10.1016/j.biopsych.2011.01.035

Olson, E. (1959, November 14). Directions to the Armorer. *The New Yorker*, p. 191.

Olson-McBride, L. (2009). *Examining the influence of popular music and poetry therapy on the development of therapeutic factors in groups with at-risk adolescents*. Doctoral dissertation, Louisiana State University and Agricultural and Mechanical College.

Olson-McBride, L., & Page, T. (2006). Poetry therapy with special needs children: A pilot project. *Journal of Poetry Therapy, 19*, 167–184.

O'Luanaigh, C. (2010). Comics put patients in the picture. *The Guardian*, July 14. Retrieved from http://www.guardian.co.uk/science/blog/2010/jul/14/medical-comics-patients. Accessed on June 16, 2010.

Opre, A., Coman, A., Kallay, E., Rotaru, D., & Manier, D. (2005). Reducing distress in college students by expressive writing. A pilot study on a Romanian sample. *Cogniţie Creier Comportament, 9*, 53–64.

Owen, J. E., Hanson, E. R., Preddy, D. A., Bantum, D. A., & O'Carroll, E. (2011). Linguistically-tailored video feedback increases total and positive emotional expression in a structured writing task. *Computers in Human Behavior, 27*, 874–882.

Pace, T. W., Mletzko, T, Alagbe, O., Musselman, D, Nemeroff, C., Miller, A., & Helm, C. (2006). Increased stress-induced inflammatory responses in male patients with major depression and increased early life stress. *American Journal of Psychiatry, 163*, 1630–1633.

Pachankis, J. E., & Goldfried, M. R. (2010). Expressive writing for gay-related stress: Psychosocial benefits and mechanisms underlying improvement. *Journal of Consulting and Clinical Psychology*, *78*, 98–110.

Page, S., & Keady, J. (2010). Sharing stories: A meta-ethnographic analysis of 12 autobiographies written by people with dementia between 1989 and 2007. *Ageing & Society*, *30*, 511–526.

Papadopoulos, A., Wright, S., & Harding, S. (1999). Evaluating a therapeutic poetry group for older adults. *Journal of Poetry Therapy*, *13*, 29–37.

Parsons, J. (2008, August). *Finding reliable on-line therapeutic writing sources: A manual for counseling professionals*. Unpublished master's thesis, University of Lethbridge, Lethbridge, Alberta, Canada.

Pehrsson, D. E., & McMillen, P. (2005). A bibliotherapy evaluation tool: grounding counselors in the therapeutic use of literature. *Arts in Psychotherapy*, *32*(1), 47–59.

Pehrsson, D. E., & McMillen, P. (2006). Competent bibliotherapy: Preparing counselors to use literature with culturally diverse clients. *Vistas*. Alexandria, VA: American Counseling Association Publication.

Pennebaker, J. (1990). *Opening up: The healing power of confiding in others*. New York, NY: William Morrow.

Pennebaker, J. W. (1997). Writing about emotional experiences as a therapeutic process. *Psychological Science*, *8*, 162–166.

Pennebaker, J. W. (2004). Theories, therapies, and taxpayers: On the complexities of the expressive writing paradigm. *Clinical Psychology: Science and Practice*, *11*, 138–142.

Pennebaker, J. W., & Beall, S. K. (1986). Confronting a traumatic event: Toward an understanding of inhibition and disease. *Journal of Abnormal Psychology*, *95*, 274–281.

Pennebaker, J. W., & Chung, C. K. (2007). Expressive writing, emotional upheavals, and health. In: H. Friedman & R. Silver (Eds.), *Handbook of health psychology* (pp. 263–284). New York, NY: Oxford University Press.

Pennebaker, J. W., & Chung, C. K. (in press). Expressive writing: Connections to physical and mental health. In: H. S. Friedman (Ed.), *The Oxford handbook of health psychology* (p. 7). New York, NY: Oxford University Press.

Pennebaker, J. W., & Graybeal, A. (2001). Patterns of natural language use: Disclosure, personality, and social integration. *Current Directions in Psychological Science*, *10*, 90–93.

Pennebaker, J. W., Kiecolt-Glaser, J. K., & Glaser, R. (1988). Disclosure of traumas and immune function: Health implications for psychotherapy. *Journal of Consulting and Clinical Psychology*, *56*, 239–245.

Pennebaker, J., & Stone, L. (2003). Words of wisdom: Language use over the life span. *Journal of Personality and Social Psychology*, *85*, 291–301.

Perilli, G. G. (1991). Integrated music therapy with a schizophrenic woman. In: K. Bruscia (Ed.), *Case studies in music therapy* (pp. 403–416). Barcelona: Gilsum, NH.

Peters, T. J., & Beveridge, A. (2010). The madness of King George III: A psychiatric re-assessment. *History of Psychiatry*, *21*, 20–37.

Peterson, C., Seligman, M. E. P., & Vaillant, G. E. (1988). Pessimistic explanatory style is a risk factor for physical illness: A thirty-five year longitudinal study. *Journal of Personality and Social Psychology*, *55*, 23–27.

Philipp, R. (1999). Evaluating the arts in health care and mental health promotion - The example of creative writing. In: D. Haldane & S. Loppert (Eds.), (pp. 96–114). The arts in health care: Learning from experience. London: King's Fund.

Philipp, R., Coppell, K., & Freeman, H. (1994). Poetry and the art of medicine. *British Medical Journal*, *308*, 63.

Philipp, R., & Robertson, I. (1996). Poetry helps healing. *Lancet*, *347*, 332–333.

Piana, N., Maldonato, A., Bloise, D., Carboni, L., Careddu, G., Fraticelli, E., ... Romani, G. (2010). The narrative-autobiographical approach in the group education of adolescents with diabetes: A qualitative research on its effects. *Patient Education and Counseling*, *80*, 56–63.

Piasecki, T. M., Hufford, M. R., Solhan, M., & Trull, T. J. (2007). Assessing clients in their natural environments with electronic diaries: Rationale, benefits, limitations, and barriers. *Psychological Assessment*, *19*, 25–43.

Picardi, A., Battisti, F., de Girolamo, G., Morosini, P., Norcio, B., Bracco, R., & Biondi, M. (2008). Symptom structure of acute mania: A factor study of the 24-item brief psychiatric rating scale in a national sample of patients hospitalized for a manic episode. *Journal of Affective Disorders*, *108*, 183–189.

Plummer, K. (2001). *Documents of life 2. An invitation to critical humanism*. London: Sage.

Possemato, K., Ouimette, P., & Geller, P. A. (2010). Internet-based expressive writing for kidney transplant recipients: Effects on posttraumatic stress and quality of life. *Traumatology*, *16*, 49–54.

Prescott, F. C. (1922). *The poetic mind*. New York, NY: Macmillan.

Pressman, S., & Cohen, S. (2007). Use of social words in autobiographies and longevity. *Psychosomatic Medicine*, *69*, 262–269.

Qualman, E. (2011). *Socialnomics: How social media transforms the way we live and do business* (2nd ed.). Hoboken, NJ: Wiley.

Quinn, J. M., Pascoe, A., Wood, W., & Neal, D. T. (2010). Can't control yourself? Monitor those bad habits. *Personality and Social Psychology Bulletin*, *36*, 499–511.

Rácz, J. (2006). Questions on the interpretation of drug users' autobiographies in a country in the 'early' phase of drug use. *Contemporary Drug Problems: An Interdisciplinary Quarterly*, *33*, 99–122.

Raison, C. L., Borisov, A. S., Woolwine, B. J., Massung, B., Vogt, G., & Miller, A. H. (2010). Interferon-alpha effects on diurnal hypothalamic-pituitary-adrenal axis activity: Relationship with proinflammatory cytokines and behavior. *Molecular Psychiatry*, *15*, 535–547.

Rapee, R. M., Abbott, M. J., & Lyneham, H. J. (2006). Bibliotherapy for children with anxiety disorders using written materials for parents: A randomized controlled trial. *Journal of Consulting and Clinical Psychology*, *74*(3), 436–444.

Rasmussen, P. T., & Tomm, K. (1992). Guided letter writing: A long brief therapy method whereby clients carry out their own treatment. *Journal of Strategic and Systematic Therapies*, *7*(4), 1–18.

Ray, O. (2004). How the mind hurts and heals the body. *American Psychologist*, *59*, 29–40.

Redick, T., Heitz, R., & Engle, R. (2007). Working memory capacity and inhibition: Cognitive and social consequences. In: C. M. MacLeod & D. S. Gorfein (Eds.), *The place of inhibition in cognition*. Washington, DC: American Psychological Association.

Reeves, T., & Stace, J. M. (2005). Improving patient access and choice: Assisted bibliotherapy for mild to moderate stress/anxiety in primary care. *Journal of Psychiatric and Mental Health Nursing*, *12*(3), 341–346.

Reiter, S. (1997). Poetry therapy: Testimony on Capitol Hill. *Journal of Poetry Therapy*, *10*, 169–178.

Reiter, S. (2010). Poets-behind-bars: A creative "righting" project for prisoners and poetry therapists-in-training. *Journal of Poetry Therapy*, *23*, 215–238.

Rennie, D. L. (1990). Towards a representation of the client's experience of the psychotherapeutic hour. In: G. Lietaer, J. Rombaults & R. Van Balen (Eds.), *Client-centered and experiential psychotherapy in the nineties*. Leuven, Germany: Leuven University Press.

Richards, J. M., Beal, W. E., Seagal, J. D., & Pennebaker, J. W. (2000). Effects of disclosure of traumatic events on illness behavior among psychiatric prison inmates. *Journal of Abnormal Psychology*, *109*, 156–160.

Richardson, I. (2007). *Learn how to do Automatic Writing: A step by step course to help you access higher realms of the mind, body, and spirit*. Frederick, MD: Crystal Forests.

Richardson, L. K., Frueh, B. C., Grubaugh, A. L., & Elhai, J. D. (2009). Current directions in videoconferencing telemental health research. *Clinical Psychology: Science and Practice*, *16*, 323–338.

Riordan, R. J. (1996). Scriptotherapy: Therapeutic writing as a counseling adjunct. *Journal of Counseling and Development*, *74*(3), 263.

Riordan, R. J., & Wilson, L. S. (1989). Bibliotherapy: Does it work? *Journal of Counseling and Development*, *67*(9), 506–508.

Ritterband, L. M., Cox, D. J., Walker, LS., Kovatchev, B., McKnight, L., Patel, K., … Sutphen, J. (2003). An internet intervention as adjunctive therapy for pediatric encopresis. *Journal of Consulting and Clinical Psychology*, *71*, 910–917.

Ritterband, L. M., Gonder-Frederick, L. A., Cox, D. J., Clifton, A. D., West, R. W., & Borowitz, S. M. (2003). Internet interventions: In review, in use, and into the future. *Professional Psychology: Research & Practice*, *34*, 527–534.

Robertson, S., & Hopko, D. (2009). Experiential avoidance: A moderator of the relationship between age and emotional expression. *Aging & Mental Health*, *13*, 611–618.

Robinson, S., & Mowbray, J. K. (1969). Why poetry. In: J. J. Leedy (Ed.), *Poetry therapy: The use of poetry in the treatment of emotional disorders* (p. 192). Philadelphia, PA: Lippincott. Why poetry is chap. 15 and begins on p. 188.

Rogers, C. R. (1951). *Therapy. Implications and theory*. Cambridge, MA: The Riverside Press.

Rolfs, A., & Super, S. I. (1988). Guiding the unconscious: The process of poem selection for poetry therapy groups. *The Arts in Psychotherapy*, *15*, 119–126.

Rönka, A., Malinen, K., Kinnunen, U., Tolvanen, A., & Lämsa, T. (2010). Capturing daily family dynamics via text messages: Development of the mobile diary. *Community, Work & Family*, *13*, 5–21.

Roosevelt, G. (1982). An examination of the effects of prepared "deep level" poems versus "surface level" poems in poetry therapy. Unpublished doctoral dissertation, International College. Please note: The sentence used in the poetry therapy chapter text was found in Hynes, 1988, p. 56.

Rosen, A., Proctor, E., & Staudt, M. M. (1999). Social work research and the quest for effective practice. In: M. Potocky-Tripodi & T. Tripodi (Eds.), *New directions for social work practice research* (pp. 39–55). Washington, DC: NASW Press.

Rosenberg, H. J., Rosenberg, S. D., Ernstoff, M., Wolford, G., Amdur, R., Elshamy, R., … Pennebaker, J. (2002). Expressive disclosure and health outcomes in a prostate cancer population. *International Journal of Psychiatry in Medicine*, *32*, 37–53.

Ross, M. M., Rideout, E. M., & Carson, M. M. (1994). The use of the diary as a data collection technique. *Western Journal of Nursing Research*, *16*, 414–425.

Rossi, E. (2002). *The psychobiology of gene expression: Neuroscience and neurogenesis in hypnosis and the healing arts*. New York, NY: Norton.

Rossiter, C., & Brown, R. (1988). An evaluation of interactive bibliotherapy in a clinical setting. *Journal of Poetry Therapy*, *1*, 157–168.

Rubin, R. J. (1978). *Using bibliotherapy: A guide to theory and practice*. Phoenix, AZ: Oryx Press.

Rubin, R. J. (1979). Uses of bibliotherapy in response to the 1970s. *Library Trends*, *28*(Fall), 239–252.

Ruiz, M. A., Drake, E. B., Glass, A., Marcotte, D., & van Gorp, S. G. (2002). Trying to beat the system: Misuse of the internet to assist avoiding the detection of psychological symptom dissimulation. *Professional Psychology: Research & Practice*, *33*, 294–299.

Runco, M. A. (2006). *Creativity: Theories and themes in research, development, and practice*. New York, NY: Elsevier.

Runco, M. A., & Pritzker, S. R. (2011). *Encyclopedia of creativity*. New York, NY: Elsevier.

Ruskin, P. E., Silver-Aylaian, M., Kling, M. A., Reed, S. A., Bradham, D. D., Hebel, J. R., ... Hauser, P. (2004). Treatment outcomes in depression: comparison of remote treatment through telepsychiatry to in-person treatment. *The American Journal of Psychiatry*, *161*(8), 1471–1476.

Ruwaard, J., Broeksteeg, J., Schrieken, B., Emmelkamp, P., & Lange, A. (2010). Web-based therapist-assisted cognitive behavioral treatment of panic symptoms: A randomized controlled trial with a three-year follow-up. *Journal of Anxiety Disorders*, *24*, 387–396.

Ruwaard, J., Schrieken, B., Schrijver, M., Broeksteeg, J., Dekker, J., Vermelen, H., & Lange, A. (2009). Standardized web-based cognitive behavioural therapy of mild to moderate depression: A randomized controlled trial with a long-term follow-up. *Cognitive Behaviour Therapy*, *38*(4), 206–221.

Salkovskis, P., Rimes, K., Stephenson, D., Sacks, G., & Scott, J. (2006). A randomized controlled trial of the use of self-help materials in addition to standard general practice treatment of depression compared to standard treatment alone. *Psychological Medicine*, *36*(3), 325–333Retrieved from http://journals.cambridge.org/action/displayIssue?jid=PSM&volumeId=36&seriesId=0&issueId=03.

Sautter, U. (2010). Reading, writing and revelation. *Ode Magazine*. Retrieved from www.odemagazine.com/doc/73/reading-writing-revelation/. Accessed on June 13, 2011.

Schauffler, R. H. (1927/1925). *The poetry cure: A pocket medicine chest of verse*. New York, NY: Dodd, Mead, and Co.

Scheuer, N., de la Cruz, M., Pozo, J., & Neira, S. (2006). Children's autobiographies of learning to write. *British Journal of Educational Psychology*, *76*, 709–725.

Schloss, G. A. (1976). *Psychopoetry: A new approach to self-awareness through poetry therapy*. New York, NY: Grosset and Dunlap.

Schmidt, U., Bone, G., Hems, S., Lessem, J., & Treasure, J. (2002). Structured therapeutic writing tasks as an adjunct to treatment in eating disorders. *European Eating Disorders Review*, *10*, 299–315.

Scogin, F., Floyd, M., Jamison, C., Ackerson, J., Landreville, P., & Bissonnette, L. (1996). Negative outcomes: What is the evidence on self-administered treatments? *Journal of Consulting and Clinical Psychology*, *64*(5), 1086–1089.

Scogin, F., Jamison, C., & Gochneaur, K. (1989). Comparative efficacy of cognitive and behavioral bibliotherapy for mildly and moderately depressed older adults. *Journal of Consulting and Clinical Psychology*, *57*(3), 403–407.

Segrist, D. (2008). Incorporating expressive writing theory into the use of autobiographies in an abnormal psychology course. *North American Journal of Psychology*, *10*, 99–108.

Semple, C. J., Dunwoody, L., Sullivan, K., & Kernohan, W. G. (2006). Patients with head and neck cancer prefer individualized cognitive behavioural therapy. *European Journal of Cancer Care*, *15*(3), 220–227.

Serpell, L., Treasure, J., Teasdale, J., & Sullivan, V. (1999). Anorexia nervosa: Friend or foe? *International Journal of Eating Disorders*, *25*, 177–186.

Shechtman, Z. (1999). Bibliotherapy: An indirect approach to the treatment of childhood aggression. *Child Psychiatry and Human Development*, *30*, 39–53.

Sheridan, D. (1993). Writing to the archive: Mass-observations as autobiography. *Sociology, 27*, 27–40.

Sherman, D., Bunyan, D., & Creswell, D. (2009). Psychological vulnerability and stress: The effects of self-affirmation on sympathetic nervous system responses to naturalistic stressors. *Health Psychology, 28*, 554–562.

Shiffman, S. (2009a). How many cigarettes did you smoke? Assessing cigarette consumption by global report, time-line follow-back, and ecological momentary assessment. *Health Psychology, 28*, 519–526.

Shiffman, S. (2009b). Ecological Momentary Assessment (EMA) in studies of substance use. *Psychological Assessment, 21*, 486–497.

Shiffman, S., Stone, A. A., & Hufford, M. R. (2008). Ecological momentary assessment. *Annual Review of Clinical Psychology, 4*, 1–32.

Shim, M., Capella, J., & Han, J. (2011). How does insightful and emotional disclosure bring potential health benefits? *Journal of Communication, 61*, 432–454.

Silfver, M. (2007). Coping with guilt and shame: A narrative approach. *Journal of Moral Education, 36*, 169–183.

Silverstein, S. (1974). Tree house. In: *Where the sidewalk ends* (p. 79). New York, NY: Harper & Row.

Silverstein, S. (1996). The voice. In: *Falling up* (p. 38). New York, NY: Harper Collins.

Simha-Alpern, A. (2007). "I finally have words!" Integrating a psychodynamic psychotherapeutic approach with principles of emotional intelligence training in treating trauma survivors. *Journal of Psychotherapy Integration, 17*, 293–313.

Sinadinovic, K., Berman, A. H., Hasson, D., & Wennberg, P. (2010). Internet-based assessment and self-monitoring of problematic alcohol and drug use. *Addictive Behaviors, 35*, 464–470.

Slavin-Spenny, O., Cohen, J., Oberleitner, L., & Lumbley, M. (2011). The effects of different methods of emotional disclosure: Differentiating post-traumatic growth from stress symptoms. *Journal of Clinical Psychology, 61*(10), 993–1007.

Sloan, D. M., & Epstein, E. M. (2005). Respiratory sinus arrhythmia predicts written disclosure outcome. *Psychophysiology, 42*, 611–615.

Sloan, D. M., & Marx, B. P. (2004). A closer examination of the structured written disclosure procedure. *Journal of Consulting and Clinical Psychology, 72*, 165–175.

Smith, M. A. (2000). The use of poetry therapy in the treatment of an adolescent with Borderline Personality Disorder. *Journal of Poetry Therapy, 14*(1), 3–14.

Smith, S., Anderson-Hanley, C., Langrock, A., & Compas, B. (2005). The effects of journaling for women with newly diagnosed breast cancer. *Psychooncology, 14*, 1075–1082.

Smorti, A., Risaliti, F., Pananti, B., & Cipriani, V. (2008a). Autobiography as a tool for self-construction: A study of patients with mental disorders. *Journal of Nervous and Mental Disease, 196*, 531–537.

Smorti, A., Risaliti, F., Pananti, B., & Cipriani, V. (2008b). L'autobiografia come strumento per la costruzione del sé: Uno studio sui pazienti psichiatrici. *Rivista Sperimentale di Freniatria: La Rivista della Salute Mentale, 132*, 145–165.

Smorti, A., Pananti, B., & Rizzo, A. (2010). Autobiography as tool to improve lifestyle, well being, and self-narrative in patients with mental disorders. *Journal of Nervous and Mental Disease, 198*, 564–571.

Smyth, J. M. (1998). Written emotional expression: Effect sizes, outcome types, and moderating variables. *Journal of Consulting and Clinical Psychology, 66*, 174–188.

Smyth, J. M., & L'Abate, L. (2001). A meta-analytic evaluation of workbook effectiveness in physical and mental health. In: L. L'Abate (Ed.), *Distance writing and computer-assisted interventions in psychiatry and mental heath* (pp. 77–90). Westport, CT: Ablex.

Smyth, J. M., & Pennebaker, J. (2008). Exploring the boundary conditions of expressive writing: In search of the right recipe. *Health Psychology*, *13*, 1–7.

Snowdon, D. (2003). *Aging with grace: What the Nun Study teaches us about living longer, healthier, and more meaningful lives*. New York, NY: Bantam Books.

Snyder, D. K., Gordon, K. C., & Baucom, D. H. (2004). Treating affair couples: Extending the written disclosure paradigm to relationship trauma. *Clinical Psychology: Science and Practice*, *11*, 155–159.

Solomons, L. M., & Stein, G. (1896). Normal motor automation. *Psychological Review*, *3*, 492–512.

Spelke, E. S., Hirst, W., & Neisser, U. (1976). Skills of divided attention. *Cognition*, *4*, 215–230.

Spera, S. P., Buhrfeind, E. D., & Pennebaker, J. W. (1994). Expressive writing and coping with job loss. *Academy of Management Journal*, *37*, 733.

Stafford, W. (1997). *"At the unnational monument along the Canadian border" stories that could be true*. New York, NY: Harper Collins.

Stainbrook, E. (1978). Poetry and behavior in the psychotheapeutic experience. In: A. Lerner (Ed.), *Poetry in the therapeutic experience* (pp. 1–11). Elmsford, NY: Pergamon Press.

Stainbrook, E. (1994). Poetry and behavior in the psychotherapeutic experience. In: A. Lerner (Ed.), *Poetry in the therapeutic experience* (2nd ed.), (pp. 1–11). St. Louis, MO: MMB Music, Inc.

Stanton, A. L., & Danoff-Burg, S. (2002). Emotional expression, expressive writing, and cancer. In: S. J. Lepore & J. M. Smyth (Eds.), *The writing cure: How expressive writing promotes health and emotional well-being* (pp. 31–51). Washington, DC: American Psychological Association.

Stanton, A. L., Danoff-Burg, S., Sworowski, L. A., Collins, C. A., Branstetter, A. D., Rodriguez-Hanley, A., & Austenfeld, J. L. (2002). Randomized, controlled trial of written emotional expression and benefit finding in breast cancer patients. *Journal of Clinical Oncology*, *20*, 4160–4168.

Starker, S. (1988). Psychologists and self-help books: Attitudes and prescriptive practices of clinicians. *American Journal of Psychotherapy*, *42*(3), 448–455.

State of the Field Committee. (2009). *State of the field report: Arts in healthcare 2009*. Washington, DC: Society for the Arts in Healthcare.

Stember, C. J. (1977). Printmaking with abused children: A first step in art therapy. *American Journal of Art Therapy*, *16*, 104–109.

Steptoe, A., O'Donnell, K., Badrick, E., Kumari, M., & Marmot, M. (2008). Neuroendocrine and inflammatory factors associated with positive affect in healthy men and women: The Whitehall II study. *American Journal of Epidemiology*, *167*, 96–102.

Stockdale, B. (2009). *You can beat the odds: Surprising factors behind chronic illness and cancer*. Colorado: Sentient Publications.

Stone, A. A., Shiffman, S., Schwartz, J. E., Broderick, J. E., & Hooford, M. R. (2002). Patient noncompliance with paper diaries. *British Medical Journal*, *324*, 1193–1194.

Stukas, A., Dew, M., Switzer, G., DiMartini, A., Kormos, R., & Griffith, B. (1999). PTSD in heart transplant recipients and their primary family caregivers. *Psychosomatics*, *40*, 212–221.

Swanbon, T., Boyce, L., & Greenberg, M. A. (2008). Expressive writing reduces avoidance and somatic complaints in a community sample with constraints on expression. *British Journal of Health Psychology*, *13*, 53–56.

Symes, C. (1999). Chronicles of labour. A discourse analysis of diaries. *Time and Society*, *8*, 357–380.

Tasca, G. A., Illing, V., Balfour, L., Krysanski, V., Demidenko, N., Nowakowski, J., & Bissada, H. (2009). Psychometric properties of self-monitoring of eating disorder urges among treatment seeking women: Ecological momentary assessment using a daily diary method. *Eating Behaviors*, *10*, 59–61.

Tegnér, I., Fox, J., Philipp, R., & Thorne, P. (2009). Evaluating the use of poetry to improve well-being and emotional resilience in cancer patients. *Journal of Poetry Therapy*, *22*(September), 121–131.

Temoshok, L., Waldstein, S., Wald, R., Garzino-Demo, Al., Synowski, S., Sun, L., & Wiley, J. (2008). Type C coping, alexithymia, and heart rate reactivity are associated independently and differentially with specific immune mechanisms linked to HIV progression. *Brain, Behavior and Immunity*, *22*, 781–792.

Tenni, C., Smith, A., & Boucher, C. (2003). The researcher as autobiographer: Analyzing data written about oneself. *The Qualitative Report*, *8*, March. Retrieved from http://www.nova.edu/ssss/QR/QR8-1/tenni.html

Thiele, C., Laireiter, A-R., & Baumann, U. (2002). Diaries in clinical psychology and psychotherapy: A selective review. *Clinical Psychology and Psychotherapy*, *9*, 1–37.

Thompson, R. I., Summerbell, C. D., Hooper, L., Higgins, J. P. T., Little, P. S., Talbot, D., & Ebrahim, S. (2001). Dietary advice given by a dietician versus other health professional or self-help resources to reduce blood cholesterol. *Cochrane Database of Systematic Reviews*, Issue 1, Art No. CD001366. doi: 10.1002/14651858.CD001366

Thornton, J. (2008). The guided autobiography method: A learning experience. *The International Journal of Aging & Human Development*, *66*, 155–173.

Trull, T. J., & Ebner-Priemer, U. W. (2009). Ambulatory assessment. An innovative and promising approach for clinical psychology. *European Psychologist*, *14*, 109–119.

Trunk, D., & Abrams, L. (2009). Do younger and older adults' communicative goals influence off-topic speech in autobiographical narratives? *Psychology and Aging*, *24*, 324–337.

Turner, F. J. (Ed.) (1986). *Social work treatment: Interlocking theoretical approaches* (3rd ed.). New York, NY: Free Press.

Turner, J. (1992). Correspondence counseling: For clients committed to change. *Employee Counselling Today*, *4*(3), 7–12.

Tyson, E. H. (2002). Hip hop therapy: An exploratory study of a rap music intervention with at-risk and delinquent youth. *Journal of Poetry Therapy*, *15*, 131–144.

Tyson, E. H. (2006). Rap-music attitude and perception scale: A validation study. *Research on Social Work Practice*, *16*, 211–223.

Tyson, K. B. (1992). A new approach to relevant scientific research for pracitioners: The heuristic paradigm. *Social Work*, *37*, 541–556.

Uher, T. (2010). Alexithymia and immune dysregulation: A critical review. *Activitas Nervosa Superior*, *52*, 40–44.

U.S. Medicine (2009). VA research proves cognitive behavioral therapy helpful in treating PTSD. *U.S. Medicine: The Voice of Federal Medicine*. Available at http://www.usmedicine.com/categories/2009-issues/november-2009.html

Van der Oord, S., Lucassen, S., Van Emmerik, A., & Emmelkamp, P. (2010). Treatment of post-traumatic stress disorder in children using cognitive behavioural writing therapy. *Clinical Psychology and Psychotherapy*, *17*, 240–249.

Van Emmerik, A., Kamphuis, J., & Emmelkamp, P. (2008). Treating acute stress disorder and posttraumatic stress disorder with cognitive behavioral therapy or structured writing therapy: A randomized controlled trial. *Psychotherapy and Psychosomatics*, *77*, 93–100.

Van Kesteren, N. M. C., Kok, G., Hospers, H. J., Schippers, J., & DeWildt, W. (2006). Systematic development of a self-help and motivational enhancement intervention to promote sexual health in HIV-positive men who have sex with men. *AIDS Patient Care and STDs*, *20*(12), 858–875.

Van Lankveld, J. (1998). Bibliotherapy in the treatment of sexual dysfunction: A meta-analysis. *Journal of Consulting and Clinical Psychology*, *66*(4), 702–708.

van Vugt, P., Paquier, P., Kees, L., & Cras, P. (1996). Increased writing activity in neurological conditions: A review and clinical study. *Journal of Neurology, Neurosurgery & Psychiatry*, *61*, 510–514.

Van't Veer-Tazelaar, P., Smit, F., van Hout, H., van Oppen, P., van der Horst, H., Beekman, A., & van Marwijk, H. (2010). Cost-effectiveness of a stepped care intervention to prevent depression and anxiety in late life: A randomised trial. *The British Journal of Psychiatry*, *196*(4), 319–324.

Vos, T., Corry, J., Haby, M. M., Carter, R., & Andrews, G. (2005a). Cost-effectiveness of cognitive behavioural therapy and drug intervention for major depression. *Australian and New Zealand Journal of Psychiatry*, *39*(8), 683–692.

Vos, T., Haby, M. M., Magnus, A., Mihalopoulos, C., Andrews, G., & Carter, R. (2005b). Assessing cost-effectiveness in mental health: Helping policy-makers prioritize and plan health services. *Australian and New Zealand Journal of Psychiatry*, *39*, 701–712. doi:10.1111/j.1440-1614.2005.01654.x

Waddington, K., & Fletcher, C. (2005). Gossip and emotion in nursing and health-care organizations. *Journal of Health Organisation and Management*, *19*, 378–394.

Waldram, J. (2008). The narrative challenge to cognitive behavioral treatment of sexual offenders. *Culture, Medicine and Psychiatry*, *32*, 421–439.

Wang, Y. (2011). *Bibliotherapy for Chinese patients with depression in rehabilitation*. Rijeke: InTech-Open Access Publishers.

Weimerskirch, P. J. (1965). Benjamin Rush and John Minson Galt, II: Pioneers of bibliotherapy in America. *Bulletin of the Medical Library Association*, *53*(October), 510–526.

Weishaar, K. (1999). The visual life review as a therapeutic art framework with the terminally ill. *The Arts in Psychotherapy*, *26*, 173–184.

Wenze, S. J., & Miller, I. W. (2010). Use of ecological momentary assessment in mood disorders research. *Clinical Psychology Review*, *30*, 794–804.

Wickramasekera, I. (1998). Secrets kept from the mind but not the body or behavior. *Advances in Mind/Body Medicine*, *14*, 81–132.

Willig, C. (2009). 'Unlike a rock, a tree, a horse or an angel'...: Reflections on the struggle for meaning through writing during the process of cancer diagnosis. *Journal of Health Psychology*, *14*, 181–183.

Wlodarczyk, N. (2009). The use of music and poetry in life review with hospice patients. *Journal of Poetry Therapy*, *22*, 133–139.

Wollersheim, J. P., & Wilson, G. L. (1991). Group treatment of unipolar depression: A comparison of coping, supportive, bibliotherapy and delayed treatment groups. *Professional Psychology: Research and Practice*, *22*(6), 496–502.

Wosket, V. (1999). *The therapeutic use of self. Counselling practice, research and supervision*. London: Routledge.

Wright, J. (2009). Dialogical journal writing as 'self-therapy': 'I matter'. *Counselling and Psychotherapy Research*, *9*(4), 234–240.

Xu, J., & Roberts, R. (2010). The power of positive emotions: It's a matter of life or death — Subjective well-being and longevity over 28 years in a general population. *Health Psychology*, *29*, 9–19.

Yalom, I., & Elkin, G. (1974). *Every day gets a little closer: A twice-told therapy*. New York, NY: Basic Books.

Yeater, E. A., Naugle, A. E., O'Donohue, W., & Bradley, A. R. (2004). Sexual assault prevention with college-aged women: A bibliotherapy approach. *Violence and Victims, 19*(5), 593–612.

Yi-Tsi Seih, & Pennebaker, J. W. (in press). Language index word count. In: L. L'Abate, & D. A. Kaiser (Eds.), *Handbook of technology in psychology, psychiatry, and neurology: Theory, research, and practice* (pp. 000–000). New York, NY: Nova Science Publishers.

Zerner, A., & Farber, M. (n.d.). *Ghost writer: Messages from beyond and magic from within*. New York, NY: Sterling Publishing Company.

Zimmerman, D., & Wieder, D. (1975). The diary-interview method. *Urban life, 5*, 479–497.

Zimmerman, J. L., & Dickerson, V. C. (1994). Using narrative metaphor: Implications for theory and clinical practice. *Family Process, 33*(3), 233–245.

Zoler, M. (2008). Dissociation can be normal, unremarkable. *Clinical Psychiatry News*, from Elkin, G. (1974). *Every day gets a little closer. A twice-told therapy*. New York, NY: Basic Books.

Index

List of Volumes

Volume 1: Theories, Models and Methodology in Writing Research
Gert Rijlaarsdam, Huub van den Bergh, Michel Couzijn (Eds.) 1996
558 pages; Paperback ISBN 90-5356-197-8

Volume 2: Effective Teaching and Learning of Writing. Current Trends in Research
Gert Rijlaarsdam, Huub van den Bergh, Michel Couzijn (Eds.) 1996
pages 388; Paperback ISBN 90-5356-198-6

Volume 3: The Cognitive Demands of Writing. Processing Capacity and Working Memory Effects in Text Production
Mark Torrance, Gaynor Jeffery (Eds.) 1999
pages 113: Paperback ISBN 90-5356-308-3

Volume 4: Knowing What to Write. Conceptual Processes in Text Production
Mark Torrance, David Galbraith (eds.) 1999
pages 190; Paperback ISBN 90-5356-307-5

Volume 5: Foundations of Argumentative Text Processing
Pierre Coirier, Jerry Andriessen (Eds.) 2000
Pages 273; Paperback 90-5356-340-7

Volume 6: Metalinguistic Activity in Learning to Write
Anna Camps, Marta Milian (Eds.) 2000
pages 228: Paperback 90-5356-341-5

Volume 7: Writing as a Learning Tool
Päivi Tynjälä, Lucia Mason, Kirsti Lonka (Eds.) 2001
Hardbound, ISBN 0-7923-6877-0; Paperback, ISBN 0-7923-6914-9

Volume 8: Developmental Aspects in Learning to Write
Liliana Tolchinsky (Ed.) 2001
Paperback, ISBN 0-7923-7063-5; Hardbound, ISBN 0-7923-6979-3

Volume 9: Through the Models of Writing:
Denis Alamargot, Lucile Chanquoy (2001)
Paperback, ISBN 0-7923-7159-3; Hardbound, ISBN 0-7923-6980-7

Volume 10: Contemporary Tools and Techniques for Studying Writing
Thierry Olive, C. Michael Levy (Eds.) 2001
Hardbound, ISBN 1-4020-0035-9; Paperback, ISBN 1-4020-0106-1

Volume 11: New Directions for Research in L2 Writing
Sarah Ransdell, Marie-Laure Barbier (Eds.) 2002
281 p. Paperback, ISBN 1-4020-0539-3; Hardbound, ISBN 1-4020-0538-5

Volume 12: Teaching Academic Writing in European Higher Education
Lennart Björk, Gerd Bräuer. Lotte Rienecker, Peter Stray Jörgensen (Eds.) 2003
240 p. Hardbound, ISBN 1-4020-1208-X; Paperback, ISBN 1-4020-1209-8

Volume 13: Revision: Cognitive and Instructional Processes
Linda Allal, Lucile Chanquoy, Pierre Largy (Eds.) 2004
248 p. Hardbound, ISBN 1-4020-7729-7

Volume 14: Effective Learning and Teaching of Writing
A Handbook of Writing in Education
Gert Rijlaarsdam, Huub van den Bergh & Michel Couzijn, M. (Eds.)
2nd ed., 2004, X, 670 p. 21 illus., Hardcover ISBN: 1-4020-2724-9; Softcover ISBN: 1-4020-2725-7

Volume 15: Writing in Context(s)
Textual Practices and Learning Processes in Sociocultural Settings
Triantafillia Kostouli (Ed.) 2005
280 p., Hardcover ISBN: 0-387-24237-6; Softcover ISBN: 0-387-24238-4

Volume 16: Teaching Writing in Chinese Speaking Areas
Mark Shiu Kee Shum; De Lu Zhang (Eds.) 2005
276 p., Hardcover ISBN: 0-387-26392-6

Volume 17: Writing and Digital Media
Luuk van Waes, Mariëlle Leijten & Chris Neuwirth (Eds.) 2006
380 pp., Hardcover ISBN: 0-08-044863-1

Volume 18: Computer Key-Stroke Logging and Writing
Kirk Sullivan & Eva Lindgren (Eds.) 2006 248 pp., Hardcover ISBN: 0-08-044934-4

Volume 19: Writing and Motivation
Suzanne Hidi & Pietro Boscolo (Eds.) 2006
346 pp., Hardcover ISBN: 0-08-045325-2

Volume 20: Writing and Cognition
Mark Torrance, Luuk van Waes & David Galbraith (Eds.) 2006
392 pp., Hardcover ISBN: 0-08-045094-6

Volume 21: Written Documents in the Workplace
Denis Alamargot, PAtrice Terrier, Jean-Marie Cellier (Eds.) (2008)
336 pp., Hardcover ISBN: 0-08-047487-8

Volume 22: Voices, Identities, Negotiations, and Conflicts: Writing Academic English Across Cultures
Phan Le Ha & Bradley Baurain (Eds.)
233 pp., Hardcover ISBN: 0-8-5724719-3